Talking Television

An introduction to the study of television

GRAEME BURTON

Visiting Lecturer, University of the West of England, UK

A member of the Hodder Headline Group

LONDON

Co-published in the United States of America by
Oxford University Press Inc., New York

First published in Great Britain in 2000 by
Arnold, a member of the Hodder Headline Group,
338 Euston Road, London NW1 3BH

http: //www.arnoldpublishers.com

Co-published in the United States of America by
Oxford University Press Inc., 198 Madison Avenue, New York, NY10016

British Library Cataloguing in Publication Data
A catalogue record for this book is available from the British Library

Library of Congress Cataloging-in-Publication Data
A catalog record for this book is available from the Library of Congress

ISBN 0 340 58964 7

1 2 3 4 5 6 7 8 9 10

Production Editor: Anke Ueberberg
Production Controller: Fiona Byrne
Cover Design: Mouse Mat Design

Typeset in 10/12 Sabon by YHT London
Printed and bound in Great Britain by MPG Books Ltd, Bodmin, Cornwall

Talking Television

Contents

Acknowledgments

The author and publishers would like to thank the following for permission to use copyright material in this book: ITN for figure 5.2; Undercurrents Alternative News for figure 6.3; Carlton Television for figure 8.6(b); Charles Green for figure 7.2(b); Radio Times and Sven Arnstein for figure 8.4 (page 184); Radio Times and Mike Owen for figure 8.4 (page 185).

Every effort has been made to trace all copyright holders. The publishers will be glad to make suitable arrangements with any copyright holders whom they have not been able to contact. Any rights not acknowledged here will be acknowledged in subsequent printings if notice is given to the publisher.

Introduction

This book is about ways of studying and understanding British television.

In some respects (such as examples of programmes, facts about ownership) it will inevitably be culture-specific. But the critical tools it applies could be used to uncover the workings of television systems elsewhere, the interactions of other audiences with their own systems, the meanings within the representations and the products of different systems.

British television is not exactly British. Apart from the obvious presence of US programmes, there is the well-established presence of *Neighbours* and other Australian product. There is the absurdist marshmallow porn of *Eurotrash* from France. There are feature films from many other countries. There is the dominant Sky satellite channel, owned by an Australian-come-naturalized-American. The BBC is in a production/distribution deal with the US factual Discovery Channel, apart from having its own cable channel in the States.

This is not to exaggerate the amount and the influence of overseas product, given that 75 per cent of programmes are of British origin [not including films]. But one does need to recognize the effects of cultural interactions and to accept that television institutions operate in a global marketplace.

This represents a change in the condition of British television over the last generation which is also driven by changes in technology. These changes mean that the study of television has to take some account of redefinitions of what 'television' means. The single screen in the living room may now have been joined by further screens in any room in the house. Those screens are simply the outlets for a range of forms of distribution – video, cable, satellite, apart from the original broadcast television. There is a multiplicity of channels to flip through. There is interactivity, most obviously on the shopping channels. What 'television' means – as a type of knowledge distributor, as a media organization, as a means of information and entertainment, as a domestic artefact, as a piece of technology – has changed profoundly. Part of the function of this book is to demonstrate the nature and significance of that change, not least in terms of power and in terms of representations.

This last concept draws attention to the fact that the study of television is inevitably about the generation of meanings about culture and society. There is a complex relationship between images on the screen and the audiences for those images. There is a more indirect relationship between television institutions and those audiences, as part of an overall entity described as a society. These relationships are to be understood in terms of different kinds of power, but not in terms of the supposed power of television over its audiences. Images have power. Carlton Communications has power. But audiences are not simply victims of that power. Such complex relationships are also the subject of this book.

A variety of critical approaches to television study will be fairly demonstrated and evaluated. But, just as I don't subscribe to the view that television does awful things to people, so too shall I avoid promoting any ideas about television as low-cultural schlock. Some television is abysmal in its production values, its condescension towards its audience, its unoriginal narratives, its cardboard representations. But some television is truly brilliant in exposing the nerves of character, in challenging preconceptions about issues, in its visual metaphors, in making coherent through a small screen the inchoate hugeness of our world geographies – social, psychological, topographical.

So there will be an interweaving of debates and concepts, many drawn from media and cultural studies in general, but sharpened on the whetstone of television material.

In terms of the overall structure of the book and of its use, I would like to draw attention to a few features. The opening of the book (chapters 1 and 2) develops ideas about the overall nature of television and approaches to studying it, as well as explaining specific critical approaches and areas of investigation. So the book starts off being about principles, concepts and ways of analysing television. The main part of the book (chapters 3 to 10) is organized under key concepts and in terms of major areas of television study. There is an underlying sense of a triangular relationship between institution, product and audience, bearing on the idea that there are meanings about the world produced by all three of these elements, but not perfectly controlled or encoded by any of them. Chapter 11 reflects on the economic, technological, social, institutional and political processes that make up the history of British television. These are embedded within it and help explain why we have the kind of television that we do have. Debates about television, changes in television management and developments in programmes are all included. There is also a final chapter which uses that history, and present events, to look at where television appears to be going and what is significant about that direction.

Because concepts inevitably overlap from one section to another, you are advised to make use of the index to track different applications of, or perspectives on, these ideas. You may also choose to dip into specific areas that you are interested in. All books are constructed with some kind of rationale for their sequence, like television programmes. But you can get ideas and information through selective investigation.

In any case, the text will be interrupted periodically to ask key questions, or to raise some key debate or issue. These points should help you think about the significance of what you have read.

Each chapter will give you a lead-in preview of its content and purpose.

Whatever television is exactly, it is nothing if not pervasive. We each watch it for upwards of 20 hours a week, on average. And whilst we may use the remote control as an electronic tap to turn on and off the stream of images and sounds, we cannot turn off our brains, which are always chewing away on television material, constructing and reconstructing meanings about the world.

A postmodernist view would say that television reality is continuous with our social and physical realities, which are all mental constructs anyway: 'Illusion is no longer possible because the real is no longer possible' (Baudrillard, 1988).

I don't agree with this. Television may penetrate our consciousness but it does not destroy our distinctions between social, experiential reality and its own simulated reality. It does, however, challenge our sense of the real and may cause us to revise it. Television may influence us, though this is very difficult to prove. It may indeed both endorse and oppose our understandings of the world. It may build on the foundations of ideology while also chipping away at those foundations. For all these reasons, television – made by people and used by people – is a medium which can be tedious and provocative at the same time. It is interesting in its variations and in its contradictions. It is to be hoped that this book does justice to this interest.

1

What Do You Mean, Television Studies?

PREVIEW

This chapter deals with:

- how we may define the word television – as an industry or as a set of programmes, for example
- a brief historical survey of critical approaches to the media and to television
- a brief comment on critical methods of research into television
- key features which describe the nature of television.

INTRODUCTION

[T]elevision today assumes some of the functions traditionally ascribed to myth and ritual (i.e. integrating individuals into the social order, celebrating dominant values, offering models of thought).

Douglas Kellner (*Media Culture*, 1995)

Television is an experience that we take for granted, yet it is also one that shapes how we think about the world. Its very availability and populist nature has in the past been made a reason for dismissing it as ephemeral and somehow 'unworthy'. But media and popular culture are now firmly on the academic agenda. The most extreme outbursts of the high culturalists against the 'worth' of television material look plain silly. Arguments about the relative merits of Catherine Cookson and Charles Dickens as dramatized on television may be interesting. But assumptions about the cultural superiority of Dickens over Cookson, or about the book over the television drama, are distasteful. Television is both a cultural phenomenon in itself, and a medium through which a range of cultural activities reach us in our homes. In any case, 'television' as an object of study is not just about its programmes.

OBJECT OF STUDY

Though television screens may be used for more than the presentation of broadcast images, many people still think of 'television' as referring to **sets of programmes** emanating through a range of channels. These sets of programmes often stand for an idea of what television is, as an object of study or a subject of discussion. They are, rather inaccurately, called genres – referring to the industry-generated categories of programmes: documentary, children's programmes, drama and the like. Discussion of genre will come later in this book. Sufficient here to say that it is not helpful to use the word genre to describe drama, for example, when within that category exist what may more definably be called genres: murder-mystery thrillers, science fiction and so on.

Another view of 'television' is that it is about **an industry and a technology**. This view would be interested in control of television companies (and power), in globalization, in the implications of changing technology for society (and audiences). Here, the object of study includes the implications of the legal basis of the television industries, especially the debate about public service and commercial broadcasting (too often set up as mutually exclusive models). Television is not merely the sum of its programmes, even though as Geraghty and Lusted say (1998), 'For most people, television is foremost the programmes that we watch.' So in this book television as an object of study is taken to comprise many important areas such as industry, audience, representation. And the study of television is taken to include at the same time key concepts such as ideology and discourse.

For John Hartley (1992) the study of television is about text, audience and meaning – 'a textual–cultural phenomenon'. He is interested in the fusion of 'textual phenomena' and 'audience practices' in order to make '*reading* and *understanding* television better informed'.

Corner and Harvey (1996) distinguish between:

1 the study of the influence of television, drawing on methodologies and concepts from the social sciences
2 the study of television as cultural process, drawing on the arts and humanities (linguistics and textual criticism).

They also refer to anxiety about television and its effects, stemming particularly from the period of early modernism and Marxism in the 1940s. This anxiety has in another way defined what television is as an object of study – a kind of demon. This accords with Geraghty and Lusted talking about 'a history of suspicion' about television. The persistence of unproven convictions about the effects of television is in itself a worthy object of study – *South Park* must be bad for you because it is vulgar and coarsely drawn.

Modernism has always been tied in with a defence of 'high culture'. Television has frequently, and uncritically, been tied to notions of popular and therefore low culture.

Stuart Hall (1996 [1971]) has broadly defined television in terms of that which is produced for television (e.g. drama) and that which is relayed on television (e.g. sport). This is akin to defining television as either an originator or a carrier. There is of course manipulation and transformation of material in both cases. This relates to the concept of **mediation**. The problem here is that this mediation has become so pervasive that a clear distinction between the two modes is difficult. Video action replays and the timing of matches for television are examples of 'production' within a sports event which is relayed. One also has entertainment programmes which are clearly produced, but which include the relaying of live pictures from (for example) some hapless viewer's home.

John Corner (1995) has produced three useful points about television. He is actually talking about the move of politics into the public area of television when he refers to the medium as:

1   'a sphere of intensive and sophisticated knowledge management'
2   one which 'represents the world through visual and aural conventions which work to invoke realist credibility rather than critical engagement'
3   one in which 'politics is dominated by strategic personalisation'.

These three areas of information management, realism and personalization are important in defining the nature of television, how it presents its material to us, how its institutions work to shape that material.

> How many topics could you list as coming under the heading of television studies?

HISTORICALLY SPEAKING

Television – also in the context of media studies – does have a critical history which helps define the nature of its study. Critical movements in various eras have all contributed to ways of interpreting how we understand television: semiotics in the 1960s, structuralism in the 1970s, popular culture and postmodernism from the 1980s. The following necessarily sketchy account also comprises the particular influence of individual commentators:

- Barthes and textual analysis through understanding of signification;
- Althusser and structural analysis infused with post-Marxism;
- Bourdieu and audience pleasures in engagement with the popular text.

This section is a history of ideas and of criticism. A more traditional history of television industry, technology and programmes is provided in Chapter 11. What 'television' is, what the study of television is about, has and will shift as interests and critical tools change and develop. In the 1950s critiques of television were much taken up with effects, with the notion of what the media do to people. The account which follows deliberately lacks elaboration of terms used, which you are advised to follow up through later passages in this book. But it is important to lay out the ground plan. I am providing a brief history of critical movements and related concepts which have a bearing on television as an object of study, and which may be referred back to as concepts and critiques are developed later in this book. It is also important not to fall into a false discourse of progress, and not to assume that because ideas about television were developed at a particular time this means that they are all *passé* and that we have somehow 'moved on'. For example, Marxism still has a great deal to say about the expressions of power within media institutions and through media texts.

In the 1950s those working out of the 1930s Frankfurt school of Marxism (Adorno et al.) decried the creation of mass culture as much as those following an English literary Leavisite tradition. Denys Thompson famously condemned the supposedly culturally debilitating effects of the 'new' media – film and television. Richard Hoggart was more sympathetic to popular culture, offering constructive analysis of popular songs. But he too, as a kind of modernist, still came down against the supposed effects of low-culture television as opposed to the uplifting possibilities of literature. William Belson produced the first of his studies purporting to prove that media encouraged violent behaviour in the young.

In the 1960s ideas about semiotics and structuralism filter through from the writings of Barthes and Levi-Strauss. This strand shifts emphasis to the text, to the programme, to images. The broad intention is to locate the meanings in the text, assuming that texts are systematically formed, and perhaps assuming that these meanings will influence the television audience. People like Hall and then Morley took on ideas from Parkin about reading that text, about readings that might be predicted and shaped by the text (preferred readings), and the possibility that viewers might read against the grain (oppositional readings).

Post-Marxism developed in the late 1960s and 1970s, with an explosion of interest in sociology. But still television was hammered in various ways in critical debates which were mainly interested in institutional power and effects on audiences. It was said that television contributed to the creation of false consciousness about the truth of power relations in society. Television was, like education, a kind of ideological state apparatus (Althusser), which contrived to spread dominant ideology by stealth. Gramsci's ideas about hegemony were woven into these critical positions – the notion that power is exerted in ways which achieve the consent of those who are disempowered. Television could contribute to this invisible process.

The work of the Birmingham Centre for Cultural Studies (run by Richard Hoggart and then by Stuart Hall) was extremely important in the 1970s for its exploration of popular culture, for its casting around for new ways of understanding the media, for consciously trying to reject by now established assumptions about the power of the media and its influence on audience. The CCS was in truth itself very much influenced by developments in Marxism. It could also be said that it was almost anarchic in its willingness to designate anything as an object of cultural study. But it was also hugely enlivening in opening up and legitimating anything from the historical formation of culture to ethnicity and representation or youth cultures. Television, as text and as medium, was part of this new thinking. In spite of some avowed rejection of 'old' Sociology, CCS still very much functioned on the basis of a sociological tradition. The work of Cohen and Young, developing ideas about deviancy and moral panics, can be seen as standing alongside that of the birth of cultural studies and as having relevance for television. Television news contributed to moral panics, though not as much as the press did.

So by the 1970s criticism of television was focused on text as much as on institutions and effects on audiences. Lacanian psycho-analysis came into the frame, alongside Althusserian discourses, and informed debates about the workings of ideology and about the nature of identity in representations. At the same time, cultural studies was trying to assert its distinctiveness from media studies. In fact, subjects like communication studies and film studies were the first into a formal roster of degree courses and A-level school courses. Media and culture followed.

But what was happening in the 1970s and 1980s was also a new interest in the nature of audiences and in how they understand texts. This new focus on audience was represented by the work of Morley and Brunsden, and became part of yet another strand: feminist or women's studies. There was examination of how families watch television. There were studies of how women use and understand television. There was investigation of women reading romantic fiction, or as audience for radio.

At this point you may rightly be wondering where the distinctions between these different kinds of study really lie. I would argue that substantially they don't exist. There is a tradition of disciplines within academic life and in education. But the divisions between these disciplines are rather illusory and not always helpful. It is more valuable to think in terms of kinds of emphasis. So a study of audience watching television may select female readers and examine a female context for that reading. But the ideas about the reading also relate to audience study in general, television study and media study in general, and very possibly to cultural studies (with its interest in context and resistance to dominant culture). A similar point about connections may be made with regard to the history within this section. We have moved into a period in the 1980s onwards of interest in culture and context, and of postmodernism – back to the text and its referentiality. But this does not mean that structural analysis or discourse analysis is suddenly useless. Nor does it mean that study of the industry and institution has been left behind, rusting on the the beaches of media criticism. It means that we should value critical tools, old and new, for their ability to enhance understanding of the object of study.

Geraghty and Lusted (1998) express the situation as follows: 'Television Studies has developed as an interdisciplinary field, each discipline bringing with it its own conventions and procedures which have, in turn, merged and developed distinct approaches of their own.' In summarizing Brunsdon's writing on the history of television studies, they draw attention to the following points:

- the distinction between writing about television as a text and the social-science tradition of writing about television as an institution
- the kind of criticism which looks at television at large (e.g. globalization) in the public sphere, contrasted with investigation of television in a private sphere (e.g. feminism, pleasure and consumption in the home)
- a move from the late 1970s and examination of genres to more concentration on audiences and on specific texts
- a convergence of interest in audience with the interest in text as read by audiences.

This could be overlaid with cultural views of audiences as:

- resisting preferred readings
- resisting blind consumption
- therefore resisting the Marxist idea of commodification of culture and of social relations.

Brunsdon herself (1998) describes television criticism as emerging in the 1970s and 1980s from three main sources of commentary:

- journalism
- literary drama criticism
- social sciences.

It may be argued that this led to some concentration on programmes (and genres), on creators (writers and directors in particular) and on social issues (with relation to realism, taste and social comment). Certainly present journalistic reviews of television work in these areas do this. Academic critiques attend to institution, audience, form and cultural process, as much as to construction and likely effect.

> What might be valued about a television soap opera by a literary critic, as opposed to what might be valued by a sociologist?

METHODOLOGIES AND ISSUES

Methods of research and of criticism also do not 'belong' to one academic discipline rather than another. They all have their uses and their limitations.

Content analysis has been used, e.g. in an attempt to quantify the kinds and degrees of violence on television. It might measure the number of violent acts on screen in a given period of time. However, it can only assume a correlation between these acts and audience attitudes and behaviours.

Ethnographic surveys have been used to describe the reactions of particular families or groups of women to television material in the context of their particular circumstances. However, the evidence is by its nature not statistically susceptible to extrapolations and generalization about the reactions of all families or all women.

Textual analysis may in turn employ semiotic analysis to identify signifiers in an image, to deduce connotations (meanings) from these signs. But there is a degree of subjectivity in these deductions, let alone in asserting the primacy of one set of meanings above another. So one can only cite such methodologies if the original question is reframed in terms of 'how does one study television?' Every method raises some questions about its validity, how it works on the evidence and how certain may be the conclusions that one draws.

John Hartley (1992) wishes to see methods as complementing one another. He argues that providing critiques of aspects of television study in isolation is not helpful. One has to see the parts together, in relation to a whole. 'Audience practices and textual phenomena can be isolated and described, but what happens when they fuse together cannot be observed without changing the circumstances of fusion.'

NATURE OF TELEVISION

It may be argued that this entire book constructs a view of the nature of television. However, there are certain features of television material in particular which bear on the study of the medium.

Flow

Charles Curran famously called television a 'seamless robe', and it is true that the producers of television abhor a blank screen.

Raymond Williams talked about the 'flow' of television. The programmes stream across the screen, channel by channel, in an uninterrupted torrent. There is no break that might allow the attention of the viewer to disengage. On the other hand, the implied argument that there is sameness and that it is impossible to disengage is not true either. People choose to break into the screen at different times because there are different kinds of programme that attract them. Audiences are also capable of disengaging from the flow, not least by zapping and channel hopping. Advertisers are increasingly uncomfortable about the evidence of this, which undermines the arguments for charging high rates for television slots.

Segmentation

John Ellis (1992) takes issue with the idea of flow, and emphasizes the narrative segmentation of television. It is true that different programmes, their different modes of realism, the punctuation of previews, trailers and commercials, all provide kinds of break and change. They offer points of entry into television. People choose the segments they want to watch – perhaps a sequence of early evening programmes for young people. But again, those same previews can be seen as bridges between programmes. The title sequences offer a period of adjustment to the next set of conventions which govern our understanding of the next programme.

Fact and fiction

In one respect Ellis almost argues for the idea of continuity, if not flow, when he asserts that there are no differences between televisual fact and fiction on the level of form. Such differences as there are exist on the level of the origins of the material. Certainly the development of 'hybrid' genres such as the docusoap have mixed up the conventions of previously distinct forms in television. The argument against distinctions between fact and fiction may be taken further in respect of narrative and of realism. Television is full of narratives – sequences of pictures and 'stories'. It makes no difference in narrative principle, one might say, if the segment of television is labelled documentary, news or drama – still, there is narrative structure. The second point may be summed up in terms of 'all realism is relative'. Television is by definition not real (if the real is measured by social experience). It is a technical medium for constructing a version of the real: all programmes are 'unreal': all programmes are just different versions of the real. These points will be developed in later chapters.

Intertextuality

All media texts have degrees of cross-reference. They are understood by reference to one another. *Tank Girl* the movie referred to *Tank Girl* the comic. Genres are especially referential. The creatures in *Alien* are partly understood with reference to other creatures from science fiction and horror. But television is especially intertextual in its nature because of its hunger for more material, because it exploits successful formulas in the chase for ratings fuelled by competition between different channels. Television genres provide examples of intertextuality in action, like the infusion of soap characteristics into police dramas (*The Bill*). The life of viruses becomes a paradigm for television genres and intertextual experimentation – accelerated mutations produce a proliferation of forms in the cause of survival. Some programmes fail. But a number succeed because of the sheer rate of experimentation and adaptation.

Actuality

In spite of the film screenings, imported programmes and repeats, it is fair to say that television is marked by its ability and willingness to create actuality material, screening events as they happen. This is exemplified in many ways – satellite links on news, live studio quiz shows, outside broadcasts, young people's Saturday morning television, ITV's *Big Breakfast*. This immediacy of material carries connotations of exciting risk – things could go wrong – and of truthfulness – seeing it as it happens.

Polysemy

Unarguably, television is polysemic in its nature. That is to say, it comprises many signs, generated through a variety of codes: visual, verbal, technical, nonverbal and so on. This polysemy makes for visual and aural complexity. There is a lot to make sense of at one time. To this extent, 'reading' television is a sophisticated activity. However, there is an argument to be resolved between two views. One is that polysemy leads to a variety of possible meanings for the audience. The other is that nevertheless television usually anchors the meaning of the image and uses narrative strategies that lead one to make sense of images and programmes in certain ways.

Transitoriness – popular culture

Television is identified as a transitory medium, because of the sheer volume of material put out, as well as because of its lack of permanence, of record. This temporary nature might be contrasted with the record offered by photographs, for example. However, one could take issue with this view on at least two grounds. Factually, it is very possible to record and keep, to purchase, copies of at least some television material. It is also the case that repeats and recycling through channels like UK Gold ensure that material does not drop out of the consciousness after one viewing. In another application of the technology people now keep video records of family occasions as much as they use photographs. Some people video record and store favourite programmes.

One could also dispute this view within the grounds of a cultural arena. It might be said that television is transitory, books are not. Television is the popular culture of mass production and collective authorship, and is therefore not so valuable. Books on the other hand draw on a high-cultural tradition of individual authorship, endorsed by the established traditions of literary scholarship in the education system – therefore they are, for the most part, of considerable cultural value. In this way the notion of the transitory becomes mixed up with cultural and indeed class traditions of consumption. The word transitory becomes a kind of subjective damnation rather than an attempt at objective description.

I would suggest that the high culture–low culture debates about the value of television (see Raymond Williams) may now be intellectually passé, but they still have social currency. For example, the column centimetres devoted to books in the heavyweight Sunday newpapers far exceed the space given to television. By any measurement of consumption one might expect the reverse to be true. The differential says a lot about the persistence of high-cultural values, perhaps mixed up with illusions about the permanent and the transitory.

Complicity – intimacy – activity

There is a particular quality to the relationship between television material and its viewers which marks out its nature. Ellis refers to a 'complicity'. One could also refer to activity and intimacy. All these qualities have a lot to do with the context of viewing – the home. Complicity has to do with images of people a few feet away from the armchair, and with the fact that a number of those people – newscasters, compères – invite complicity through direct address to the viewer from the screen. The viewer is made complicit with privileged information in, for example, documentaries showing snooker or wild animals, through the voice of the interpreter – we are there with the commentator. It is a short step to intimacy when viewers declare a sense of 'closeness' to the commentators or with the characters in soap operas. And activity – ironing or conversation – may mark out the domestic and social nature of television in terms of the viewing experience.

A family medium

Referring to conversation also raises the assumption that the 'nature' of television includes family viewing. I would dispute this. It may involve families. It certainly takes place in something called 'the home'. But the evidence is that families do not always watch television together. More importantly, only 25 per cent of British households consist of two parents with one or more children. And 64 per cent of all households have more than one television set (1996). So even the concept of the 'family home' needs fresh consideration. Issues surrounding the experience of family viewing are not invalid when discussing of the nature of television and perhaps of its effects. But they need to be kept in perspective.

A domestic medium

Furthermore, John Hartley (1992) suggests that television is by its nature a domestic medium. He argues that the home is simultaneously an economic and cultural construct, important to broadcasting and cultural consumption as we know it. He suggests that the home as an individual family unit is a creation of the twentieth century which deals with the potential for social and political disruption caused by the compressed urban masses of the nineteenth/early twentieth century. Entertainment and pleasure moves in emphasis from the streets, from pubs, from music halls, even from cinema, into the domestic arena – which is identifiable and controllable.

A cultural agent – cultural commodity

This phrase is used by John Fiske (1987). He goes on to talk about television as a 'provoker and circulator of meanings'. For Fiske it is these meanings which are the focus of study: 'television makes . . . meanings that serve the dominant interests in society' and 'circulates those meanings among a wide variety of social groups that constitute its audience'. He distinguishes his own interest in and definitions of 'television' from those who, for example, see it as 'an industrial practice or as a profit-making producer of commodities'.

It is indeed Fiske himself who elsewhere (1991) defines television as **a cultural commodity**. A programme is on a financial level a product which has a price and is sold to the audience. But on a cultural level it becomes another kind of product, where the audience makes use of its meanings and defines it in terms of cultural value.

So television inhabits the spheres of art and commerce at the same time. It makes the distant object close for us and the strange experience almost familiar. It produces trash and quality with equal facility and it challenges our sense of what those words mean. To make sense of its variety and its contradictions one may employ critical approaches such as those described in the next chapter.

2

Critical Approaches to Television Studies

PREVIEW

This chapter deals with:
- the development of critical approaches to television
- traditional general models or critical overviews for describing the media/television in relation to society
- some key concepts within television studies
- some particular critical and analytical approaches.

INTRODUCTION

Critical approaches to television are in some respects shaped by perceptions of the medium and therefore are particular to it. But they are also part of a general thrust within media studies and indeed within propositions about culture and society. So, for example, a great deal has been written about the supposed power and influence of television, above that of other media. The medium has also been written about especially in terms of its genres, where news has received a lot of attention. Taking the wider view, one might cite the influence of semiotic analysis of images or the culturalist approach to viewing pleasures as examples of criticism which may be applied to the media overall. Yet these also yield insights specific to an understanding of television.

For Robert Allen (1992) a key question about television is 'How are meanings and pleasures produced in our engagements with television?' This places criticism firmly in the area of audience interaction with text and of the formal properties of text. We are also in the area which cultural studies has particularly adopted.

However, I would argue that answers to this question do not preclude critical examination of related questions, for example about the commercial and political forces which shape the television with which we engage. To this extent, a sensible model for criticism would be one which has to do with process, which recognizes the interrelationships between institution, text, audience and cultural context. Allen recognizes this complexity when he comments on the unsatisfactory nature of quantitative research (perhaps content analysis) in trying to make sense of television. He refers to the different agendas of social scientists and to the considerable body of research which is taken up with the supposed influence and effects of television. He argues that 'the relationships between viewer and television are so complex and multidimensional that they resist all attempts to reduce them to phenomena that can be explained by the same procedures that work for the chemist'.

Perceptions of television drawn from the tradition of journalistic criticism referred to in Chapter 1 changed in the 1990s. One can agree with John Hartley (1998), that negative views exist about television as a medium. These stem from the kind of Leavisite high-cultural tradition of literary textual criticism, but have nothing to to do with the kind of textual analysis referred to in the section below. Nor are they apparent in the critiques of television presented in the broadsheet newspapers, which at least show awareness of form and meaning, and which do not automatically devalue television as a medium. Whether or not Hartley is correct in asserting that there are elitist social perceptions of television among the classes or groups which have most influence within our society is another matter. One would have to find ways of objectifying this idea. He talks about

> the home-talk of the knowledge class; the class which wants to take power over information media and cultural technologies like television, not only by running the culture business on behalf of the shareholders and stakeholders, but by regulating it, and controlling the literacies and discourses by means of which it is understood.

But one cannot be sure that assumed criticism of the medium – even contempt for it – actually exists. In any case, this is not necessarily part and parcel of wanting to control the medium. Furthermore, the explosion of television technology and access to a variety of forms and channels of television is not so much opposing some classist critique of the medium as simply bypassing it. Questions of control and of effects remain on the table.

Is television as a medium regarded as lacking cultural value, or is it only certain programmes which are seen in this way?

MODELS OF THE MASS MEDIA – THEORETICAL APPROACHES

In the first place, one may look at established critical frameworks for understanding the media in general, as they operate in relation to the society of which they are a part. This itself raises an important point about how one conceives the relationships between objects of study, between what we call television and society, for instance. Whether or not they entirely fit each of the theoretical approaches below, I would argue for the following points:

- television (and those who operate the television system) is a part of society and culture, and not a separate entity which impinges on society from 'without'
- nevertheless, television makers and performers are placed in a special position within society by virtue of their access to television production
- culture and society are largely indistinguishable from one another: social structures and relationships are driven by cultural values, are an expression of these values
- culture is manifested through the artefacts and the behaviours of a society: social interaction is a form of cultural behaviour: television is a form of cultural behaviour
- we assume meanings, values, ideologies within these artefacts and behaviours
- we construct those meanings under the influence of the very ideologies which we are attempting to define
- therefore critical detachment is a difficult mental feat: it may even be argued that our notions of objectivity are themselves subjective.

All this is not to bring criticism of television – or anything else – to a grinding halt, sunk in a morass of subjectivity. But these points do draw attention to the following:

- that talking about television requires scepticism about objectivity
- that views about television may co-exist and not be mutually exclusive
- that all the concepts expressed within this book stand in some relation to one another and not alone
- that whatever the particular points made about television – perhaps its technology or its programmes – the central thrust of criticism seems to reflect on what meanings are produced how, by whom, and with what social and cultural significance.

Granville Williams (1996) summarizes two views of the role and function of media in society as being either:

1 media which impose commercial values on everything, and their views on the audience, which functions as a consumer, or

2 media which are diverse and pluralist, creative and aware that too much
media power can work against the interests of democracy.

This is essentially a contrast between determinism and pluralism.

As Williams says, the latter view reached its apogee in the 1980s under
Thatcherism in Britain and Reaganism in the USA, at least in the views of
media owners and politicians: a promoted illusion that everything was OK. It
has become clear once more that this is not so. It is also the case that these
two views are not the only views on the media, and need not be simply
opposed to one another.

What Williams does present is a useful set of dichotomies which emerge
from these two views and from the problems created by embracing
marketplace consumerism as a model for running for the media, including the
BBC.

```
SOCIETY      – MARKET
CITIZEN      – CONSUMER
NEED         – WANT
VALUE        – PRICE
COMMUNITY  – GLOBALISM
REGULATION – EFFICIENCY
```

What are the arguments for, and what is the evidence for either of these views?

Marxism – determinism

Marxist views of society and then of the media developed throughout the
course of the twentieth century. They remain hugely influential and useful, if
not finally definitive. They focus on economic determinism, class relations
and the exercise of power and control within social structures. They are
sometimes described as control theories.

Television does partly exemplify the idea that society is driven by the
interests of capital and by economic forces. Commercial television is funded
by a capitalist system. Television programmes discuss the influence of
economic forces (e.g. the current debate about joining the Euro).
Developments in television – whether these be new kinds of programme or the
digital expansion of new channels – are driven by economic interests: creating
new markets, making more money.

Television represents class relations more or less explicitly. The sitcom
Keeping Up Appearances makes fun of Mrs Bouquet's middle-class
aspirations – therefore contributing to the circulation of ideas about class. The

news creates the idea of elite persons by showing some people and not others, and by showing them in certain ways – the royal family, for example.

Television represents power relations explicitly in, for example, the ways that programmes show men treating women. Implicitly, it may be argued, it is a way of exercising power over large sections of society, by representing certain ways of thinking and behaving as 'natural' and others as not. Different treatments are all expressions of ideology.

It was the Frankfurt school of Marxists, in the 1930s and after, who developed ideas about the media and culture in particular. They conceptualized a malign influence of mass media creating a passive mass audience. They assumed that the media do things to people. Although none of these ideas now stand up to analysis, they are very persistent, and are freely used by rightwing commentators to criticize television. Other more sophisticated ideas that were developed, notably discourse and hegemony, will be discussed elsewhere. There are long-standing concepts, such as that of **false consciousness**, which remain useful for explaining how television may create an illusory view of social relations and of where power lies, concealing the realities of social practices and of power. What is clear, if one takes the example of Milliband (1973) and others in the 1970s, is that even post-Marxism continues to take an adverse view of television, in terms of its institutional power and the effects of its material on the audience.

It is cultural studies and postmodernism which have broken away from good–bad, reception–effects, high-culture–low-culture models. Even post-Marxism sought sophisticated explanations for the exercise of power through media which were not based on them and us, on straightforward cause and effects or on paranoid views of those controlling television intentionally seeking to control us.

Pluralism

Pluralist views of the media are often contrasted with Marxist views. They could be seen as having a generosity of attitude towards choice in the media, as opposed to the dire warnings of the Marxist about what the media are doing to our culture and our freedoms. However, such views, and their opposition, are simplistic. The pluralist is not necessarily a fellow traveller with capitalism, nor is the Marxist necessarily condemning television out of hand. The pluralist view is about the notion of variety and choice – of channels, of programmes, of opinions. This choice exists, but within limits.

The development of new channels has actually been about rather more of the same – whole channels for children (Fox), for sport (Sky), for documentary (Discovery), for music (MTV). There isn't a channel for Asian communities, or for the disabled. The same is broadly true of programmes –

the number of chat shows expands, but generally to a formula that grabs more ratings (let's talk sex) or to agendas defined by the programme makers. There isn't a programme in which children talk freely about adults. Plurality of opinion is also limited by editorial control, the imperative of the ratings, as well as the dominance of television output by the conception of 'entertainment'. Programmes about the cinema are dominated by comment on stars and new Hollywood releases. Currently there is no critical discussion of cinema as such, no series reflecting on television itself. Television has plenty of space for self-reflection within its thousands of hours of output, but its pluralism does not extend to this.

Libertarianism

This is another view of the way that media do and should operate, which approximates to the notion that absolute freedom is right in principle and will sort out everything in the end. It will sort out freedom of ownership, freedom of speech, freedom of access. The notion of **liberal pluralism** covers pretty much the same ground. The idea sounds right in democratic principle, but is nonsense in material fact. You are not free to start up a television station because you feel like it. The capital costs favour existing rich players. Anyway, the government will impose considerable constraints on whether and when you start up, let alone on what you may 'say'. Similarly, as an audience you do not have any right of access to television producers: you do not, it may be argued, have access to a notably wide choice of programmes.

Social responsibility

As a way of modelling pluralist principles behind the media this critical view would argue that television has a freedom modified by a sense of responsibility. The theory was originally applied to the press – a kind of wishful thinking, one might say, given the ways in which some of the press operate, for example doorstepping people to the point of desperation or outing Mary Bell as a murderess to her unsuspecting daughter.

Anyway, the government which allows television to happen is also apparently not optimistic about the notion of 'natural' responsibility. Through the broadcasting acts and other mechanisms it provides a constraining framework within which television is forced into the government's notion of responsibility – in relation to what is broadcast to children or to how the news is produced, for instance.

> What flaws can you see in these views of how the media and television work in relation to society?

PROCESS MODELS – KEY CONCEPTS

If one takes terms such as institution, product, audience, context, then a process approach would argue that understanding of one element is a product of understanding of all elements and their relation to one another.

If one wishes to look at the production of meaning in television as being part of a related sequence of events and key elements, then again a process model would view that sequence, from conception through production to audience and into understanding, as being part of something continuous (*see* Fig. 2.1).

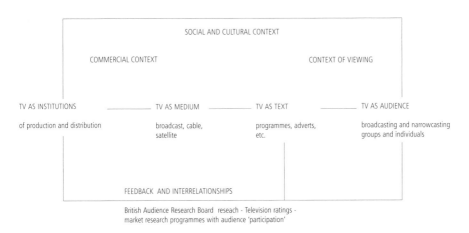

2.1 A process model: the interrelationship of some key areas in television studies.

The demerit of some critical approaches is that they look at the parts rather than at the whole. The history of audience studies is an interesting example of how the approach has moved from assuming that television does things to its audience, to looking at what the audience does with television, to realizing what is 'done' depends on various kinds of context. It would be a mistake to assume that just because there is evidence that audiences *can* make sense of television material in their own ways, the same material may not *also* shape the ways in which sense is made.

IDEOLOGIES

The notion of ideology – systems of ideas about the world – both emerges from and informs any study of the media. Where the ideas are systematic enough they will be given labels – capitalism, for instance. And in this sense, religions are also ideologies. These ideas include the values and beliefs which drive our social behaviour and which define our convictions about power relations – who should have power, who should not. An ideology is part of our consciousness because it is what we have grown up with. It is something that we share with others in our culture. It is a collective thing – one cannot have an individual ideology. The very notion of individualism is itself part of our ideology. Our formative growing-up experiences include the ways in which our family talks to us, ways in which we are educated, ways in which television makes sense of the world for us. These 'ways' are ideologically determined.

Television is an agent or a carrier of ideology. It is what Althusser would call an ISA – ideological state apparatus. It is a means by which the interests and values of those who have power are made part of the thinking of those over whom power is exerted, though the exercise of that power is largely invisible (*see also* hegemony, p.38 below). So it is impossible not to consider ideologies when making sense of television, in all its aspects. The core meanings which are commonly teased out of television product are actually those same beliefs and values. In October 1999 ITV ran a drama entitled *Births, Marriages and Deaths*. This title simultaneously encompasses three discourses, three core areas of cultural experience, three key sets of values within our ideological framework. The story presents conventional ideas about masculinity (the dominant ideology and its view of the world). It also to some extent challenges those ideas (exposes ideological contradictions between ideas about male dominance and the ineffectiveness of this dominance in given situations). Ideology is not political in a partisan sense – it does not belong to leftwing views in particular. Rather, all social relations have a political dimension because they all have dimensions of inequalities of power, and of the beliefs which inform those inequalities.

Television, in a variety of programmes, represents ideology in action. It cannot help being ideological. It may not consciously promote or reproduce inequalities, but the fact that it actually does so means that it cannot be regarded as 'innocent'. So just as ideology is held to permeate our thinking and our behaviours, so also it permeates television, whose sounds and images also become part of our consciousness.

Rosalind Brunt in Goodwin and Whannel's *Understanding Television* (1990) ties together the ideas of ideology and of text through a reading of one specific programme. She describes ideologies as 'explanatory systems of belief' and ties this to 'a recognition that television communicates meanings, values and beliefs'. In support of her reading she proposes a number of questions about ideology which are useful and which in adapted form read as follows:

- How do ideologies come together and hold together as systems of belief?
- Who believes them and why?

- What meanings about social groups do they construct through representations?
- How and where do they manifest themselves?
- What historical circumstances have given rise to the sets of ideas which are ideologies?
- What political, economic and institutional factors work to support the continuation of an ideology?

The answers to all these questions involve to some extent the institution, production of and audiences for television.

Ideology is like colourless, odourless gas which permeates our social relations, and which inhabits television production and material. But the views and values of ideology are not entirely consistent. Indeed it may be said that the key values of dominant ideology operate precisely to cover over those contradictions. For example, in 1999 Britain was engaged (with the USA) in bombing targets in Serbia. At the same time it was talking – on television, on radio, and in the press – about keeping the peace. Ideology proposes the values of democracy and of peaceful solutions, yet contains an **ideological contradiction** when it also proposes the value of using force. Government statements argued that they had no quarrel with the Serbian people, but still Serbian soldiers were dying – they are also Serbian people. This is not an argument for or against the action. But it is a demonstration of contradictions. And it is dominant ideological values of humanitarianism or of patriotism (the interests of Britain) which plaster over these contradictions (*see* Fig. 2.2).

COMMODIFICATION

Strictly speaking, the idea of commodification is a further extension of Marxist rationale. But it deserves separate examination in the light of its critical development over many years.
In the context of television it applies to:

- the cultural artefacts which television programmes are
- what lies behind the social behaviours and exchanges which television depicts (for example in drama and advertising)
- audiences themselves, who are measured and described by ratings research, and sold as commodities through the rate cards to those who spend their money on television slots.

Television programmes, including news, are commodities or goods which are bought and sold. They have a material value. This in itself is interesting in light of the fact that we are encouraged to think of them as pieces of creative

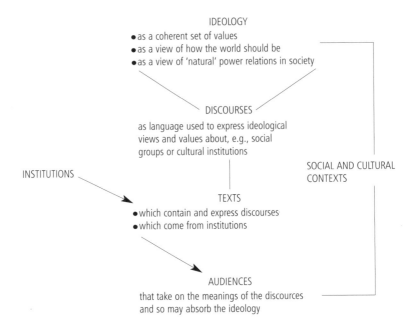

IDEOLOGY
- as a coherent set of values
- as a view of how the world should be
- as a view of 'natural' power relations in society

DISCOURSES

as language used to express ideological
views and values about, e.g., social
groups or cultural institutions

INSTITUTIONS

SOCIAL AND CULTURAL
CONTEXTS

TEXTS
- which contain and express discourses
- which come from institutions

AUDIENCES

that take on the meanings of the discources
and so may absorb the ideology

A key question is, how far do audiences take on meanings uncritically, or unknowingly?
It may be argued that they can make alternative or oppositional readings of texts, which
don't go along with the dominant meanings of the discourse (or the dominant ideology).
See also Chapter 9, on audiences.

2.2 Audiences: ideology expressed through texts.

expression (say, through the BAFTA awards), rather than as functional objects
such as a soft-drinks can. This thinking about programmes conceals the
practices behind their appearance – production processes, accounting and so
on. The concealment denies the commercial nature of television and
encourages valuation in terms of art or of social significance. Furthermore,
programmes may become cultural goods in themselves. This refers to their
acquiring a kind of cultural value, so that, for example, keeping up with
episodes of *Friends* becomes a cool cultural activity. Also, those making and
appearing in *Friends* earn money which stands for that cultural value, which
is far more than the base costs of time, materials, equipment and average
salaries for a sitcom. Culture has a price on it. Goods or commodities acquire
a cultural value. Television further encourages this equivalence of culture and
cash within its programmes, but most obviously within its advertising. The
way goods are sold is about the way that beliefs and values are sold. So beauty
is in a bottle of lotion that has a price far beyond the cost of its materials, the

workers' labours and even some notional 20 per cent markup for profit. Beauty becomes a commodity – the bottle. Loving relationships are commodified – the advert which gives the couple value in terms of the car they own. But all the time, the fact that these goods become more than just a bottle, just a car, conceals the truths about mass production behind them – the social inequalities which mean that the workers on the production line get paid far less than the owners and executives who control the production line, or indeed than those who run the television companies which screen the adverts about the goods.

Cultural goods in some societies – a religious painting, for example – simply are not conceived of in terms of material value. They only have a cultural (in this case a religious) value. In this sense they are priceless. Commodification is something which television has encouraged because television itself is an expression of a materialist society.

John Fiske (1991) draws attention to the idea of **television as cultural commodity**. He refers to 'a cultural economy within which meanings and pleasures circulate'. He argues that 'in the cultural economy the audience rejects its role as commodity and becomes a producer, a producer of meanings and pleasures'. In this case Fiske is colonizing the notion of commodification into cultural studies and putting another angle on it. He does not ignore the traditional sense of commodification. But he does argue that one does not always have to return to the financial value of the programme to the producer, of the audience to the advertiser, of the cultural goods to their manufacturers. If you like, the classic Marxist view of commodities and exchange is a pessimistic one in which dominant groups and ideologies rule over the working class. A culturalist view is more optimistic: the people turn the material commodity of television into cultural commodity by deciding for themselves what programmes mean, what they enjoy, what they want to do with their viewing, how they will talk about television.

REPRESENTATION

Analysis of representation in television is also a key critical approach to understanding the significance of the medium and the meanings which it constructs for its audiences.

The term representation refers broadly to **the depiction of social groups and institutions**. It has to do with stereotypes, but is not simply about these. Most importantly, depiction is not merely about appearance and description, it is about **the meanings (or values) behind the appearance**. The appearance of representations is a cloak concealing the true form of meanings beneath. Because television is a visual medium it provides us with icons, with pictures of people and groups which at least look like life, even if they are only electronic constructs. It is is easy to apply processes of social perception to these televisual images. Our perception of others in life is also dominated by an inclination to assign them to categories and to make judgements about those categories. It is these judgements which inform our readings of television representations. There are three experiences through which these judgements may be formed:

1 we read the utterances and the non-verbal behaviour of people on television as we would of those in life – social experience
2 there are also the judgements we may be inclined to make through our media experience of reading television 'characters' or television narratives
3 layered onto this is the encoding of television material by its makers (through use of camera, for example) – an indirect experience.

It may also be argued that representation should cause one to attend to matters of form. It is the way that television is used that causes the audience to construct meanings which are the essence of the representation. To this extent representation is also about symbolic production – the making of signs within codes from which we make meanings. In studying representation one studies the making, the construction. Representation is therefore also about re-presenting: not the original idea or the original physical object, but **a re-presentation or a constructed version** of it.

More will be said about the concept of representation in Chapter 8.

MODE OF ADDRESS

The idea of mode of address has its origins in linguistic theory and in an emphasis on the active communicator, on the use of language, on the context in which things are said. However, it would be misleading to emphasize only the notion of addressing, of television as a kind of talking head in the corner. Rather, one should pick up on the idea of an addressee and understand this phrase to include a kind of **relationship with the viewer**, set up through the ways in which the medium is used. Indeed the way that the text is created actually sets up a view of what the audience is like – we talk in certain ways to different people. Morley (1992) refers to 'what is distinctive about the specific format and practices of a programme'. The relationship – very obvious in examples such as game shows such as *The Generation Game* – creates the **illusion of social interaction** between the viewer and the text. In some cases – soap operas, for example – one could say that we are drawn in to a kind of **false community**. Andrew Tolson (1996) talks about 'intimacy at a distance'. Television operates in a public sphere, but actually enters our domestic sphere, our homes. It creates an illusion of intimacy or a false

2.3 Model relating modes of address, personalities, audience positioning.

relationship between the addresser on the screen and the addressee (ourselves) at home (*see* Fig. 2.3). Those who emphasize the primacy of textual analysis argue that 'addresser and addressee exist only in texts' (Thwaites et al., 1994). In other words, we read the nature of the presenter and of the audience into the style of the programme, which includes the style of the presenter.

The notion of style also has connotations of language, and is helpful in describing mode of address as being **something like a spoken or written style**, but in this case constructed through all television codes, including visual codes. So the mode of address of a children's programme like *Alive and Kicking* can be defined in terms of the impression it constructs, how it constructs this impression, and how this construct creates a relationship with its audience (in and out of the studio). Its impression, its style, is about fun, humour, energy, but above all, complicity. It addresses the audience in such a way as to suggest that 'we' are all part of this youth world. The presenters' clothes, delivery and jokesy relationship is one element. The constant movement on screen, lively camera work, with a continuous flow of short items is another element. Activity involving the studio audience, not least with pop-music personalities, is another. Phone-ins emphasize the complicity of studio and viewing audience. Mode of address is about all these things. Reference to presenters should draw attention to the fact that **television is much about personalities and talk**. Tolson (1996) refers to the 'pervasive use of direct address in broadcasting'. There is a dangerous tendency to characterize television in simplistic terms, as a straightforwardly visual medium.

Television sound, and above all its talk, should not be underestimated. Robert Allen (1992) talks about television's 'capacity to emulate live performance'. Many programmes depend on talk, and specifically on personalities talking to the audience out of the screen. Chat shows, quiz shows, the news, some documentaries, current-affairs programmes, all involve people talking to us (compères, announcers, hosts), creating an impression and a kind of relationship that is in itself the building of a 'television personality'. These programmes actively encourage responses from both studio audiences and the viewers at home. They seek to give themselves value

MODE OF ADDRESS	AUDIENCE RELATIONSHIP	AUDIENCE ROLE	EXAMPLE
DIRECT	Semi-formal	Aquaintance/client	Consumer-affairs programme
OBJECTIVE	Formal (but equal)	Listener	Documentary
AUTHORITATIVE	Formal/submissive	Learner	News
FAMILIAR	Friendly	Friend	Game show

2.4 Examples of modes of address.

and to characterize themselves by creating a simulated personal relationship with the audience. They move into our private spheres and even private spaces such as the bedroom. Mode of address positions the viewer in relation to the programme and its potential meanings:

> [W]e need to be concerned with the modes in which programmes address us, as audience, and with how these 'modes of address' construct our relation to the content of the programme, requiring us to take up different positions in relation to them. This emphasises the role of television discourse not just in reinforcing pre-established subject positions but rather in actively constructing these viewing positions.
>
> (Morley, 1992)

This positioning influences the audience's understanding of the text. It causes them to adopt a certain role in relation to the text (*see* Fig. 2.4). We 'join in' quiz shows, but we position ourselves as 'learners' for a documentary. If this positioning is taken for granted – naturalized – then it actually stops us questioning how the programme may be influencing us, what it may really be saying. This is analogous to accepting what people 'in authority' say to us simply because they are in authority. To this extent, mode of address may become a vehicle for ideology. Its positioning of the audience/reader helps naturalize the ideological meanings in the programme.

This ties in wth the concept of interpellation proposed by Althusser. It refers to the meanings which are implied through the mode of address, which in this sense exert a power over the audience.

> Through mode of address we take on a subject position or role, but do we have to take on the ideological meanings which come through that address?

TEXTUAL ANALYSIS – IMAGE ANALYSIS; SEMIOTIC ANALYSIS; STRUCTURAL ANALYSIS

Text

The concept of television images and programmes as texts to be read is well established as a critical approach. It is an extension of the process of reading literary texts. But it also co-exists with the emergence of semiotics in the 1960s and structuralism in the 1970s. So one moves on to the question of *how* television texts are to be read – the critical methodology. In a general sense it could be argued that each of the critical approaches discussed in this chapter is also a way of breaking into the text. But historically the concept of text as applied to *any* cultural artefacts has much to do with the unpicking of meanings in images. Texts are seen as coded systems of signs. One needs to make sense of structures or organizing principles behind the texts. So this section will present these three approaches in relation to textual analysis.

One qualification needs to be made. 'Analysis' has connotations of precision: indeed it should be careful and accurate as a process. But it would be dangerous to assume that such analysis yields absolute truths. All the critical approaches in this chapter are valid in their own way. This is not a matter of using a tool to open up the oyster of absolute truth and find the pearl of meaning within.

Indeed Fiske (1991) would emphasize the idea that television texts are ambiguous, that the medium is polysemic (full of many codes and their signs). He describes television as a **producerly text**. He says that it 'delegates the production of meaning to the viewer-producer'. Others would disagree with him, still arguing for the existence of **preferred readings** in television programmes – dominant ways of understanding the programme which are written into the way that it is put together. In fact, Fiske does not reject the workings of dominant ideology within the text and on the audience. But he wants to redress the balance, as it were, and attend to the relative freedom of viewers to make meanings, not least because of the intertextual nature of television – that its meanings depend so often on how one understands references within one programme to various other programmes, in terms of form as much as of content.

Norman Fairclough (1995) draws attention to the text as representing the views and interests of their producers: 'media texts . . . constitute versions of reality in ways which depend on the social positions and interests and objectives of those who produce them'.

Image analysis

On one level the notion of analysing an image is a strange one for television, which is actually about a multiplicity of images resonating off one another, streaming across the screen in what we construct as a visual narrative. On the other hand, the shot is part of visual language. It is something we take in. It is something that we absorb. Some shots may impress themselves on us more than others – such as the iconic image of the old-fashioned English bobby wearing the tall helmet, in the titles sequences from *Heartbeat* on page 74.

One well-established approach to gauging the meanings within, and the possible effects of, images is to distinguish between:

- what makes up the image
- what it may mean
- what helps fix the meanings.

That is, **denotation, connotation, anchorage**.

This approach is predicated on the fact that we tend to concentrate on some aspects of images rather than others, but may in fact unconsciously take in other points and consequent meanings.

So in the example of frame 5 from the *Heartbeat* title sequence one may notice the following elements in terms of denotation: the main frame includes elements such as the rural village backdrop and the grazing sheep in the foreground; the insert frame includes elements such as the helmet badge, the open mouth, the downward gaze. These elements or signs provide connotations such as tranquillity, the country location, the period setting, some issue involving law and order, and so on. Different viewers may privilege different meanings, or emphasize certain connotations. The image is polysemic, and yet it is anchored by the insert image of the police character. It is pretty clear that we have to make sense of the whole image in terms of police work, not for example as some neutral documentary of country life. This is an example of how one reading of an image or text may be preferred above others. It supports the argument that the producer controls meaning by controlling the encoding of the material.

However, another approach to image analysis, which I have proposed elsewhere, looks at three other elements in the search for meaning. These elements are:

1 the positioning of the viewer in relation to the text, through the positioning of the camera in relation to its subject
2 the treatment of the image in terms of devices of form, such as focus, foregrounding, framing, colour
3 the content of the image in terms of what is depicted, how these items are juxtaposed, what symbolic connotations they may have.

All three elements contribute to our constructing meanings from the image. So in the case of the frame referred to above, it matters that we are located within the foreground of the village scene (positioning), and are simultaneously confronted by the half-body shot of the policeman looking at something surprising out of frame. This frame within the frame (form) teases us by denying us information about what it is that the policeman is dealing with. And yet the conjunction of bobby and countryside (content) forces us to take on the unfamiliar location of crime in the countryside, while the title music signals the comfort of more law-abiding times. In this case I would argue that the emphasis on form and technology is helpful.

Semiotic analysis

This approach draws on theories about sign and meaning which were developed by Roland Barthes in particular in the 1960s. In principle, the central concepts of **signifier and signifieds**, together comprising a sign, tie in with **denotation and connotation** (*see* Fig. 2.5). Thus the part of the sign which signals to us – the signifier – is like one of the items described in denotation. This might be a camera pull-in on the face of a male character in a drama. This signifier then has meanings (connotations), some of which we may consciously construct. In the example given, it could be:

(a) a signal to notice expression/reaction
(b) a signal that we are about to go into subjective mode
(c) a signal that the character is about to take action.

Meanings are not specific to signs. The actual signification or chosen meaning is chosen by the viewer.

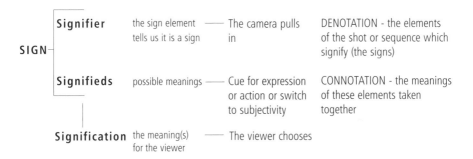

2.5 Signs and meanings in the image: the relationship between sign, denotation and connotation.

The importance of this approach to text is that it draws attention to detail, to signifiers, which one might otherwise miss. This detail enlarges one's sense of what the television text is 'saying' to us. It helps explain how we adduce the meanings that we do. It draws attention to the polysemic, complex nature of television as a medium. In asssociation with what we know about visual perception, it suggests that we may take or make meanings from a text on an unconscious level. In the example of three signifieds above, it would be the case that all these possible meanings are taken in. Indeed the momentary possible uncertainty about which signified should predict the next image and action by the character would be part of the interest, the pleasure, we get from viewing.

The connotations that we may draw from a process of semiotic analysis are also the meanings of ideology, the ways in which we are meant to understand the world. Connotations are also about what Barthes called **myths**. Television is a great producer of these myths if only because of its huge output of material. A recent piece of mythologizing involved the coinciding pregnancies in early 1999 of two members of the female pop group the Spice Girls. Television contributed to a mythology of 'starring motherhood' as a fun experience in which the real practices and experiences of discomfort and of physical change were suppressed.

Codes are another semiotic concept which is relevant here. Codes are coherent systems of signs, made coherent and meaningful by conventions or rules as to how they are used. Television is code-rich as much as it is polysemic or sign-rich. You will come across some variations in the categorizing of these codes. For example, the signs given by use of camera and shot may variously be described as technical codes, camera codes or visual codes. Technical could also apply to sound. Personally I prefer to use the phrase visual code, applied to any of the visual media, and understand it to include all the rhetoric or language of shot, of editing, of other visual signifers such as depth of field. This is analogous with the undisputed codes of speech, writing, non-verbal behaviour. In addition to these you may refer to dress codes (of characters). Anything which seems to have its own coherent 'language' is a code whose signs contribute to the total meaning of the television shot, or sequence, or programme. And the signs resonate off one another, so that the possible meanings from a collection of signs interacting are far more numerous than the meanings obtainable from a single sign (or indeed a single shot).

Structural analysis

Structuralism has travelled alongside semiotics, stemming notably from the work of the French anthropologist Levi-Strauss in the 1960s. It also has a great deal to do with the organization of and the meanings in narratives (*see*

Chapter 5). Lorimer (1994) refers to 'the underlying pattern both of single texts and of genres'.

Two concepts of particular use are those of **binary oppositions** and of the **syntagm**.

A **syntagm** is conceived of as a coherent collection of signs, perhaps from different codes, which form a definite unit – a building block of narrative. We recognize that instinctively when referring to shot, sequence, scene, episode, story. If television has structures within its output, then these represent not only ways of organizing that output, but also ways of organizing our engagement with and understandings of the text.

Oppositions, perhaps most obviously symbolized by opposing protagonists – heroes and villains – are a way of structuring ideas and plot lines. Hope and despair may be opposed in a television drama: our engagement as audience is with the struggle between these two and with the outcome of that struggle. Will there be a happy ending or won't there? Structuralism in isolation is concerned only with the text, not with the producer or the audience. In this respect television output is susceptible to this kind of analysis, yet cannot be understood only through its structures. One also has to recognize that television is a moving target. The structures of one programme are not the structures of another. The structures that one perceives in one part of a programme or within one image from a programme may also change as the images flow on.

DISCOURSE ANALYSIS

This assumes an understanding of and the ability to identify discourses in the first place. The concept, again particularly developed by Louis Althusser in the 1970s, refers to collections of meanings about a given subject. These meanings are generated by the special ways in which we use language about the subject. The language, the meanings, the discourse may also be understood by its difference from other discourses, by its contrast with them. Discourses also have a great deal to do with ideology because their meanings are ideological. 'A discourse is the language used in representing a given social practice from a particular point of view' (Fairclough, 1995).

So, the way that television may 'talk about' women within the discourse of female gender takes an ideological position on women, on their place within society in terms of power or lack of it. The 'social practice' could be in the way that women are treated and expected to behave in a sitcom such as *Men Behaving Badly*. This programme shows the long-suffering girlfriends as having supposedly female attributes of domestic competence or romantic aspirations. This ties in with notions of women being soft, emotional, caring. These attributes are articulated through language used about the females, how they use language themselves, how they behave in given situations. Humour is derived from the fact that the men are not like this. But the ideological outcome of the stories is not to condemn the men for social incompetence, but rather to indirectly endorse their power by condoning the incompetence. 'It's OK because this is what real blokes are like – they're just great boys, aren't they?' But the real blokes aren't punished for their boorishness. And we all know that out there it is men who run the banks, run the hospitals, run the government. Discourse analysis reveals meanings about the dominant ideology and about social inequalities.

The notion of contrast illuminating discourse may also be seen in examples such as the young and the old. You only have to draw up lists of words describing the young and the old (respectively) as generally seen in television–

active	inactive
cool	boring
sharp	senile
technophile	technically incompetent

– and the point is made.

You will also realize that in discussing discourse about types of people, one is also discussing representations. This reinforces my point that concepts and critical approaches interlock and overlap with one another. It is useful to grasp these relationships.

GENRE STUDY

In spite of the fact that some books on television have structured themselves around major television genres, there is a problem with using genre as a critical approach. There is a relative lack of critical writing around the idea of genre. Genres may be seen as being dominated by representations – so why not regard them as a function of representation and its conceptual apparatus? Genre seems to be a descriptive term – to be about typologies – so that once the categorizing has been done there is nothing left to say.

I would disagree with this view. The very fact that so much of television product may be categorized is highly significant in terms of understanding the relationship of the audience with it and the commercial structures which produce it. To this extent, and without wishing to pre-empt the development of ideas in Chapter 4, I would suggest that genre study leads to

- understanding of audience pleasures
- revelation of cultural myths

- understanding of finance and marketing within television institutions
- understanding of intertextuality and postmodernist forms of television.

Indeed in terms of a taxonomy, it could be argued that many key areas of study plus their key concepts are really extensions of an explanation of what genre is about and why it matters.

Genre is most visibly an expression of popular culture, of shared pleasures, of interacting modern media – as opposed to the relatively individual productions and more solitary pleasures of high-culture products: painting, Booker prize novels, modern opera. I am not suggesting that there are no typologies or movements in 'high-culture' material. I am not arguing on the basis of, for example, absolute sales figures for an art novel. Nor am I ignoring the fact that there are industrial production systems behind these products. But it is impossible to ignore the fact that the media with the widest audience reach – and television is pre-eminent among these – are dominated by 'genre-ness'. Nor can one ignore the fact that this audience reach occurred in the twentieth century, was not there previously, and depends on technology (as well as social changes in work, leisure and literacy). It is not useful to study television simply through description of its evolving and intermingling generic forms. Genres have key elements and conventions which produce a formula of some kind for each one. But what matters is what these elements signifiy – what they say about social preoccupations, or about beliefs and values. What matters is how genres transmit and reinforce such values – ideologies – so widely. The meanings are made attractive. It is the interpretation of what one may observe which counts.

So genre study may expose programmes' endorsement of mythologies about material security and happiness. It may lead to understanding of how financing and costs in television relate to a reduction in risk-taking and an increase in both similarity and variation in product. It may elucidate audience pleasures in material which has a tension between predictability and the unexpected, in material which explores social concerns such as divorce and the breakdown of relationships.

The very process of categorizing, of identifying a category of television material, is in itself a cultural statement. The category does not have its label ready-made, waiting for recognition by audience or critic. The category/title is a made thing. We invent a phrase such as Situation Comedy to recognize not so much the similarities between some programmes as the importance of those similarities. So genre criticism needs to attend to the implications of categorizing: that at a given time in history a commentator finds it significant that there are many examples of closed social situations from which humorous social comment is drawn: that the comment is itself significant in respect of what it is able to say about that society.

AUDIENCE STUDY

Studies of audiences for television shifted broadly during the second half of the twentieth century, away from concerns about how the mass audience (or specific audiences such as children) is affected by television. These embrace influence or effects theories – usually malign – and are dominated by interest in sex, violence and politics. The shift was towards an interest in:

- how particular audiences understand television
- what they do with it
- how they construct meanings about the world.

Assumptions about effects on audiences certainly have not gone away. Research into effects is still being carried out by, for example, the Independent Television Commission (ITC) Research Division. Popular convictions remain that television can cause people to be violent or to shift their voting habits. But the formal evidence for this is limited and hedged about with caveats regarding the kind of person influenced and the conditions which affect possible influence.

The broadcasters, mainly through the Broadcasting Audience Research Board (BARB), are active in audience research. This organization conducts continuous research into audience response and programme preferences on behalf of the BBC and of ITV companies. Its agenda is concerned with aspects of audience which are important to television producers, for example:

- How many of what kind of audience are watching at a given time? (This helps construct the television ratings – or TVRs – on which advertising rates are based.)
- What attracts audiences to certain kinds of programmes and programming?
- What do audiences object to in given types of programme?
- How do audiences vary regionally or by gender in terms of what they prefer?
- Are factual programmes regarded as being objective and impartial?

The research is dominated by the interview and questionnaire approach, coupled with selective electronic checks on the broad picture of which programmes or channels are being watched at a given time.

In relation to audience, the idea of 'critical approach' works on two levels:

1 to examine the nature of audiences and their responses to television material as a way of understanding television itself
2 to examine audience behaviour in reading texts in context.

One simple example is in the shift from assumptions about passivity to a view of the audience as actively engaging with material. The 'couch-potato' metaphor dies hard, but in fact viewers are making complicated readings of multiple codes when they sit and watch television. In any case, there is evidence that people don't just sit and watch. They do all sorts of things, from ironing in front of the television to talking about programmes as they are watching them.

A research approach increasingly used in the late 1980s and the 1990s was the ethnographic survey, in which researchers watch television with their sample. They ask open-ended questions to generate discussion about the viewing experience and what goes on around it. This approach coincides with the development of cultural studies, with an interest in popular television material and in the context within which television is understood. The approach is not looking for effects of programmes directly, or institutions indirectly, on the audience. It is interested in the programmes as texts, but again would not regard the text as a collection of given meanings. The text may indeed be inflected. But different audiences will read different texts in different ways at different times. An 'audience-centric' view of television would see meaning as something created in the mind of the viewer by interaction with the programme, and certainly not as something to be plucked whole out of the programme like a sweet out of a packet.

So the concept of audience is not one that can be taken for granted. It is a term that changes its meaning according to the critical perspective taken on audiences. It should no longer be assumed that audience study automatically means effects study (though you will find the two yoked together in Chapter 9). Most of all, approaches to the nature of audiences and to how audiences view are also approaches to what television is, how it is a part of popular culture and how it provokes certain kinds of understanding of social relations.

GENDER STUDIES

Gender studies have been largely synonymous with women's studies, though there is now some work on masculinities. In relation to television this critical approach is in effect an appraisal of existing forms of analysis in terms of the social position of women and of their relative lack of power. Obviously the notion of representations is important in this case.

The use of existing critical tools is exemplified by E. Ann Kaplan's description of feminist modes of criticism in *Channels of Discourse Reassembled* (Kaplan 1992). She identifies Marxist feminism and radical feminism in the 1970s, and post-structuralist feminism in the 1980s, all of them attending variously to structures of power, to assertions of difference and to the power of language to discriminate.

With regard to key concepts relating to television, institutions might be appraised in terms of the dearth of female technicians and executives as well as in terms of the difference that might occur in management and production if something to be defined as a 'female perspective' were given expression.

In relation to television texts, this critical approach is obviously interested in ideological positions on gender incorporated within material (representations again). It is also concerned with the relationship between audience and text, with ways in which women read texts, and with texts which 'appeal' to women.

Laura Mumford (1998) refers to a consensus that television 'plays a significant role in teaching and maintaining the political and social status quo'. This would include a status quo of attitudes towards women's roles, women's status and women's identity – on the part of women themselves, as well as on the part of males. But she also points out that feminist criticism disagrees about just how significant that role of television is – 'how free viewers are to reject or resist television's ideas about gender, sexuality, identity and other issues'. She summarizes criticism as attending to three areas: production, text and audience. But she points out that little criticism takes on all these areas at once, as they relate to one another.

There has been a tendency for feminist criticism to take a negative stance on texts and representations, drawing on pessimistic views of the media as producing negative effects. This is not necessarily justified. Certainly work on the pleasures that women draw from certain kinds of viewing can be seen in a more constructive and positive light, not least because of the extending pervasiveness of soap-opera hybrids among televison genres generally. One tiptoes round the morass of gender clichés in saying that analysis of present television schedules provides evidence of a great number of programmes – drama, genre hybrids, make-over factual programmes, kinds of docusoap, chat shows – all of which are 'sympathetic' to a female audience.

So, if pleasure and identity are key terms in feminist criticism, then it may be observed that there is a lot in television material for women to take pleasure in and to identify with. It is another matter as to whether that pleasure is tainted because the material, for example, reinforces ideas that women's territory is dominated by the home or by the idea of romance. Mumford (1998) refers to this when she talks about programmes which 'inscribe a position for women viewers that evokes the cultural skills associated with femininity'.

Taken further, there is also an argument that programmes which are explicitly made for women are not helpful to the position of women in society precisely because they draw attention to difference, rather than simply providing 'neutral material' which also happens to be accessible to women.

CULTURAL STUDIES

Television is a form of culture, an expression of culture and a medium through which culture is mediated to its audiences. Television texts are cultural artefacts in themselves, ripe for analysis – consider the science fiction sitcom *Red Dwarf*, with its different 'takes' on masculinity. But they also carry and transform cultural activities such as sport, which are not originated by television itself. So television both generates and mediates cultural experience. Thus culture achieves meanings at the point at which the audience interacts with the screen, but in the context of social experiences and relationships which exist outside the screen.

The term cultural studies does not describe a critical method so much as a critical perspective, with particular areas of interest and particular concepts used to make sense of those areas. Cultural studies is interested in:

- **differences and similarities between social groups**, and in what defines these differences. Television provides powerful definitions.
- **the identities of social groups** and how these empower or disempower the group concerned. Television contributes to our understandings of these identities.
- **the way languages are used to construct representations and meanings**. Television, through its multiple codes and languages (visual and verbal) 'talks about' what youth is or what is news is, for example.
- **cultural production**, that is, the creation of popular culture material which appeals to large audiences (though not necessarily what we call a mass audience). Television clearly manufactures popular culture in its programmes. It also recycles culture – in a postmodernist way – in that there are programmes about programmes and programmes about popular culture (e.g. *The Adam and Joe Show*).
- **consumption and commodities**, as described in Marxist terms. In this case it is easy to argue that television contributes to a cultural process in which goods are invested with a value beyond their basic financial worth. Cars are goods sold in adverts. But the television advert may help invest a make of car with a status value that makes it desirable beyond the cost of its function of carrying passengers from one place to another. Similar adverts turn even human relationships into commodities which are consumed – buying the relationship between the man and the woman who feature in a number of car adverts.
- **regulation**, because this shapes production and consumption. The forces which regulate, constrain and control television necessarily influence in what respects the medium is allowed to work on its audience.
- **social practices** which are around and behind the process of consumption. Some television programmes may be about fashion or music, for example,

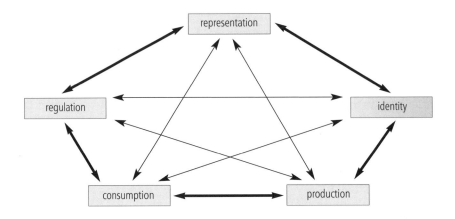

2.6 The circuit of culture – key concepts.
Source: Du Gay et al., 1997

but it is the practices of presentation through clothes in society, or the practices of going to gigs or buying CDs in society, which give a context to those programmes. Other practices of production and marketing are themselves concealed behind the Virgin music megastore or the shopping-mall fashion store (*see* Fig. 2.6).

O'Shaughnessy (1990) links the study of popular culture with the concepts of ideology and especially of **hegemony**. He argues that if ideology is about a dominant view of the world held by powerful groups and projected onto 'the rest', then hegemony is more about how that dominance is maintained. He argues that 'the hegemony or power of the dominant groups can only be maintained through a struggle and tension between dominant and subordinate groups'. Popular culture, especially that expressed through television, may be seen as the culture of subordinate groups. The validation of that culture becomes part of the struggle. What television programmes mean, who controls their meanings, also becomes part of a struggle.

It has to be said that other views of hegemony are less optimistic. They would see it as an invisible exercise of power, a process in which the dominant obtain the consent of the subordinate to their dominant ideas, their control, by subtly proposing those ideas as being 'natural' and acceptable. In this case, television would be a prime means of obtaining consent by stealth. The idea of a 'struggle' becomes more theoretical than real.

Critics like Fiske (1987), on the other hand, would argue for a celebration of popular culture and for a meaningful struggle. Fiske would see the audience as using material produced by ideologically dominant insitutions for their own pleasures and purposes. If you like, this is the argument that the audience is in control as much as the producers.

Some cultural theorists would indeed go so far as to set aside issues raised by ideology and hegemony, arguing that the whole social and cultural situation is too complicated to be seen in terms of class struggle. Yet it is difficult simply to ignore issues raised by the ideas within ideology and hegemony. It is quite clear that there are disparities of power within society, and that television reproduces these but also sometimes challenges them.

The issue may be set in the context of sport on television. From one point of view this endorses ideas about 'winning at all costs', 'individualism is good', 'cultural chauvinism is OK' in support of your team and so on, not to mention validating consumption (of programmes) as a form of cultural activity. Behind all this are the enormous sums of money paid by and accrued to television through advertising and sponsorship – capitalism in full flower. But from another point of view, television sport is the stuff of popular culture. It is a response to the 'demands' of the people. It encourages shared pleasures, shared experiences. It encourages live sport as a social activity. It validates the increased leisure time that working people have 'won'. Its pervasiveness is a sign of the power of people to demand what they want, and implicitly a sign of the lack of power of institutions to impose what people don't want.

POSTMODERNISM

This is also not so much a formal method of critical analysis, with propositions to be tested, as a critical approach to media material. It is very much tied in with cultural studies. This approach will emphasize certain features of television above others. A postmodernist is also a cultural critic, more interested in the popular text and how it works for the audience than in grand theories about media and society.

Postmodernism is sometimes defined in opposition to modernism, and these two terms are themselves described in terms of Fordism and post-Fordism. The point here is that the modernist structured world of the Ford production line, cranked up in the 1930s, is a world of mass production and of mass consumption. The post-Fordist world is one of niche markets, market research, of variety for a variety of consumers. This metaphor works for television in its state of development at the beginning of the twenty-first century. There is a multiplicity of channels and of audiences. The 'take-it-or-leave-it' world of the 1960s, with two channels and limited viewing time, has gone. Broadcasting has turned to narrowcasting. Broadcasters desperately seek viewers. Programmes feed off one another. Channels proliferate.

Postmodernism is not uninterested in ideas about the power of the text, but would understand this to be constructed through the use of language. Hence discourse is a key term: meanings produced through particular uses of language. The postmodernist approach understands texts in relation to one another – intertextuality – indeed celebrates the pleasures that television audiences may get from picking up references in one programme to other programmes and other media. Postmodernist criticism is more interested in form, in how the medium is used – again, how the codes are used. So in respect of television this approach would look at how the medium is used in a given programme, rather than being concerned with programme structures or even with institutions and their exercise of power. In respect of form, structured views of realism and of a social reality separated from television reality are suspended as being meaningless – because actually, it is argued, the experience of television is as real as life experience. For example, what the news tells us is reality as far as we are concerned.

> How would the emphases in a postmodernist analysis of a television programme differ from those in a feminist analysis?

3

Institutions and Power: the British Television Industries

PREVIEW

This chapter deals with:
- which institutions run British television production and distribution
- the characteristics of the institutions and of their operations
- different systems for bringing television into homes
- public-service broadcasting and related issues
- the place of government and the ITC
- questions about the power of television and its institutions.

DOMINANT INSTITUTIONS: THE BALANCE OF POWER

In the first place, a few facts are in order. In terms of programmes and production, the phrase 'British television' covers a huge range of organizations which fall into the following categories.

Small independent commercial production companies such as Tiger Aspect or Hat Trick Productions specialize in a small range of programmes which they sell to the dominant distributors of commercial and BBC television. Examples of programmes would be *Whose Line Is It Anyway?* (Hat Trick), *Birds of a Feather*, *Goodnight, Sweetheart* (SelecTV), *Poirot*, *Bugs* (Carnival Productions).

The BBC itself makes and distributes programmes through its two main terrestrial channels, BBC2 having a minority programming policy. The BBC takes in about 25 per cent of independent productions (compelled by the 1990 Broadcasting Act). It runs its own network of transmitters. It runs BBC Worldwide, one of whose divisions sells programmes to other countries, another of which licenses and sells spin-offs from programmes. It also co-owns UKTV (in partnership with Flextech), including for example UKGold, a satellite channel devoted to re-runs of BBC's back catalogue. It is in partnership with the US Discovery Channel, distributing factual programmes, and runs BBC America. It also runs the teletext service known as Ceefax.

The BBC is administered by a board of governors, who are appointed by the home secretary. It is run by a director general, answerable to the governors, also a government appointee. It is funded by a licence fee, payable every year by any home with a television set. This fee is set by parliament but is collected and administered by the BBC itself. In these respects the BBC is an independent public body but is answerable to government and is expected to operate in the marketplace.

Large independent regional commercial production companies, known collectively as **ITV** (channel 3), also buy in programmes for screening from other countries. They are also compelled to buy at least 25 per cent of independent product.

The smallest of these 15 companies, such as Border Television or Channel Television, are relatively poor, and are dominated by the big three. These are:

1 **Granada Television** which covers the big cities in the northwest of England and has the London Weekend Television contract. It also controls Yorkshire and Tyne Tees Television in the northeast. It is now bidding for the Scottish Media Group (Grampian Television and Scottish Television), which covers the whole of Scotland. The SMG also owns 18 per cent of Ulster Television in Northern Ireland.
2 **Carlton Television** which owns Central Television covering the Midlands and has the London weekday contract (Carlton Television). Carlton also owns Westcountry Television, Good Morning Television (GMTV) and like the others has a stake in ITN, the news producer, as well as Ondigital, the new commercial digital channel.
3 **United News and Media** which owns Meridian Television (south) (also owned 20 per cent by Carlton), HTV in the west and Wales, and Anglia Television in the east. Carlton and UNM agreed a merger in September 1999 (Carlton 52 per cent, UNM 48 per cent) which would create Britain's biggest media group, worth £7.86 billion. However, it is likely that the government will demand some selling off of other interests before agreeing to such a monopolistic move.

The huge income of the big companies, mainly from advertising but also from sponsorship, sales and spin-offs, means that they dominate the programmes on offer, and effectively determine what the schedules are: what goes out and when. This dominance is formalized through **ITV Network Centre**, set up in 1993 by the ITV companies to coordinate:

- commissioning new programmes
- purchasing programmes
- scheduling programmes.

C3 is obliged by contract to produce or commission at least 65 per cent of its programmes. C3, C4 and C5 all have to produce at least 25 per cent of independent programmes, including repeats.

The Independent Television Commission, which is a non-commercial organization set up by the government (but independent of it) to oversee the operations of the commercial companies. It views and vets all nationally screened advertising. It operates codes of practice for advertising and other areas of ITV broadcasting; these codes in effect control programming quality (see also Chapter 10 on regulation and censorship). In case of any doubts on the part of the contractors, the ITC has to be consulted over programmes and programming in general, though it does not formally vet programmes before transmission. This is in the light of the fact that it issues contracts to the companies to produce programmes. These contracts include clauses designed to enforce a range of programmes, especially those for regional communities, for minority interests and covering factual matters. Foreign imports are limited to up to 25 per cent of output.

The ITC is paid for by a levy on the commercial companies, scaled in relation to their income. It monitors programmes and complaints, and may impose sanctions on 'offending' licensees or producers by:

- requiring an on-screen apology
- imposing financial penalties
- revoking licences to broadcast.

Questions of taste and decency represent the majority of complaints (which are still relatively small in number). In 1997 the ITC made four interventions over questions of 'bad language' in programmes, and gave warnings to the producers concerned. The greatest number of complaints in 1997 (30) were about matters of 'racial offence', though most were not upheld.

The ITC has a Cable & Satellite Division which regulates those services, licenses local delivery (cable) and licenses satellite broadcasting. It also has codes regulating teletext on commercial television, which is run by a separate company.

The ITC is run by a board of governors, half of whom are appointed by the home secretary.

The transmitters which broadcast ITV programmes used to be owned and run by the ITC but since 1990 have been run by a private company called National Transcommunications Limited. However, this network is still paid for by levies on the commercial contractors, and is still effectively a client of the ITC.

Teletext Ltd (fomerly Oracle) runs the teletext service for C3 and C4. It is owned by the Daily Mail and General Trust media conglomerate.

Independent Television News is a separate non-profitmaking yet commercial organization set up to feed news and some documentaries to ITV companies, including Big Breakfast News, Channel 4 and Channel 5, as well as producing specialist news services such as one for world airlines. Again, it is funded pro rata by the commercial companies. News is also a legally required part of commercial output, defined by the statute which enabled commercial broadcasting (1953) and by the contracts issued through the ITC.

GMTV is a commercial organization given the contract to operate the early morning slot on the ITV1 channel. Its dominant shareholders are Granada and Carlton.

Channel 4 (1982) is a commercial organization set up to produce minority programming, for example in specialist sport or the arts. Most of its programmes are bought in. In a sense it is a commercial parallel to BBC2. Under the directorship of Michael Grade (1988–96) it achieved considerable success in attracting profitable audiences, to the point where some said that it had become 'too commercial'. This change was forced though by the 1990 Broadcasting Act, which legally recast C4 as a public corporation but one which had to be self-sufficient on its own advertising. Previously it had been protected by receiving income from the main ITV companies and had existed as a company owned by the then Independent Broadcasting Authority (IBA). Now it is out on its own.

Channel 4 is obliged to provide 'a service which contains a suitable proportion of material calculated to appeal to tastes and interests not generally catered for by C3' (ITC web page, December 1999).

Channel 5(1998) is a commercial organization set up to introduce more competition into the mainstream commercial sector. It is owned by a consortium of media companies – Pearson, UNM, CLT (Luxembourg). As yet it is not very profitable or successful in terms of audience reach (4.6 per cent). Its programming is necessarily cheap and populist in a quirky fashion – *The Pepsi Chart Show*, *Sex and Shopping*. It is hard to programme competitively on a budget of £110 million.

Satellite television is Sky Broadcasting (BSkyB), run by Rupert Murdoch's Newscorp (though it has only 40 per cent of the shares). A further 25 per cent of shares are owned by the multi-national media and tele-communications business Vivendi. BSB is picked up either directly by dish or via cable links operated by other providers. It offers a range of subsidiary channels under licence, such as MTV, as well as its own Sky Sport, for example. It has been particularly successful in buying up the rights to major sports and sports events, and so getting a larger share of the audience. It dominates the subscription television market, gathering 79 per cent of these revenues.

BSB is continually seeking ways to expand its market share – for example, it has a deal with the German Kirsch media group through which BSB owns a share of the European Premiere channel. BSB has also done a deal with the youth channel Rapture, which will let that channel move from weekends only to full weekly broadcasting, with access to 6 million homes. Rapture's content is dominated by clubbing, gaming, movies and fashion.

Cable television: there are other channels available through area cable providers such as Telewest. These include European channels from countries such as France and Germany.

Cable has a curious history. The first experiments with cable took place in the 1960s and 1970s, with companies such as Rediffusion licensed to operate in specific cities such as Bristol. The idea was that they would generate community programming as well as carry the national channels. It didn't work. There wasn't the money, the will or the means of recovering costs to justify a commercial company seriously investing in local cable television.

Cable was relaunched in 1984 by a Cable and Broadcasting Act. It was overseen by a Cable Authority. This time companies were allowed to carry more than domestic material, so a fair amount of US product was imported. It was clear that government would let more or less anything happen in order to encourage commercial investment, but there was at least the intention of providing urban or local television.

Even this condition was abandoned in the 1990 Broadcasting Act. What is more, there are no longer restrictions on ownership, so American companies like Nynex have moved in and grabbed large slices of what was and is a limited market. What success cable has had is on the back of the wiring of Britain in the 1990s with optic cable. Customers could buy in pefect reception of existing channels, even satellite, without the inconvenience of having a dish. Only about a fifth of British cable operators offer any programming of their own, and this is limited. The further intention of creating an information revolution and allowing services such as interactive shopping (QVC, shopping channel) through the same cable systems has also, largely, not been fulfilled. Cable has in effect fragmented the market still further, generally seeking upmarket customers for its special channels and services.

The other dominant cable operator is Flextech, which is mainly owned by the American cable and telecommunications giant AT&T. Flextech owns the channels Living, Bravo, Challenge and Trouble. It co-owns UKTV with the BBC, which comprises the channels Style, Horizon, Gold, Arena and Play. It manages the Discovery Channel in Britain (also in a merger with the BBC), plus Discovery Home and Leisure.

Nynex (NTL) is at the time of writing trying to merge with Cable and Wireless, another huge telecommunications distribution and cable production company. So in this area, as in others, television is dominated by fewer and fewer global players.

Government: on the face of it the British government has nothing to do with the institutions of the television industry. But if you have picked up my comments above it is clear that government does play a part in deciding who broadcasts what to whom and when. Indeed, it could be said that government holds the real aces. It licenses the right to broadcast in the first place, under Wireless and Telegraphy Acts passed by parliament, through the charter which set up the BBC and through the statutes which set up all the institutions of commercial television. It appoints most of those at the top of the BBC and ITC organizations, and the BBC and commercial television still have 75 per cent of the UK audience. It created the Broadcasting Standards Council (1989), of whose judgements on the quality of product the industry has to take account.

More will be said about the relationship between government and television in Chapter 10. But any comment on power has to take account of the legal and political influence of government and parliament.

The lightest touch of government is on satellite television – mainly Sky. It does fall within the remit of the ITC, but does not have a record of attracting adverse critical attention. This is for a number of possible reasons: its programming is generally uncontroversial in most respects, including that of taste, it has been regarded as marginal because of its small audience; it is technically difficult to control because channels and material are sourced outside the UK. Programming and advertising on satellite are not vetted in the same way as for ground broadcast commercial companies.

But it may be argued that the power of satellite television should not be underestimated. The audience is growing and very profitable. The new digital providers are offering satellite channels as a matter of course. Satellite has to be looked at in a global context – the influence of CNN 24-hour news on our perceptions of the 1991 Gulf War is a prime example of this. Critical examination of the nature of power and influence appears elsewhere in this book. But if one summarizes this as the ability to reach audiences and potentially to shape their view of the world through television material, then satellite is becoming a major player, particularly in its monopoly of some sports.

Concern about power and its balance is in terms both of control of institutions and of their ability to influence the making of meanings for the audience. The notion of balance applies to the relationship between those who produce programmes, those who distribute them and those who in various ways may allow or disallow this making and distribution. There is a kind of balance, or tension, between government and the industry.

There is also competition for power within the industry. There has been a shift in production power from monolithic big producers to a range of smaller providers, fuelled by government demands for a percentage of independently produced programming. There has been a diluting of the power of the traditional commercial and BBC organizations, with the arrival of new channels and of satellite.

These changes have also brought about a power shift analogous to the changes in Hollywood in the 1950s and 1960s: a loss of power over production, but an enhancement of power over finance and distribution. The new channels are as much distributors as originators of material. Television becomes increasingly a game of looking out for audiences, of trying to establish channel image, of finding niche markets.

> Does the British television system of ownership fit a pluralist model of media, or not?

CHARACTERISTICS OF OWNERSHIP

So the notion of 'ownership' of British television is complicated by the range of players, by the non-commercial model of the BBC and by the point that 'owning' distribution is as important as owning means of production of programmes. Having said this, and having seen changes which may become greater in the future, it is still the case that the BBC and major commercial companies dominate viewing and audiences. It is also true that even the newer players fall in with certain patterns of ownership.

Conglomeration: television companies tend to extend the scope of their ownership in order to give themselves a more secure position in a competitive marketplace – see the example of Carlton above (p. 42). Even the BBC is in partnership with commercial companies, so offering specialist subscription channels such as UK Arena (Arts) – part of UKTV. By the same token, where institutions are themselves owned by conglomerates (bigger corporations or groups of companies), then they are an example of these corporations following the path of strength through acquisition.

This achievement of industrial and financial power clearly has implications for control of the television market: fewer people control more. Nor should one forget the huge technical infrastructure behind television. The people who make the equipment, the optic-fibre cables, who launch the satellites, are also conglomerates such as Cable and Wireless, and are also in this sense part of the television industry (though as far as people like AT&T are concerned, television is but one aspect of their telecommunications business).

Vertical integration describes the control of all aspects of the business of a company from sourcing of materials through to customer consumption. Some would argue that this notion of total control is part of a modernist age of big manufacturing companies with production lines. It may not apply so much to service industries such as television. Certainly, even the monolith of the BBC has been broken up with 'producer choice'. And yet if British television is not about total ownership, it is about an attempt to achieve integration of control. Small producers – like manufacturers of car parts – don't have much choice about whom they sell to. Those who pay for programmes and who own the channels call the tune. Sky can access the parent company's material from Fox Television and Twentieth Century Fox. It runs its own news channels. It has bought up the right to sports such as premier-league football. This is integration. I would argue that **modern vertical integration is about control** of the business, not necessarily about outright ownership of every aspect of it.

Multinationalism: this in effect follows from the above. Co-production deals with channels in other countries are now commonplace, where they were unusual before about 1980.

The maintenance of television's institutions depends, like other industries, on their going global. This is the only way that they can maintain the financial resources, the access to a range of product, the appeal to paying audiences, which enable them to stay in business. Governments are unwilling for economic reasons (and partly unable for technical reasons) to block international growth of the telecommunications industries. Once that growth has taken place, and one company gets an edge in terms of size, breadth of base, strength of cash flow, degree of control, then others have to follow.

Cross-media ownership is of a piece with the previous three points. The media feed off one another: television news editors read the newspapers first thing in the morning; radio programmes such as *Have I Got News For You* are filched by television; classic novels are adapted for television and in turn help to sell the original; there are programmes which showcase films and pop music. So another characteristic of television is its buying into other media industries, limited mainly by government rules on the proportion of cross-media ownership allowed. The Tory government actually amended the 1990 broadcasting act in 1993 to allow more cross-media ownership – an ITV company can own two franchises and up to 20 per cent of a third one. From a commercial perspective it makes sense for a television organization to have a stake in other television companies and other media. It enhances power and security.

Horizontal integration would be a variation of the above, in which a company concentrated on buying into one of the media as its main business activity. Globalization and the convergence of media industries works against this kind of specialisation in broadcasting.

These characteristics of ownership are exactly the same in principle for television as for other industries, which supports a view that television is no different from any other business. It may feel different because it is located within our homes and so has a personal place in our lives. It occupies a considerable portion of people's leisure time. It has some connotations of creativity which seem to set it apart from, say, motor manufacture or the holiday industry. Yet, as with those industries, its power lies in the extension of its financial base and in the scope of its control.

FINANCE AND THE PRODUCTION BASE

About 20 per cent of programmes shown on television in the UK are not made in Britain but are bought in from other countries, mainly the USA. The British production base has been diffused to some extent among independents. These tend to specialize in certain niche markets or categories, such as documentary. Even those programmes made by the big players may contain the work of freelance camera operators or small editing outfits. Co-productions such as *Walking with Dinosaurs* (BBC/Discovery/Television Asahi with Prosieben and France 3) are common, where costs are high and potential foreign sales are good. Whatever the source, high costs will mean that a programme will be tailored to an international market. Three or four companies make the majority of British original commercial television output, not least when measured in terms of money spent.

The BBC is still a major producer. But in the 1980s a huge shake-up in the organization not only got rid of many permanent staff but also brought in **producer choice**. This gave producers – those who manage the making of programmes and who often initiate and get ideas for programmes approved – the choice of using BBC staff or not. If you can get freelance staff from outside to do the job as well and cheaper, then you can use them. In effect this puts the BBC in a production marketplace. It has become more cost-efficient, but it has lost a protected freedom to be original. It is argued that while these changes have brought in fresh ideas from small companies, they have undermined the ability of British television to take risks with original work, especially drama, where the costs are high.

Costs are one part of the financial equation; income is the other. It is possible to buy in programmes at anything from £40 000 to £80 000 an hour on average. But then it is hard to make quality drama for much less than £230 000 an hour. Cheap local cable programming can cost as little as £2000 an hour, but then quality documentary will cost £100 000 upwards. Television isn't cheap. Even the arrival of increased competition and the increase in numbers of young freelance workers hungry for experience cannot change this significantly.

Income for the BBC and ITV is dominated by the licence fee and by advertising rates, respectively. Increases in the licence fee have lagged behind the rate of inflation for many years now, and the BBC is hard-pressed to maintain its promises of quality in all areas at the same time as funding innovations such as its own 24-hour news service and a digital service. Even

ITV, with a greater income, is under pressure from the competition of channels 4 and 5 and Sky. It has also suffered from competition within advertising, where television – though still popular and profitable to ITV – is not the golden medium that it once was. Niche markets have made a medium of mass distribution look less interesting, compared with, say, the young audience for independent local radio or the cheapness of hoardings and buses for the urban market. So television is having to achieve more with its income – £2.8 billion (inc. Worldwide) for the BBC in 1997/8; £4.7 billion for all ITV in 1997 (four-fifths of which accrued to C3, C4, C5).

POWER OF DISTRIBUTION

In support of points already made, it should be said that television should not be seen simply in terms of its programmes and of their manufacture. Advances in technology have changed the ability of institutions to get programmes to audiences as much as changing the way that those programmes are made – cable, satellite, video cassettes, and now the digital encoding and distribution of television material. The importance of control of the means of distribution was recognized when in 1953 the government gave the ITC the power over transmitters, to counter the power of the programme generators. The deal between the BBC and Discovery in 1998 was important to both for the access it gave each business to means of distributing their material, as much as for access to the material itself.

Similarly, I would argue that the arrival of new channels in the 1990s is of significance in terms of choice of distribution to various audiences. It does not signal a flood of new production. Indeed, if anything, the 1990s were characterized by caution in big-budget production but the expansion of low-budget production, from chat shows to docusoaps. The base market, the mass market, was accessed and saturated by the early 1970s. Expansion since then has been in terms of specialist audiences: late-night viewers, youth audiences, sports audiences, film audiences. Indeed the satellite channels by genre are a good indicator of the nature of this expansion, and of the importance of finding new means of distribution for getting to these audiences. It is significant that as new channels opened up in the 1990s, so did the BBC (and to a lesser extent ITV) share of viewers go down. There is increased competition, but through targeted distribution.

COMMERCIAL INTERESTS – PUBLIC-SERVICE BROADCASTING

In Britain until the 1980s there was a pretty clear distinction between the notion of commercial television represented by ITV contracting companies and funded by advertising revenue, and public-service television represented by BBC1 and BBC2 and funded by a universal licence fee. The situation was describe as a duopoly. The arrival of C4 (S4C in Wales) changed that.

Until the 1970s the BBC was well established as the model for PSB because of the 'neutrality' of its income base, because of its programming (not least the specialist programmes on BBC2), but most of all because it had cultivated an image of serving the public. This image was based on policies implemented by the first director general of the BBC, Sir John Reith, in his period of office from 1927 to 1936. In essence, he supported broadcasting that maintained standards of good taste and which served to bring a range of good culture, decent entertainment and educative purpose to its public. He saw himself as a guardian of taste and of culture. This view later gave rise to the soubriquet 'Aunty BBC' precisely because the corporation took on a role of protectiveness and well-meaningness, in which the notion of 'we know what is good for you' was clearly implied. This position now seems unspeakably condescending and paternalistic. At the time it accorded well with the classist nature of society and with well-intentioned notions of how one should serve the public and one's country.

Reith is quoted in *Media Cultures* (1992) thus: 'It is occasionally indicated to us that we are apparently setting out to give the public what we think they need, and not what they want, but few know what they want, and very few what they need.'

Graham Murdock (1992) refers to four key roles played by public broadcasting in its classic form:

1 to provide a public forum for political parties and for legitimated interest groups
2 to act as a source of surveillance and feedback for those in power, regarding public thinking
3 to help cement a bond between notions of citizenship and dominant definitions of nation and culture
4 to redraw the line between public and private spheres, bringing participation and 'public events' into the home.

I would suggest that these descriptions are still part of current thinking about PSB, not least on the part of politicians. This thinking explains why PSB survives pressure from proponents of market forces and the arrival of multi-channel television.

By the 1970s society had changed significantly in its structure, and the idea of what one would call high culture being the benchmark for cultural validity was seriously challenged. ITV had been going for 20 years, had half the audience, and its programmes were well established as forms of popular culture. Driven by competition, BBC1 (indeed BBC radio) had changed as well. By any kind of measurement television had replaced cinema as the dominant populist medium. By the end of the decade a Tory government was in power, committed to materialism and capitalism and the primacy of the market. The market would profit from giving people what they wanted. What they wanted on television was comedy, genre drama, quiz shows and the like.

The debate about what constituted public-service broadcasting was not dominated by the view that one served the public by giving them anything that they wanted – even blood and circuses. But the assumption that the BBC had got it right or was a definitive model was challenged. Government didn't want to rubber stamp rises in the licence fee; it wanted 'value for money' (however one defines that). Commercial interests wanted to challenge the position of the BBC. Critics challenged it intellectually, arguing that the sourcing of income alone did not guarantee public service. There were bigger questions of who was being served and how – for example, ethnic minorities. There were questions about what was being done with the money. It was also the case that, whatever some adverse arguments about its policies and contracting decisions, the ITC (then the IBA) was at least as successful as the BBC in preserving programme 'standards'. An example of this might be the drama series *The Jewel in the Crown*, produced by Granada in 1984. It was a classic story, adapted from a novel, of life in the days of the British Raj. Audience research showed that many people assumed it was a BBC production because it was high-quality 'costume drama', period stuff, superbly acted and directed.

So came C4 (1982) and a fair model of how to achieve public service with commercial cash. The Annan Committee report on broadcasting (1977) had conceptualized a new channel that would would act like a publishing house for new material. Ironically, it was this same report which privileged the BBC, describing it as 'the most important single cultural institution in the nation'. This was not the way that the Thatcher government felt about the BBC. They wanted commercial underpinnings and a public-service superstructure. The new Channel 4 got off the ground because the government in effect told the rich ITV companies that they were going to pay for it until it could manage on its own advertising revenue. It produced an imaginative range of minority pro-gramming because it was legally forced to look to small providers – indeed these appeared because they had a new market. It supported new British film as a matter of policy and of economic good sense. Its in-depth news at 7.00 p.m. achieved such a reputation for impartiality that miners in the infamous 'battles' with the police over closure of the Midlands coal fields (1983) would in the end only let in C4 crews – the rest were seen (textual analysis would support this; see Philo, 1990) as generally supporting the government line. The act which brought C4 into being directs it towards minority interests and away from seeking mass audiences.

It would show complacency to overstate the good qualities of one television channel. Debates about, for example, public access to, and a voice in, television have not yet been answered effectively. But C4 did prove that there was another way to skin the cat. Just as the licence fee could not of itself cause the BBC to recognize a changing public, even to question the idea of public service, so too commercial funding is of itself not necessarily a bad thing if the money is compelled to be spent in the public interest.

In one sense commercial interests prevailed in the 1990s, as Sky moved into big profits and the 1991 Broadcasting Act loosened restrictions, allowed takeovers, enabled C5 and opened up satellite and cable. These new broadcasting institutions would argue that they do supply a public service because if they are successful then they must be giving the public what they want. However, the counter-argument is that they are not giving the public a real choice and that anyway the public don't know what they want because they haven't seen it – nor are they likely to in an environment where accountants play safe with 'more of the same'. Public service, by this argument, includes taking risks and making mistakes. There is also the important point that commercial interests – television funded by advertising – must please the advertisers. There are a lot of people out there, however one categorizes them, who don't have much disposable income and so are not of interest to advertisers.

Public service, it may be said, involves serving all the public, not just those who make money. Some of the public live in remote rural areas, hence the original requirement that ITV had to transmit everywhere and could not cherrypick urban areas. The public are sometimes old, and so might have a conservative idea of what television should be like. Some of the public are Asian and might like to hear some programmes in their own languages. For public-service broadcasting to be true to its ideal it must employ a broad, inclusive concept of the public as well as an appropriate concept of service.

The expansion of channels in the 1990s has then not silenced the debate about public service. Nor has the debate about the future of the BBC been resolved. Would its programming policies necessarily be compromised if it did take some advertising revenue or sponsorship? If its share of the audience continues to fall, at what point may government or audience say it is no longer reasonable for everyone to pay the licence fee when only 35 per cent of viewers actually watch the BBC?

It seems people feel that public service is a good thing, but they cannot always define it. PSB has been defined in terms of an opposition to commercial television, but this is too simplistic a model. For example, the BBC did a deal with Sky in 1995 over the rights to screen the then premier football league matches, including highlights. However, the growing strength of the new commercial television providers is such that some definition of public service will have to be agreed and 'enforced' if a range of programmes is to be preserved, if experimentation is to continue, and if unprofitable minority audiences are to be provided for.

Karen Siune and Olof Hullen (1998) have defined PSB in these terms:

- having some form of accountability to the public
- supported by some element of public finance
- being closely regulated
- providing a universal service – for an audience seen as citizens rather than as consumers
- having regulated entrance, so that the number of competing PSB channels is controlled.

James Curran (in Curran and Liebes, 1998) largely dismisses concerns over the survival of public broadcasting. He recognizes concerns as represented in the writing of Katz – 'the public is being dispersed and fragmented by the multiplication of channels' (Curran and Liebes 1998) – but is sceptical about the impact of channel choice, not least in Britain. He points out that the BBC and ITV channels still have two-thirds of total viewing hours (BARB, 1996). He argues that the evidence is that most people are not willing to pay for new channels, given what is on offer for free and from the licence fee.

Pressures on PSB and the BBC are identified as follows:

- there is no longer a problem of scarce airwave frequencies
- the BBC is no longer seen as a manifestation of a benign state
- there has been an erosion of the coherent social and cultural values which have underpinned PSB
- pluralism in society undermines coherent definitions of 'quality' or of 'good broadcasting'.

Even so, PSB television remains largely intact, not least in C4 – 'an imaginative way of reinterpreting the public service tradition' (Curran and Liebes 1998). People still see PSB as being independent and trustworthy. It still gives a range of views on public affairs. It offers a cheap and reliable way of fostering cultural continuity and innovation.

> What are the arguments for and against protecting the BBC as a haven for PSB in Britain?

REGIONAL TELEVISION

In Britain this has been a concept more honoured in the intention than in the action. In terms of the BBC, regionalism exists in BBC Scotland, Wales and Northern Ireland, matched by commercial equivalents in companies such as S4C (part of Channel 4), HTV Wales, Grampian Television. The BBC also has regional centres in places like Bristol, Birmingham and Manchester. The BBC spends about one-third of its programme budget in the regions. The regions have their own news and magazine programmes. They also specialize in certain types of production – the crime series *Taggart* is a popular example from Scotland. Even so, one cannot say that programming offers a strong local identity.

This is even less the case with ITV, where the regional system of companies was in many cases a commercial convenience as much as a recognition of real cultural boundaries and coherence. In any case, the freedom of ownership has created larger providers who have no great commercial interest in the regions. Ironically in the light of this, all ITV companies have, since 1990, a legal obligation to provide regional programming. They do this in varying degrees, commonly through, for example, local arts programmes, documentaries about regional centres and issues. But prime-time television comes from ITV Centre.

There is no regional television as a full-time choice for viewers in the regions of Britain. This in no way damns the quality of what is provided. But the pull of London as the cultural centre and the basis of financing television makes it difficult to go regional when the logic is in big audiences, economies of scale and profitability.

CHANNEL IDENTITY AND PROGRAMMING

Television channels only have identities in broad brushstrokes, considering the huge numbers of people they wish to appeal to. Five million is a respectable but fairly small audience for a television programme. Yet even the best-selling newspaper in Britain (the *Sun*) only manages about 4 million copies a day. Identity is also circumscribed by factors such as contracts which require a range of programmes. On satellite it is easy to identify Film Four as a fairly upmarket film viewers' channel. But in terrestrial television one talks in more general terms about the high-culture profile of BBC2 and to some extent Channel 4. C4 has some distinction for promoting gay programmes over the years, and especially for its funding of British films (with prior distribution on 4) now running at about 4 million a year. Channel 5 has been struggling with an identity problem, trying to appeal to a younger age group with incomes attractive to advertisers. The problem has been not having the income to buy programme quality, and trying to promote a range of programmes with that audience appeal over many hours. Identity is relatively easy if it is by genre, as with Sky Sport. It is even more manageable if it is by region – say, the distinctive Welsh language and content for S4C, HTV Wales and BBC Wales. But the scale of output and of audience reach for a separate channel can give it problems in achieving an identity in the minds of the audience.

In the end it is programming which helps create identity and perhaps develops an appeal to at least similar types of audiences. Programming is about the policy behind programme acquisition and production, while scheduling is about the reasons for the timing of particular programmes. Programming has to do with the purchase and commissioning of television material. For example, the BBC has nurtured a strong base of wildlife documentary production in the west of England (some freelance). It maintains a reputation for excellence in this kind of programming, both appealing to a certain kind of audience (around the world), and contributing to the public image of what the BBC channels are like. Its two-part adaptation of *Great Expectations* (BBC2) is a similar example of maintaining a tradition and an identity that includes the notion of 'good-quality' programmes, of 'cultural excellence'.

SCHEDULING AND COMPETITION FOR THE AUDIENCE

Scheduling is more directly competitive activity, in which channels try to maximize appeal to certain audiences at certain times. They also try to take and hold as large a share of their target audience as possible. Saturday-afternoon sport is an example of such scheduling and competition – the attempt to have the most attractive sport covered in the most appealing manner. Saturday afternoon is a culturally traditional time for sporting activities, although other slots such as Wednesday-evening football have emerged.

Scheduling as competition is in any case modified by the fact that channels have varying obligations to provide programmes of specialist interest, for example for children. Also, the BBC is as much concerned with its overall audience share – trying to hold it up to 40 per cent – as it is worried about individual programmes' viewing figures. Until the aggressive purchasing policy of Sky, both ITV and BBC were inclined unofficially to ease off competition, especially about control of sporting fixtures.

Scheduling is television's response to the rhythms of our culture. From 4 p.m. to 7 p.m. is 'come-home-from-school time'. It is full of programmes for the teenage (and sub-teenage) audience, from *Neighbours* to *The Fresh Prince of Bel Air*. Lunchtime is chill-out time for housewives, some students, some unemployed, all those who will be available and attracted to the baroque revelations of sexual misconduct on *The Jerry Springer Show*. Nine o'clock is 'watershed' time, as agreed by the government and the television powers that be – when all good children are supposed to go to bed so that their parents can enjoy sex and violence without embarrassment. Saturday morning is chill-out time for the kids, when they can watch hours of 'their' television and the parents can have a lie-in and generally not be bothered. Christmas is film-blitz time, when the audience is meant to be inert from overeating and keen to enjoy the pleasures of domestic relaxation. Television colludes in these cultural myths or clichés.

Scheduling aims to enhance the idea of cultural rhythms, of viewing patterns. In 1967 it used to be *Sunday Night at the Palladium*, now Sunday evening is drama-episode time, but still with the intention of getting the audience to make a regular commitment to viewing, to fall into patterns which endorse the domestic familiarity of television viewing. This is about continuity. The timing of cult series like *The X Files* is crucial to scheduling and to legitimating television viewing as an accepted cultural activity. The longevity of some programmes, such as *Coronation Street* or *Panorama*, is a confirmation of deeply conservative tendencies in our culture and of the ability of television to provide a sense of security supportive of that conservatism.

The problem here is that even when viewing figures are consistent, research shows that the audience for a series shifts from week to week. Also people have other leisure activities to pursue – which is why Saturday in particular is a bad time for schedulers, and they don't waste their 'best programmes' on an audience that may well be out anyway. Scheduling is as much an attempt to stabilize audience behaviour as a truthful recognition of that behaviour. It is an attempt to naturalize television viewing as cultural pursuit. It is predicated on the need to convince advertisers about audience share, and therefore to maximize television companies' profits. It is a device for wooing the audience to the altar of television, to the sofa. It doesn't always work.

Specific devices that have been tried are:

- **hammocking**: when a less popular programme is slung between two more popular ones in an effort to keep its viewing figures up. This is now dangerous practice, with audiences inclined to use the remote control to switch channel as soon as they get bored.
- **inheriting**: placing a programme after a known popular one, for example to try and get the viewers hooked on a new series
- **trailing**: actively selling programmes during the evening, including choices of programme on other ITV or BBC channels.

One should also note a purely functional element to scheduling, which is to allow for the standard programme lengths of 52 minutes (against an hour) for British programmes and 46 minutes for US programmes, designed to allow for trails and advertising. Even the BBC will operate with these in mind because it wants to sell material, and when it has to allow for imported material.

> In what ways does television scheduling respond to audiences, or actually create audiences?

TELEVISION AMONG LEISURE INDUSTRIES

This and the next section are meant to offer contextualizing comment. It is important to remember that from one point of view, television is just another leisure and entertainment industry. Television has an important interactive relationship with those other institutions, in which the attraction and value of each to the public becomes the product of a web of mutual support.

The holiday industry appears in programmes such as *Wish You Were Here?* (ITV), the motor industry in *Top Gear*. Television is also a major medium of advertising for holiday and car firms. Sport is shown in many slots. Entertainment events such as the Oscars are shown on television. Movies are discussed in relevant programmes, but are also validated merely by being shown so frequently on television. Indeed for many people the movie experience is of watching television as much as of going to the cinema. Music programmes effectively publicize that industry, as do programmes about fashion. The list of interactivity becomes almost tedious. But consider removing these programmes (and advertisements) from the schedules, and the gaping holes this would leave look very significant. Equally significant is clear evidence that television promotes book sales, encourages participation in sport, generates activity in fields such as archeology and antique collecting. In these respects television has played a dynamic role in social changes, especially in definitions of work and leisure. Viewing is a leisure activity, but one that makes sense in relation to the other leisure industries which it both supports and is supported by.

To this extent the power of television resides in its ability to cause people to use it for leisure and its ability to promote other media and leisure activities. The extension of this argument is familiar within cultural studies – the power of television lies in its pleasure.

TELEVISION AMONG INFORMATION INDUSTRIES

The fact that television can be seen as a source of information as well as of leisure pleasure is consistent with a view that entertainment material is also informational, and that informational programmes are constructed in ways that make them entertaining to watch. Information and entertainment on television are in the end not to be distinguished. It is indeed an interesting cultural inheritance that causes some to argue that only tragedy has weight, while comedy is inherently 'light' : that information is worthy, but entertainment is suspect because it is fun (and therefore self-indulgent). Enjoyment comes in various forms: a current-affairs programme may be as enjoyable as a sitcom, but in a different way.

It may be supposed that the power of television exists in its factual face – hence the interest in the ideological force of news on television (*see* Chapter 6). However, I would argue that the force of news lies in the special understanding that it has created about its priviliged factuality, rather than in the facts themselves. In a straightfoward understanding of the term, television is an information medium because of the range of programmes described as factual: news, documentary, current affairs. It offers information through teletext, through channels such as Discovery, through segments such as the Learning Zone on BBC2. It can be argued that the special nature of television – in the home, multi-channelled, a simulacrum of reality – means that whatever information it does supply has a special impact, possibly a kind of believability which, for example, cannot be achieved through a visit to the cinema.

What is true, as with entertainment, is that television information exists in the context of other information industries. News depends on the news-agency businesses – UPITN, Reuters, Associated Press, et al. Weather depends on satellite information-gathering and European supercomputer fact-crunching. Advertising depends on market research. Programming depends on BARB audience research. Certainly television also employs its own reporters and researchers. But the power of television lies in its ability to pay for information sources, in the ways that it uses those sources, in what it does with the information from those sources, in the view of the world that it presents from its use of those sources. This view, this ideology, is not only constructed by news. It is the sum of the information parts of television, which may for example both make programmes about the work of information creators such as credit-rating agencies and use the work of information creators.

BRITISH TELEVISION AND GLOBALIZATION

I have already referred to this process in terms of the production deals done with companies in other countries, and in terms of the internationalization of media ownership. Rupert Murdoch (and Newscorp) is of course the high-profile example here. Murdoch not only owns the dominant satellite business in Britain, he also owns the biggest-selling national and Sunday newspapers, not to mention owning elsewhere Fox Television, Twentieth Century Fox cinema, Star satellite (beaming television to most of Asia) and a dominant share of Australian newspapers and television.

But there is a danger that the attention paid to Murdoch, not least by our own news media, deflects attention from the broader picture, of which he is only a prime example. This picture is dominated by the ever greater concentration of ownership (and power?) in fewer and fewer hands. British television ownership has already been described, along with reference to the restrictions which limit that concentration and the degree of overseas ownership. But these kinds of restriction do not apply to other countries, least of all the USA. Here, for example, Turner Broadcasting Services (best known for CNN) bought Hanna-Barbera animation in 1991, giving Ted Turner control of a huge proportion of this entertainment material. It is no surprise then that most such material broadcast in Britain and indeed in Europe comes from the USA and from Japan. But in any case, TBS is also in a deal with Time Warner, itself a media mega-corporation. TW has financial control but not outright ownership. The consequences, for the control of distribution of product, are obvious.

In terms of product there are again protective restrictions. Apart from the British quotas, the European Parliament has also taken a strong line: the Television Without Frontiers Directive (1996) insists on the majority of programming being of member-state origin and covers all kinds of television/video sourcing of material (see Williams, 1996). This reminds one that given the legal ties among European states, one does have to look at national television to some extent at least in a European context.

NATURE AND LOCATION OF POWER IN TELEVISION

> [T]elevision . . . is the single most powerful form of public communication, as well as the prime site of the social negotiation of ideas, values and lifestyles.
> Michael Skovmand and Kim Schroder (*Media Cultures*, 1992)

Assumptions are made about the power of television, not least with reference to ongoing debates about the effects of television. This notion of power and influence is worth examination in different contexts because it is so pervasive. A great deal of research into and critical commentary on television is driven by concerns about it having some kind of power over our minds and lives.

I would not argue that television has no power, but I would suggest that this power is overrated and not that well demonstrated. One needs to ask questions about what kind of power to do what to whom, how and under what circumstances? The fact that politicians, for example, behave as if television has power does not mean that it does have it. This is rather like argument by assertion. The fact that political campaigns are orchestrated around elements such as photo opportunities, carefully timed press conferences and sound bites says as much about the power of the parties to control information as it does about the power of television to shape that information or to put a spin on it. To this extent television may have become the whipping boy for other sources of power and responsibility which also influence how we think about political and social issues.

Certainly whatever power television does have needs to be seen in at least two spheres of influence: that of the other media and that of our social environment. Whatever audiences do with television material in their heads happens in a context, not in isolation.

Potentiality and actuality

There are differences between arguing for what television might do and what it does do. The concentration of ownership and control might allow media groups to promote certain political and commercial causes. Whether they do or not is another matter. One should not be complacent about the potential for misuse of power, but nor should one (in defence of objectivity) assert that misuse does occur without evidence.

Conrad Lodziak (1992) asserts that it is 'a relatively unproblematic matter to establish that the ideological output of television . . . is in support of the "interests of dominant groups" '. But he also points out that it is another matter to prove that television 'effectively manipulates the audiences ideologically'.

Good or bad

Some commentators – for example, Neil Postman in *Amusing Ourselves to Death* (1986) – have referred to the power or influence of television in an almost fashionable mode of condemnation. There is loose talk about advertising as propaganda when it is no such thing in any accurate use of that term.

Condemnatory attitudes coalesce around television for children. For example:

- it stops children reading (the contrary has been shown)
- it teaches dysfunctional behaviours (so own up all you adult *Simpsons* watchers!)
- too much television is bad for you (so is too much exercise or too much food).

So what happened to the good things in television? I am not letting it off the hook of criticism when I point out that it is an effective means of communication for public information campaigns, even though it hasn't actually revolutionized attitudes towards, for example, safe sex. Michael Moore and John Pilger do get a voice, even though some of the things they say are uncomfortable for some of those in authority. Documentaries may carry culturally skewed views through their discourses, but it isn't reasonable to damn them all off the screen. They offer a huge amount of information about our social, geographical, political environments which gives us a chance to understand more about our world than was true for previous generations. Some television drama does raise issues about our social behaviours, our moral inconsistencies and the cultural status quo.

Power points in the process

It may be thought odd that not much has been said about the power of institutions, in a chapter about the industry. But I would like at least to question an implicitly hierarchical model which would have the audience as 'victims' of the programming decisions and materials put out by companies such as Carlton.

For a start, there is the problem of what one means by 'Carlton'. It is easily personified through its chief executive, Michael Green. But what about the board of directors and the shareholders? And in any case it is others who make most decisions about what Meridian commissions, and how programmes are put together. What is power in this case? The decision to go ahead with a programme? Decisions about the format for a programme? Decisions about editing? Power within institutions seems both to be collective and to exist in various interacting spheres, so that if it does have an effect it is as a form of composite power. Also, one may take a view of the production of meanings through television as being part of a process. The decisions and activities of the institution are only the beginning of a process which works through the programme, through transmission, through the minds of the audience. The work of other institutions such as the ITC may impinge on this process, as may the influence of cultural context.

The audience has some autonomy, some power to determine what it watches, what sense it makes of material. It is too simplistic to locate the power of television only in the institutions of ownership, to model this power as a kind of shockwave that has its epicentre in the executive boardroom and is carried outwards via the production workers and the programmes into the minds of the audience. This view should qualify what is said in the rest of this section (*see* Fig. 3.1 on aspects of power).

Meier and Trappel, in *Media Policy* (1998), also argue that there are alternative views on television (media) institutions with regard to arguments about monopoly or competition. They point to evidence that large monopolistic groups are also able to oppose competition and to protect their independence. They argue that 'there is no empirical or scientific evidence that editorial quality has declined under monopolistic conditions'. Equally, they argue, there is evidence that competition is desirable because, for example, monopoly reduces the number of information sources available to the

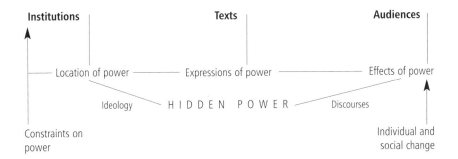

Institutions	Texts	Audiences

Location of power ——— Expressions of power ——— Effects of power

Ideology   HIDDEN   POWER   Discourses

Constraints on
power

Individual and
social change

The power of television may be said to be:

- located within institutions and their operations
- expressed through the exercise of kinds of control and through texts
- revealed in its effects through audience attitudes and behaviours.

As a hidden force it is exercised through the working of discourses, and is shaped by ideology.

3.1 Television and aspects of power.

audience. They also refer to evidence that the range of news coverage benefits from competition, that local and regional news diminishes under monopolies. From these remarks it could well be argued that monopolistic conditions in British television – a centralization of power – have worked against truly regional programming.

Reach

Television, with its images and sounds, reaches into 96 per cent of British households. Television is available to every section of the population. It is available 24 hours a day. Our homes are environments in which generally we feel safe and comfortable, even trusting. So whatever television 'says' to us has a particular kind of acceptability. The extent of the reach of television and the domestic context of its reception gives it a peculiar kind of power. It enhances that through its mode of address, which in the case of many programmes is friendly, direct, the face and words of an attractive television-show host talking to us from the screen, in private.

Intentionality

The way that one may feel about the power of television has something to do with how far it is believed to intend to use that power. It is clear that advertisements intend the viewer to acquire a favourable attitude towards a product or service, even to buy it. Programmers and schedulers intend us to be attracted to watching certain kinds of programmes at certain times. But there is no evidence that the controllers of television or the makers of programmes intend us to adopt certain political views or to acquire certain attitudes towards social groups. We may indeed adopt views and attitudes, but for other reasons.

This does not diminish the degree of power that *may* be exerted. Indeed it may be said that because this power is not apparent through intentions it is the more subversive.

Cash resources

In a material sense the power of television is located in its income. Cash is only potential for action. Nevertheless, it does pay for the people and the equipment which make the programmes which are, one might say, an expression of that power.

Technical resources

Similarly, because production and transmission technology is hugely expensive it is ownership of that technology which gives television its power. If television has reach, it is because of this. If programmes exert influence by constructing meanings in the minds of audiences, then it is because of this. Technology is behind the forms and conventions of television programmes: it enables things to be 'said' in certain ways.

Policy or executive

Within the institutions of television there is a distinction to be made between the broad power of those who make company policy or editorial decisions and the hands-on power of those who make the programmes. One can see the programme as the meeting point between institution and audience. So then one asks who within the institution has the power to do what to the programme?

The more one examines answers to this question the more collective (though not necessarily less significant) the power of institutions seems to be. If one looks at the BBC for example, the board of governors make policy and may even disapprove projects within the organization. But it is the director general who is the chief executive – and even this person does not actually make the programmes. There are heads of programmes for generic areas such as drama, who express the power of the governors but still do not direct programmes. They would regard themselves as executives because they get programmes made. But it is only at the level of producers and directors (and other programme workers) that one sees people exercising hands-on power by actually manufacturing what comes on air. So different kinds of television workers have different kinds of power. Some have the power to cause a programme to be made. Some have the power to determine what kinds of programme will be made. And some have the power to shape the nature of the programme which is made.

Professionalism and power

The notion of workers as professionals has resonances of expertise and responsibility. The concept of professionalism is usually (and will be) discussed in relation to the behaviour and responsibilities of journalists. But I would argue that many groups of television workers see themselves as professionals and not, for example, as technicians. This situation is formalized through professional associations such as the Directors' Guild.

For all the analogies with the production line which may may be applied to television in some respects, in other ways producing television is nothing like mass-producing rivets. Television is a knowledge industry, a meanings machine, not an objects producer. Television workers know this. They may be in the pay of those whom we define as owners, but they also have their own kind of power. They articulate ideas, they conceive and manufacture images. They choose how to narrate, how to set up or to deny issues. They may not be entirely at one with the governors, the directors, the financial controllers.

When television workers define themselves as professionals they express a sense of their own knowledge, expertise and desired status within society. I would argue that they also thus recognize their power to produce ideas through programmes. Implicitly, power brings responsibility, at least in a Western social-libertarian way of looking at things. But of course it does not necessarily bring the exercise of that responsibility. So there are issues around the assertion of expertise and privilege under the umbrella of professionalism. Is that assertion matched with the kind of responsibilties and obligations that, for example, the professional associations of doctors or solicitors impose on their members?

In one sense this kind of responsibility is recognized, even enforced, through the codes of practice relating to material for children, or to pornography, for example. How far it is taken on board when the commercial imperatives of the television institutions are at stake is another matter. The production practices of television are complex and pressured. For a television worker the most immediate critics are their peers or their immediate line manager – not the audience. As Philip Schlesinger says about news practices in *Putting Reality Together* (1987), there is 'an intense obsession with the packaging of the broadcast and with the comparative evaluation of others' goals'.

Power of meaning

A programme means nothing unless it is seen. Power is made real in the expression of it, even though it may be believed to exist potentially. When a programme is seen, the audience is interacting with it. It may be that the power of the programme is in its encoding, especially the ability to privilege some meanings above others. It may be that power is also within the viewer who constructs meanings out of that interaction. But either way, it is the meaning which may or may not translate into a reinforcement of beliefs or a change of attitudes or a determination to act.

So although the location and exercise of power in television is complex, one might agree that the ultimate focus of power in television lies in its ability to produce meanings.

If 'power as meaning' is importantly inscribed in 'programmes as texts' then one may note that the producers of such texts have this power in respect of:

- provision of content – inserting matter selectively
- excision – keeping out or taking out material
- shaping – control over textual features or form
- repetition of material – repeats, videotape duplication
- distribution of material – videotape, DVD, broadcast, cable, etc.

> What are the arguments for and against seeing the idea of the power of television as an illusion?

DIGITAL REVOLUTION

A profound change is taking place in television with the rise of digital technology. This technology centres on the encoding of information – pictures and sound – in terms of numbers. This is machine code or basic computer language. It is replacing kinds of encoding (images on film stock, magnetic particles on video tape arranged as images) which are described as analogue. It is part of a process in media and telecommunications which has been happening for several years and which means that increasingly all communications technology is 'talking the same language'. It means that one can use computers to control and change what passes through telephone systems, broadcast systems and so on.

Digital television is creating new television institutions and changing the way the existing ones work. It started in 1998 with BSB, the BBC, ITV and Online vying to attract customers. It has had limited success because the transmission technology and definition is not yet better than many analogue television sets, and because people are reluctant to spend money buying into the digital packages which include some channels they can presently get for free. But it will be the television standard of the future, and government has made plans to phase out analogue television transmission.

The advantages of digital television, depending on whose view you take, are as follows:

- improved picture and sound quality, as the public buys updated television sets
- the use of widescreen format (still only a minority of programmes). European companies are also moving towards a high-definition standard of 1250 lines. Governments will endorse this at some point, and there will be no more transmission of television on the present system.
- the ability to receive many more channels (up to 500 according to BSB)
- the ability easily to make these channels partly interactive (see the shopping channels)
- the ability easily to 'mix' channels and sources – e.g. to access computer material at the same time as viewing
- the ability to introduce strategies such as 'pay per view'. This is the real driver behind technological change. Companies would like this to become the new way of paying for television (and a way of getting rid of the licence fee).

However, there are also issues and problems for television institutions in terms of their 'old-fashioned' roles as broadcasters:

- Competition and choice will become so great that channel image and channel loyalty will become difficult to sustain. The phenomenon of channel hopping by those with satellite/cable access is already worrying advertisers.
- The BBC in particular will become even more vulnerable to the effect of falling audience figures. Many channels, including its own UKTV, are already paid for on a subscription basis. There will be pressures to move entirely down this route – or to adopt pay per view.
- Institutions will have to operate even more in a global marketplace. The

BBC, for example, already runs BBC Worldwide, an associated but separate business. It is a commercial profitmaking organization, paying its own way based on deals with Flextech and with Discovery (1998). It also owns an American channel, BBC America. British television will have to sell itself abroad to survive, and will have to accommodate global deals and foreign product coming onto British screens.

- The expansion of channels will create demand for product, which may be good for producers, including small companies.
- But it may also drive costs down through competition, and in fact reduce quality. If nothing else there are likely to be more repeats and more specialist channels. Anything to fill the space.
- If this happens then more power will be in the hands of the distributors who control the channels
- There is also the issue of regulation: it will be harder and harder for government to control access and quality on these new digital channels because more owners will be based outside the UK and material can be originated outside the UK. If more and more channels are available on satellites broadcasting within the UK 'footprint', then it will be easier and easier, especially with digital technology, to pick up these signals. If an originator cannot be physically stopped from originating a porn channel, then it seems unlikely that government would be able to stop receivers from accessing it. As an aside, one wonders what would happen if black-market decoders were to appear, allowing people to access channels without paying.
- It appears that digital should offer more choice, but the evidence of new channels is that they will offer more of the same – Sky's various movie channels or the Comedy Channel.

For further discussion of this topic, see Chapter 12.

4

Television Product: Points of Contact

PREVIEW

This chapter deals with:

- television programmes in terms of ways that they engage the audience
- pleasures derived from programmes
- the ways that titles work on us
- the importance of personality
- intertextuality
- adverts
- genres, myths and meanings.

INTRODUCTION

This chapter is not a survey of British television programmes. Rather, it is about some ways in which television material makes contact with and makes meanings for its viewers.

There are sections elsewhere which refer to particular genres or kinds of programme. What I would argue is that one needs to understand television product in terms of its functions and its interactions with the audience. It mostly makes sense at the point at which the viewer interacts with it. The survey, the descriptive approach, does not in the end deal with issues of why television product has any significance, nor how it can be engaged with critically.

One aspect of that critical engagement lies in the continuity between product and audience: one leads to the other. So it follows that at least some of the material in this chapter could equally well be placed in Chapter 9, on audiences. The significant difference is only in one's starting point.

PRODUCT AND PLEASURE

One might start with the sheer availability and accessibility of television in the home; with the volume of programming; with the succession of audiences during the day. Viewing has been described as pleasure. The scale of interaction between product and audience adds up to a lot of pleasure.

This notion of pleasure is often associated with a view of television as an entertainment medium. Examples of this approach include the work of Mulvey (1975) and others on cinematic viewing pleasures. But unlike cinema, which consists almost entirely of fiction, television includes a large proportion of factual product. Analysis of the five terrestrial channels in a randomly chosen week indicates that 39 per cent of programming was factual (of programmes as items in the period 20 to 26 June 1999, including news and sport).

Equally, one could question the conflation of entertainment and fiction. What does 'entertainment' really mean? Viewers may achieve diversions and satisfactions from watching a gardening programme as much as from watching a drama. And in any case the division between factual and fictional programmes is now hopelessly blurred. Even gardening programmes have been invaded by the make-over type, in which degrees of dramatization attend the race against time by our cast of characters to transform the garden concerned.

John Hartley (1992) argues that television is a capitalist venture, a means of social control and a popular source of pleasure, all at the same time. He criticizes a Marxist tradition which takes a negative view of television, conflating 'leftwing' and radical criticism of the medium with rejection of enjoyment in viewing. His view is that 'the hegemonic is popular, the dominant regime is a regime of pleasure'. If one wants to make sense of the relationship between audiences and television then one has to accept that people do like watching television, that it is not the business of critical debate to stop that enjoyment. This is consistent with my argument that one use of a book like this is to extend the range of pleasure in the viewing experience, to enable critical faculties (even intellectual rejection) to co-exist with enjoyment.

The familiar phrase about things 'giving pleasure' compounds confusions about what television product is 'doing', or about how it should be understood. Programmes don't do anything as such: audiences take pleasure. This is not meant to deny discussion of the text or the idea of inscribed meanings. But it is meant to lay weight on the 'programme as object', the 'programme as potential meanings', rather than assume the programme to be 'the creator of pleasure'.

Pleasure of recognition: familiarity

In one sense there is a pleasurable familiarity in the act of returning to television watching in general, evening after evening. But specific pleasures are to do with the familiarity of the programme or of the personality concerned. Recognition brings security. Habits of viewing are securing, apart from the pleasure of re-engaging with subject matter and personalities that we find attractive and approvable for other reasons.

This kind of pleasure has to do with repetition of material, repetition of viewing practices, genre-ness, series and serials. At its heart are the longest-running programmes on television: the soaps, like *Coronation Street* and *Emmerdale*; the nightly news; even the children's programmes. There is nothing so effective in opening conversation among adults as to talk about the television programmes which they watched as children – repeatedly and with enjoyment. Nostalgia gives edge to the pleasure of revisiting the familiar mooring points of childhood lifestyle.

Pleasure of reflection: talking and thinking

People like talking about television. At least some programmes have become a common social and cultural experience. Television material has become part of social interaction. Because people enjoy talking about people, so they enjoy talking about characters in dramas. Audiences take pleasure in reflecting on their viewing experience, in revisiting conversations, motives, dramatic outcomes.

Pleasure of continuation: coming back to it

This kind of pleasure has to do with recognition and repetition. But in this case one draws particular attention to series and serial phenomena in television. The uncompleted or open-ended narratives of these forms create a sense of there always being something to return to, something which is waiting for the viewer. There is a pleasure in returning to that which is familiar and which has previously been enjoyed. There is a pleasure in continuing, returning to engage with unfinished business.

Pleasure of engagement: thinking it out

This draws attention to the active quality of television viewing. Meanings are not simply absorbed through the eye; they are built in the mind. This act of engaging with the text may in itself be pleasurable. Some texts privilege such engagement: for example, various kinds of quiz show in which the audience may identify with the participants (as studio audiences do, loudly) and try to answer the questions for themselves. Other examples of this engagement would be: trying to work out the guilty person in the murder-mystery thriller, playing at being referee, coach or manager while watching a football match.

There is also that general kind of engagement which involves talking to the screen or talking to another viewer while the programme is on, for example about the motives and behaviour of one of the screen characters.

Pleasure of submersion: living it out

This links to a degree of involvement in the material, whether it is a screen drama, a screen competition, or even the vicarious pleasures of sharing a journey through remote places as part of a documentary. This is the pleasure of suspending one's relationship with everyday reality and slipping on the garments of another world and other experiences. It is living out other realities without the accompanying responsibilities.

Pleasure of knowing: information and satisfaction

Fiction provides its own kinds of pleasure when one knows that the material is 'safe' in being not true. There is a pleasure opposed to this which depends on believing that what one is watching is true, that the sense one is making is based on truth. Sometimes this information pleasure is derived from extraordinariness, as with programmes about remarkable features of natural history. Sometimes it is derived from actuality – for example, satellite link information on the news. Sometimes it is derived from sheer factuality as when we watch explanatory science programmes. In each case the viewer derives satisfaction from knowledge as well as from the manner of its presentation. It may be that this satisfaction has something to do with curiosity – interest in how things are and why they are, for the sake of knowing it. It may have something to do with security – the feeling that understanding empowers.

These various kinds of pleasure are a consequence partly of the variety of television product, but mostly of the ways in which viewers respond to that product. They are not just about the pleasures of 'feel-good' or of something loosely called 'relaxation'. They are more positively about the 'satisfaction' experienced through different ways of engaging with the text. They make television in general an attractive medium for the audience. They make particular programmes attractive. They provide a point of engagement with the text. They promote a mental environment in which the audience is either disposed to take on meanings inscribed within the text, or inclined to build meanings for themselves. However, even in the process of constructing their own meanings I would argue that the audience does not have complete autonomy because these meanings are built within another context, a social and cultural context – a way of understanding the world – which is already inside our heads as a product of social conditioning.

Fiske (1987) argues that 'pleasure results from a particular relationship between meaning and power'. The viewer feels pleasure when they feel in control of the meanings gained from the material, when they feel they are resisting the structures of domination that exist within televison texts, when they stop being subordinate to those structures. So women take pleasure in the way that females are empowered by their roles within soap operas. However, I do take issue elsewhere with the legitimacy and extent of that empowerment. One also has to recognize (see the examples of types of pleasure on pp. 71–2) that whether they 'should' or not, people take pleasures outside the context of politicized and critical debate. Women may enjoy a good romantic weepie in which objectively the male hero still holds a dominant position. But I wouldn't want to deny or invalidate the pleasure that the female audience takes in this material.

Roland Barthes (1977) would actually distinguish between the two kinds of pleasure referred to in the example above. Having a weep over the situation in some television melodrama would be described as **jouissance** – a kind of gut pleasure, something spontaneous and of the emotions. But if the viewer identified with the heroine's situation, perhaps in terms of being a woman and in terms of how she would want to conduct the central relationship, then this would be something more rationalized – **plaisir**. The distinction is not always easy to make in examples. It is discussed by Barthes and others in terms of how far these kinds of pleasure may represent the viewer escaping from structures of social control which come through the text. Perhaps plaisir is a kind of resistance to these meanings in the text, and jouissance a kind of momentary freedom – liberation through emotion. Pierre Bourdieu (1984) would see the pleasure of watching television as being tied up with the meanings one gets from the programmes. And he would argue that these meanings and pleasures relate to class and social power. In terms of popular culture his view is that what the audience gets out of watching a football match or a game show actually works in the interest of those who are subordinate, who lack power. They get pleasure, a sense of identity, self-worth, groupness, in spite of the fact that the dominant system works in the interests of those who are rich and powerful. Bourdieu sees cultural product such as television programmes as kinds of goods in circulation – the equivalent of financial capital or the money you have to spend. So for him

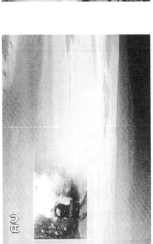

4.1 These selected shots from the titles sequence for *Heartbeat* (ITV) are a series of composite frames mixed into one another, with the music of the Buddy Holly track 'Heartbeat' from the late 1950s played over. The titles sequence locates this popular programme back in time and as a hybrid police/soap genre. The frames identify the key characters from the drama in the context of the English countryside.

television is mostly about popular culture and therefore mainly about ordinary people, and about a struggle for power based on politics, money and class. Enjoyment makes you powerful. Feeling powerful adds up to a kind of resistance to those who want to 'keep you in your place'.

> Do viewing pleasures endorse the value of television programmes?

TITLES AND UNDERSTANDINGS

The titles of television programmes are designed to create a certain mindset, to make predictions out of which the viewer adjusts to and anticipates the programme to come. They are intended to work for new viewers as much as for those already committed to a series or a genre. They also work for prospective purchasers of programmes. In particular the naming of the programme and of its principal creators is not so much about identity for the viewer – though it may be that the name of a writer like Jim Allen or of a director like Gavin Millar will attract some viewers. This naming is as much for the trade (like the closing credits), to enhance the reputation of the programme makers with their peers.

Titles are the first element of a programme which addresses the viewer and tries to set up a relationship between material and viewer. This is establishing a mode of address. Titles want to engage the viewer, to throw out a hook which the producers hope will become more firmly embedded as the rest of the programme continues to absorb attention.

Characteristics of title sequences

Signalling change: attention grabbing

Titles signal a change in the sequence of programmes, the beginning of another segment. If one is watching through then this change is in itself a signal for attention. Equally if one is switching in as part of programme selection then the titles are a confirmation of 'place', of the identity of the programme, saying that one may now attend to the chosen programme.

Catch-up narrative: continuity setting

In a serial, sometimes a series, the title sequence is composed of referential shots (probably with voice-over) which catch up with the story so far. This is not only for the benefit of the committed viewer, but also for the channel switcher and sampler who hasn't watched the story so far. Such a use of titles helps create continuity for the whole serial. It is an integral part of minidramas shown over two or three nights.

Character establishing

Titles establish personalities and characters in dramas. If the actor is known, then this also serves a promotion purpose, not least at trade fairs. But in any case, they may help preview the key players in a drama. This device is not peculiar to drama. Titles may also use a personality such as a programme compère, as with Rolf Harris and *Animal Hospital*. Such programmes are built around a personality and that personality's cult. Barry Norman was an example of this, fronting a programme about cinema for over 20 years. The appearance of the personality in the titles simultaneously validates and identifies the programme; it accrues certain qualities to the programme (the persona of the presenter); it reinforces the importance of the personality.

Mode predicting

Titles prepare the viewer for a certain mode of treatment, a certain set of conventions. The most familiar of these modes are realism and genre; other examples are comedy or melodrama. If a title sequence can signal such a mode, then it can also position the viewer. This is an adjustment of expectations about content and treatment. It helps provide a framework within which the programme will be interpreted.

In this area I would include mode of address. The titles sequence establishes a way of 'talking' to the viewer and a kind of relationship with the viewer. This overlaps with the other prediction areas. The titles 'say' things like 'sit back and enjoy yourself' or 'you need to pay attention, we're going to explain something' or 'we want you to take part in this programme'.

Mood setting

Titles may produce an emotional response in the viewer. This can reinforce the mode of the programme. The portentous music of news or the lighter musical touch of comedy are examples of this.

Referentiality

Titles may use referentiality via symbols, icons or intertextual references to borrow qualities from another source and attach them to the programme. A classic example of this is from the documentary series *Horizon*, which at one time used the Da Vinci image of a naked man with superimposed compass set within a circle. The image invoked art and science, discipline and creativity, and most of all the 'quality' of a high-culture reference.

PRODUCT CONTINUITY OR FRAGMENTATION

This is about the flow–segment debate and how the audience uses television.

By signalling difference, title sequences work against the idea of undifferentiated flow. They draw attention to the programme as unit of television and to the relationship of that programme with its audience as being important to producers, in economic terms if nothing else. Flow as continuity is a different matter: certainly the screen is never 'quiet'. To remark on flow is perhaps to remark on a difference of engagement with the television medium, when compared with, say, a visit to the cinema or the picking up of a magazine.

However, the television audience also makes similar choices to 'pick up' television. The one kind of engagement is an analogy with print media, when viewers make a selective programme choice (and are helped in doing this by the titles). The other kind of choice is when television is picked up at random. This can take the form of households where the television is left on more or less all the time, to examples where viewers turn on the television with no clear idea of what they are going to watch (for example, coming home after the pubs have shut). And then there is channel hopping, where again the idea is to watch television, not a particular programme. In all these cases, the functions and effects of the titles sequences are marginalized.

There is a view that the audience has fragmented the product into a splintered collection of television. In the case of channels such as MTV or CNN the producers collude with this process. The notion of separate programmes and so the use of titles is largely lost, if not removed altogether. It more or less does not matter where one switches into such channels, if all you want is some news or some music.

It has been argued that channel hopping is a product of a diminishing attention span among a viewing public which is used to its media fare being predigested and made 'bite-sized'. But it is equally arguable that this is due to an increasing proportion of material which fails to hold attention through lack of originality, distinctiveness or even 'usefulness' to the audience.

PRODUCT AND PERSONALITIES

Television product both supports and is supported by an array of personalities. The concept of personality refers to television performers who are invested by the audience with distinctive and attractive qualities, who nurture such qualities through their performance. There seems to be a separation from the idea of stardom which is based on the difference between cinema and television as media. Cinema invokes a sense of distance through the occasional viewing experience in a special place. Stars are invested with mythic qualities, not least through their material. But television is made intimate and familiar through the frequency of viewing in home territory. It is also the case the television has such a volume of output that its personalities are unlikely to achieve the rarity value of the filmstar, who is probably seen only for a few hours of the lives of the cinema-goer. Clint Eastwood was a television personality as Rowdy Yates, but only became a star through cinema. As John Ellis puts it, television personalities are 'celebrities rather than stars . . . they are familiar rather than remote'.

Programmes need personalities because television needs programmes, and personalities are the life force of programmes. Audiences like to engage with images of other people because their lives are about engagements with others. Generally speaking, we are social and interactive, in one degree or another. There is no difference in principle between the gossip of teenage girls on the telephone and the images of young women gossiping in teen soaps such as *Hollyoaks*. There is some screen time which is not occupied by personalities – for example some dramas, documentaries, animations. But successful programmes are all supported by personalities in some way. Television exposure helps create the cult of personality, but the human material must also be there in the first place. Satirical programmes such as *Spitting Image* are as effective as long-established institutions such as Madame Tussand's for indicating when certain personalities are sanctified by fame.

The range of personalities is considerable. Some, such as the comedian Jim Davidson, are media performers who have careers outside television. Some are pretty much tied to television – Adam and Joe fronting their own take on popular culture in *The Adam and Joe Show*. Many are hosts and compères of quiz shows, for instance Dale Winton. When it comes to drama they may be described as 'stars of', but there is no discernible difference between this kind of stardom and established personalities. People like Martine McCutcheon knew this, leaving a very successful role in the soap *EastEnders* to attempt a career in pop music which would have the kind of scope that television could not offer.

Factual programmes are equally full of personalities – Trevor McDonald of ITN News, Carol Vorderman of science programmes. Children's television rapidly endows and discards stars such as Zoe Ball. Television may further transform personalities into cultural icons. Again, Vorderman, moving from a role as an accessory in a relatively upmarket quiz show to one as presenter of popular science, has been transmogrified into an acceptable symbol of 'brainy and beautiful'.

David Lusted (1984) suggests that 'the cult of the personality is a product of *the myth of the individual*'. Our culture is so wedded to the idea of individual achievement and people 'making it' that television personalities are constructed in the minds of the audience as an expression of that belief – never mind that the creation of a television programme is clearly a collaborative enterprise.

Keith Selby and Ron Cowdery (1995) see the personality as a 'media commodity' – goods with a value. They also argue that those who are personalities or television stars have 'specific qualities which transcend the qualities of the characters that they play'. So one could say that David Jason has a kind of reliability and decency of the common man that comes through in his role as the detective Frost, even though it is mixed with roguishness in *Only Fools and Horses* or *The Darling Buds of May*. There is something in each of the characters he plays which the audience can recognize and like. The various personalities are renewed and validated as a product of the television industry.

Andrew Tolson (1996), on the other hand, refers to the television personality as 'another kind of constructed persona'. He agrees that the nature of the medium makes television personalities different from movie stars, but disagrees that they are any the less interesting or complex because of this. In effect he talks about the personality that we believe we know not actually being the real person at all. He discusses the particular genre of chat shows and the way in which presenters such as Michael Parkinson establish personalities which make them effective and liked as interviewers. Tolson might also have pointed out that the chat show has a double commodity of personality – the guests are also part of this phenomenon. Sometimes this gives rise to friction. An interesting example was when the abrasive personality Clive Anderson interviewed the BeeGees pop group, who interestingly might be described as something more mythic and remote – as stars. The group finally walked out on the programme when they became upset by the familiarity of Clive Anderson's questions. Perhaps the contrast between the television studio and the rock stadium was too much for them.

In what ways is the 'personality' not a real person?

INTERTEXTUALITY OF PRODUCT

In terms of the development of new product, and of understanding what is on offer, one needs to realize that the media are self-regarding, incestuous and prone to cloning.

Television is part of these tendencies. The fact that it borrows from the texts of other media may be signalled in generic titles such as 'magazine

4.2 Angus Deayton hosts the successful quiz show *Have I Got News For You* (BBC2). The intertextual references to mainstream news conventions in this shot include face to camera, desk, sober dress, images as backdrops. The viewer understands this programme by referencing other programmes.

programme', or in the subject matter of a film review programme. The fact that it interbreeds its own genre combinations is a commonplace. One of the more obvious examples is the marrying of the crime thriller to the soap in programmes such as *The Bill* or *The Sopranos*. The viewer has to understand this dual referentiality in order to anticipate the development of narrative and how this is to be understood. However, this marriage of genres and their features does not work at random or at the behest of television programmers desperate for ratings. *The Bill* works because it is already based in a community, a prerequisite for soaps. Its themes and storylines are those of soaps. Its crimes may be serious enough, but they are rooted in that which is acceptable to the audience, what one would describe as the human face of crime and personal troubles. The introduction of a murder into the plot line of the soap *EastEnders* in early 1999, on the other hand, met with a lot of critical rejection. I suggest that murder is not seen by the audience as a valid point of contact between the genres. It is not a matter of direct experience for most viewers, and so loses credibility in the pseudo-realist context of soaps. Shoplifting, breaking and entering, domestic violence, by contrast, are valid points of contact. As crimes they can work intertextually.

But most of all it is in content and use of form that television refers both outside itself and within itself. The viewer needs to pick up this reference to understand the text. This is intertextuality: mixing up and cross-referencing of texts.

Advertisements lend themselves to this intertextuality because the referencing can make a point quickly but also engage the interest of the audience. An example is an advertisement which uses a comedian (Vic Reeves) known for his surreal humour. The narrative of the advert exploits this. Yet the referentiality is also to the comedy programmes of Reeves and Bob Mortimer, including *Vic Reeves' Big Night Out* and *Families at War*, as well as Reeves's book of humour, *Sun Boiled Onions*. But *Vic Reeves' Big Night Out* is intertextual in itself because it is a parody of a particular kind of quiz show and can only be understood and found amusing if one knows about quiz shows. The intertextual references come thick and fast. There is a further layer of reference to programmes such as *Neighbours from Hell*, which dramatizes and documents conflict between families warring over problems such as noise and tree planting.

Comedy especially exploits intertextual reference in the modes of parody, pastiche and satire. But perfectly serious programmes also interlock in a complex web of cultural practices and understandings. For example, in five days of British television (26–30 April 1999) there was a programme called *Crash*, about car safety and accidents; there was an item about a car crash and rescue within a series about true accidents called *999*; there was a programme about a motorcyle stunt rider and the consequences of his near-fatal crash; there were also four programmes about cars, including one about motorway usage and one about car clamping and the conflicts which result. In the previous week there had been the end of a series about motorway crashes caught on surveillance cameras. The audience's understanding of this sequence of programmes became a rich mixture of references and meanings, which reached out even further to the hundreds of images of cars in television drama and film fiction: cars which crash, explode and are driven furiously; cars that are custom built and driven by stuntmen for effects that are not of the everyday. Yet the black-and-white images of others' driving taken from, for example, inside police cars combine the reference of actuality with the description of people driving fast and dangerously. We are invited to be as excited by these antics as by those of the stuntmen. The stunt-rider story pivots on heroism: the adventure of the stunts and the person's heroic attempts to become mobile after being largely paralysed. The notion that his life was based on stupid and dangerous actions which might have been simply forbidden is not entertained.

The intertextual properties reinforce the dual meaning position which brings together excitement and danger with regard to car driving. These two qualities are then brought into into realist programmes which should promote censure of dangerous behaviour. But I would argue that reference introduces excitement which then overwhelms boring old moral censure. One can only speculate about the connection between these cross-referential images and antisocial youth behaviour such as joy riding.

Commentators such as Fiske (1989) take the view that intertextuality is dominantly but not exclusively concerned with popular culture. Fiske distinguishes between the intertextuality of high culture and that of popular culture on the grounds that the former is more about the idea of the author or artist – understanding the work through what one knows of the creator's other works – whereas 'in popular culture the object of veneration is less the text or the artist and more the performer'. This emphasis on performer would of course 'fit' much of television in respect of the primacy of the personality. It is true that a majority of programmes are dominated by personalities, including screenings of football matches. In this case the personalities perform on the field and are used in the studio as commentators. But, as Fiske might say, they are understood through the intertextual context of all the other references to these star players and commentators. Our view of them comes not just from television but also from newspaper reports, fan magazines and so on. High-culture intertextuality and criticism would be more in the order of commentary on the work of a film director.

These remarks also carry the implication that television is in itself a popular-culture medium. This view may be supported by the reach of television into almost every household, and by the scale and range of audience profiles. At the same time, if one wants to make the distinction, it also has appeal to and product for a wide range of minority audiences. In terms of cultural events and cultural formats there is little that television has not covered. One is then on dangerous ground if one begins to associate product, taste, class and validity. It would be one kind of classism to argue that ballet is better than a musical because of its origins or because of the socio-economic background of its audiences. It would be equally classist to argue that watching football on television has a kind of validity because it is a popular activity (is of the people) and that reading poetry has less validity because it is a minority activity.

None of these comments denies notions of social differences or of the unequal exercise of power in society. But they argue against opposing the material of high culture and popular culture in terms of an idea of validity which is measured by popular appeal. In this respect Fiske's further comments on intertextuality and popular culture might be seen as descriptive rather than evaluative. His metaphor would have the material of popular culture as a kind of liquid, flowing from one text to another and from media reality to social reality: 'all popular texts have leaky boundaries; they flow into each other, they flow into everyday life'; 'Popular culture can be studied only intertextually, for it exists only in this intertextual circulation.'

Thwaites, Davis and Mules (1994) would agree that 'textual groupings and their social meanings are not static'. They would relate intertextuality to semiotics in respect of the polysemic properties of television. That is to say, television offers a multiplicity of signs (and codes) which offer an interlocking choice of meanings. Our experience of watching television – a certain type of television – may help pin down the meanings. But then intertextual reference opens up even more possible nuances of meaning or understanding.

These writers identify three elements in thinking about the relationships between text – here we might say between products:

1 the signs and meanings within the texts
2 the intertextual references that texts may set up amongst themselves
3 the responses of different readers of texts, in terms of what they may see within and between texts (as opposed to all the possibilities that may be there).

Intertextuality is a kind of cross-referencing system which may be seen in the text. But its significance, what it means to each of us as a television viewer, depends on how we read that referencing, what we notice and what we don't notice. In this respect the kind of liquid indeterminacy that Fiske refers to does not matter to the individual reader, who makes their own decisions about the pleasures and interests which they draw from the text.

ADVERTISING AS PRODUCT

The ITC monitors commercial television advertising via its **Advertising Advisory Committee** and its **Code of Advertising Standards and Practice**. There is also a **Broadcaster Advertising Clearance Centre** set up jointly by commercial broadcasters with the ITC, to which scripts of ads have to be sent for prior approval.

In one sense, advertising cannot be regarded as being like other programmes because of its intention to persuade, and because it is the point of contact between commercial interests and the audience as consumers of products and services. Its special position is signalled by the constraints surrounding it, many embodied within codes of practice specifically relating to advertising. For instance, there cannot be more than 7 minutes of advertising in any hour. There are products and services which may not be advertised – religions and doctors and fortune tellers, cigarettes and other tobacco products. Alcohol may not be glamorized for youth audiences. The National Lottery, slimming products and alcohol products may not be advertised around children's programmes. The advertising of women's sanitary products is not permitted until after 9.00 p.m.

At the same time, advertising is like other programmes because it:

- comes out of the same production base, technologies and production practices
- has the same basic narrative structures, but compressed
- uses genre material as a point of recognition and attraction for the audience
- makes intertextual references to other television material
- uses television performers (and their voices) whom we know from other programmes
- creates its own 'stars' and popular 'series'.

All this exists, ironically, in the context of the ITC ruling that there should be a clear distinction between advertisements and programmes.

It is arguable that something to be described as advertising exists outside the category of conventional paid-for videos, which themselves include persuasive items such as government information films. There are also the ubiquitous programme trails which advertise programmes themselves.

Sponsorship exists in various forms (such as HSBC for ITV drama productions, in which the bank is trailed at the beginning and end of every break in the drama). Sponsorship has been allowed on British television only since 1991, and is not permitted for news and current-affairs programmes. Sport is full of sponsorship, whch is announced through coverage and in news programmes, even on the BBC. Sponsorship deals were worth £60 million to all broadcasters in 1995. However sponsorship is not relatively a major income provider if one considers that ITV income from this source in 1997 was only £36 million, against a total advertising income of £2.6 billion. The dangers of the influence of sponsors have been evident in the USA, and it is now a matter of concern in Britain that the content and angle of the sponsored product is determined by the needs of the sponsor. Granville Williams (1996) quotes an unpleasant incident in 1996, when Heineken as sponsors of Planet 24's independently produced *Hotel Babylon*, complained to the producers that there was not enough beer being drunk on screen and that there were too many black people in the audience. Heineken were forced to apologize in the ensuing row.

Other examples of sponsorship deals seen on television are *Friends* (Wella hair products), *Formula 1 Racing* (Texaco petroleum), *C5 Films* (Stella Artois beer) and *Frazier* (Douwe Egberts coffee products). Shows sponsored by magazines are also permitted – e.g. Granada/BSB has the *Good Housekeeping Show*, C4 has the *OKTV Show*.

Indirect promotion is about kinds of indirect advertising such as the billboards artfully placed for the cameras at sports events, especially in sports stadiums. Product placement is not allowed on British television, though the schedules are full of films which may include this kind of promotion.

Programming and scheduling on commercial television is at least partly driven by the interests of advertising. Advertisers want to be associated with programmes which attract audiences and which fit their image and marketing objectives. Programmers want to purchase and commission such programmes to sell time to the advertisers. Schedulers want to arrange programmes so that they maximize these selling opportunities. It is the terms of commercial contracts which contain unbridled market forces.

John Corner (1995) sees television commercials as 'a kind of essential television' which both borrows from and gives to other kinds of programme. A number of ads set up a soap-opera situation in miniature, especially for products like soap powders and foodstuffs. Equally, some short sections of travel/holiday programmes are nearly indistinguishable from the holiday-company commercials which have influenced their segmented glossy appearance.

Corner suggests that television ads are distinctive as product because they exploit what they cannot do in other media such as magazines. The three features which they exploit are speech, music (FX) and action. Music establishes the mode of the product – how we are meant to understand it. Music also melds the elements together and provides a motif. Action may demonstrate or illustrate aspects of the product. But it can also produce the dramatic impact of a microdrama – that which attracts and maintains attention. Speech is interesting as television ads use a high proportion of direct address – something which we see a great deal elsewhere in television, not least in 'truth-telling' forms such as news and documentary. In this case Corner suggests that speech in ads can help identify product (e.g. repetition of brand name), describe product and affirm product (and its good qualities). In respect of this reference to speech I would suggest that it draws attention to the fact that far from being a dominantly 'visual medium', television is a very 'talky' medium. There are a number of programmes – chat shows, discussion programmes, soap operas – in which much essential information is carried verbally. I am not suggesting that pictures are redundant, but nor are they always dominant. Just as one can make sense of some programmes with the sound turned down, so also one can make sense of some by listening to them from another room.

It is arguable that as television product advertisements have a particular, dual nature. They are regarded as separate from programmes because of their brevity and their function of marketing. But I suggest that they are in another sense 'programmes in miniature', and as much a part of television's cultural output as anything else. People discuss advertisements as much as they talk about other programmes. They have narratives and production histories, like other programmes. I am not denying differences, but I am emphasizing similarities. And in terms of potential effects and understanding, ads can be understood like other television material. So they are both distinctively persuasive and typically full of stories, characters and views of the world and of their times like other programmes. For this reason they also reveal discourses and carry ideology. Judith Williamson made this point in *Decoding Advertisements* (1978) – advertising 'creates structures of meaning'; it 'in many ways replaces that (function) traditionally fulfilled by art and religion'. That is to say, the ways in which the world was pictured and explained through religion in the past are analogous to ways in which advertisements picture our world to us today – pictures of childhood and age, home and foreign places, and explanations of our place in the world in terms of our lifestyles and of what we own.

> How is advertising on television similar to or different from other television products in the ways that it tries to engage with the audience?

GENRE PRODUCTS

In this section the word genre is used in two senses. The dominant definition covers those programmes which work to a formula which includes repeated characteristics, protagonists, themes, backgrounds, situations. This refers to a lot of fiction material, but also includes examples like news and quiz shows. The other sense of genre is a much looser one of category, in which there is nothing like a substantial formula but there are very general repeated features. In this case I would prefer to talk about a programming category, for example sport or costume drama. In these cases we know something about the content and look of the material. But there isn't a great deal that is specifically predictable. This may be shown by looking at the programme categories as defined by the ITC. These are: Drama, Entertainment (including comedy, music, game shows), Sport, News, Factual Progarmmes, Education, Religion, Arts, Childrens' Programmes. These are production divisions, not genres as such.

Jane Feuer (1992) discusses the problems caused by the loose and various ways in which the term genre is used. She refers for example to a literary tradition which might apply the term to comedy and tragedy. This tradition itself originally drew on the classics, and on notions of comedy and tragedy which were in fact much more rule-bound than they are today. Our 'problem' is that television and film have built up what Feuer would call their own history of types of material. A situation comedy on television has consistent and repeated elements such as the location of the action, the cast of characters, this week's little crisis and the tension between certain key characters. *Birds of a Feather* has three contrasting types of women, the situation of two of them having (absent) criminal husbands, and a set location in one of their houses. There is a formula for situation comedy which there is not for comedy in general. From here on genre will be taken to refer to formulaic material with a substantial number of elements which differentiate it from other genres.

The dominance of genre product on television is an economic and a cultural phenomenon, in the following ways.

Economics and production

Programme genres dominate television output. One reason has to do with volume – so many hours have to be filled, so much money is involved in purchasing and making programmes, that it makes economic sense to put out programmes that have either been successful in a previous series or which are like some programme which has succeeded. Costs temper a desire to be innovative for the sake of creativity or potential great profit. Genre material brings down costs when it enables sets to be built and people to be contracted for a run of programmes, or even for more than one series. Of course actors' fees go up if a genre hits gold (see George Clooney in *E.R.*). But then the associated increase in rates and programme sales compensates for this. So genre is attractive to the television industry for production reasons, as well as for marketability and for likelihood of success. (*See* Fig. 4.3.)

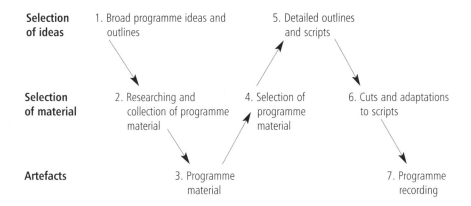

4.3 Production as process: selection and stages of programme broadcasting. Source: Elliott,1979

Marketing

Programmes have to be sold – to backers and producers, to audiences, to other television systems. Genre product is easy to market because its features are already known and understood by its 'buyers'. These features, which will include personalities, can become marketing tools in themselves. An actor such as Nick Berry is a classic example of a marketable feature for British audiences, having become a successful character in a soap opera (*EastEnders*), then popular in a soap crime series (*Heartbeat*). He was heavily featured in the promotion trails for a new series, *Harbour Lights*, also a kind of soap in which he took the lead as the local harbourmaster. The series was not in fact a success in terms of ratings. It is easier to sell a known successful series at a trade fair than a new one, but a new series is more marketable if it exploits an old formula. An example of this is *Jonathan Creek*, which is stuffed to the gills with clichés, starting with the idea of the brilliant intuitive detective and his assistant. The marketable variation here is the persona of comedian Alan Davies, as the hero and professional deviser of illusions, and his on–off romantic relationship with a female journalist played by Caroline Quentin. The usually one-off episodes update the classic English mystery formula. They are tailored for a family audience. They exploit English backgrounds and types. This is prime material for marketing abroad, and indeed the series has been successful in overseas markets.

The crossing of cultural boundaries is more likely with genre material. Detective action stories appeal to all urban populations. Youth soaps, their types and their themes make sense to most young people with 'Western-world' values and backgrounds: variations of local detail add spice and cult status. Programme categories such as sport have wide cultural accessibility – you don't need to have much English to understand what is going on, even if dubbing isn't available. This opens up a debate about:

- the archetypal nature of genres and their elements – i.e. all cultures have heroes and villains in their stories
- the global influence of television, in which the accessibility of genre material is partly built on familiarity with previous material: more means more.

Pleasures

Genre products are especially relevant to ideas about audience pleasures. I don't want to repeat points made above (p. 70) about the possible nature of those pleasures. But it is valid to attend to those characteristics of genres which actually appear to hit the pleasure spots.

Genres work to **formulas of repeated elements**, which are also sometimes described as **conventions**. These formulas have some flexibility in terms of what elements are used and how, but generally they hold true enough to be one way of defining a genre as a genre. So one might still expect to see the attractive female assistant in many game shows as a stock character. One expects to see the authoritative desk and high-tech set dressing in news programmes – the familiar background and decor. One expects to see something like a courtroom scene or a police-station interview in a crime drama – a stock situation. The ways in which the formulas are used are also about conventions, or rules of the game. One expects to see protagonists opposed to one another, in conflict over some issue. One expects to see the studio audience used to evoke humour or excitement in quiz shows or game shows.

In all this the key word is **expectations**. We enjoy seeing our expectations realized, though we get bored if too many of the same old conventions are used in the same old ways. We also get pleasure from having expectations frustrated. So if the couple set up to have an affair in a soap opera don't have one, this can also be satisfying to the viewer trying to second guess motivation and plot.

Pleasure lies in anticipation, involvement, complicity, and is an expression of the relationship between text and audience.

Pleasure may be enhanced when it is shared with others in discussion, something which television especially allows one to to do. Viewing television is a shared experience, as opposed to the solitary pleasure of reading a magazine. Viewing takes place in a safe environment which the viewers own and control, as opposed to, for instance, theatre. Precisely because genres are formulaic, we can both know them and not know them. We can reasonably anticipate what might be said and done by characters and with what outcomes – as we try to do through the process of perception in everyday life. Yet just as people defy our expectations, so genre characters may slip away from anticipated behaviours. But again, whereas in life this may cause us anxiety, in the simulated life of television it doesn't matter. We can play the pleasure game without suffering any consequences.

The repetition of the genre formula reinforces conventions. It creates familiarity and degrees of predictability which teeter on the edge between pleasurable recognition and plain tedium. It reinforces expectations that elements will appear and will be used in conventional ways. Pleasures may be revisited, as with the sparring dialogue in characters from a sitcom. Pleasures may be renewed – for example, if one of the characters unexpectedly tries to break away from the anchorage of the sitcom location.

Genres exist in a social and cultural context with which the television audience interacts. This context influences how one makes sense of programmes. It also changes over a period of time, as do the genres. Genres adapt or collapse. They also supply a kind of self-supporting context in which one genre product refers to another. Our understanding of one chat show depends on our understanding of others (intertextuality again). For example, an English chat show such as *Vanessa* relates to the example of the American show hosted by Ricki Lake. Both are fronted by large personalities, include personal and intrusive material and are a long way from early examples of the genre which might typically contain friendly and admiring conversations with minor stars or with compliant studio audiences. Audiences have become accustomed to intrusion and personal revelations through 'kiss-and-tell' stories in the populist press and magazines. So the genre has developed its conventions and its style. It has its own history. But it is also in a dynamic relationship with the cultural conditions of its audience. The one affects the other.

Soaps as genre

Soaps are a dominant example of a television genre, and are referred to elsewhere in chapters on realism and audiences (Chapters 7 and 9). They have developed since the mid-twentieth century, drawing on a tradition of realism and naturalism in British television. They are rooted in slices of British culture, mostly urban. They address a female audience through narratives which are significantly interested in relationships and emotions. The place of television in the home and its availability to women is linked to these characteristics of soaps. Soap qualities have crossed over into other genres such as the cop show. They may also be understood in relation to the strong strand of romantic drama which is a staple part of television programming.

Mary Ellen Brown, referred to in Fiske's excellent discussion of gendered television (1987), produces a useful list of soap-opera genre characteristics, as follows:

1 a serial form which resists narrative closure
2 the presence of multiple characters and plots
3 the use of time which parallels actual time, and the implication that action continues to take place whether we are watching or not
4 an abrupt segmentation between parts of the narrative structure
5 an emphasis on dialogue, problem-solving and intimate conversation
6 having male characters who are 'sensitive men'
7 having female characters who are professional and otherwise powerful outside the home
8 being set in the home, or some other place which functions as a home, providing the setting for the show.

I would in fact dispute the notion that a significant number of soap characters are professional females. Women are empowered in the domestic sphere and in relation to their ability to deal with relationships, in a way that men largely fail to do. But otherwise, Brown's version of a formula refers to a kind of domestic drama that mimics the rhythms of home life and 'real time'.

The pleasures of the genre are in some way measured by the huge ratings, by the fact that an early-evening soap is a familiar programmer's device for attracting and holding the channel's audience. The repetition and reinforcement of the formula has not caused the attraction of soaps to pall – *Coronation Street* has been going for 35 years. Indeed soap failures are often a punishment for breaking the rules of the game. The BBC's relative flop in the early 1990s, *Eldorado*, suffered because it was located in Spain, not Britain – reality is not about always being 'on holiday'. British soaps have never had a taste for the exotic.

Ideology

In ideological terms this pleasure – which may be variously described as a relationship with the text or a condition created out of the text – may be seen as a sign of the secret workings of power. Rather than being a sign of audience autonomy, it may be a sign that the very complicity of pleasure, the joining in with the game of conventions, actually shuts off other ways of looking at genre material. By this argument, genres can never be subversive or easily read as oppositional. They draw the viewer into worlds in which the dominant ideology rules. This dominant ideology is composed of dominant positions, attitudes and values which are represented through the construction of the text. These positions are taken on significant cultural elements which help define social place, social relationships, the exercise of power. In this case we are talking about gender, kinds of work or labour, class, law, education, childhood and so on.

So the meanings of genre products are deeply ideological. The very repetitive nature of genre means that it also reinforces ideological positions. The pleasurable familiarity of genre material operates, it can be argued, to deflect attention from what it is really saying about social differences and about the exercise of power. In textual-analysis terms, it creates a climate in which preferred readings are made and oppositional readings are difficult to enter into.

For example, an episode of *Ricki Lake* (broadcast in Britain on 24 April 1999) includes a segment which is about the reunion of two young women, ex high-school friends. Both domestic and studio audiences are complicit in the pleasure of this reunion. The show's hostess invites us to enjoy her power to bring about this special occasion. The spin on the situation is that both females are overweight, but the one who has been hidden from her friend on set (but not from us), has taken control of her excess and has lost 140 pounds. So far, and typically, the show is about the empowerment of women, about coming to terms with weight, excess and a sense of self-worth. It is to a degree challenging the dominant view that the value and power of women is measured in the shape and weight of their bodies – something that ties in with meanings shot through the fashion and entertainment industries.

But I would argue that darker meanings are concealed. First, the camera and narrative conspire to put the two young women on show, on stage for an audience, actually drawing attention to their weight problem (one of them might fairly be described as obese). As much as being shining examples of friendship and positive attitudes, the visual language of television and the genre context of such shows actually sets them up as being 'odd', exceptions to an unspoken 'rule'. This rule is that women should 'normally' be slim to be considered attractive. 'Attractive' is something that is measured in relation to attracting men. The norms of ideology as meanings can't so easily be dismissed, even by Ricki Lake. Second, the intertextual nature of television, combined with the repetitive nature of genres, tends to reinforce all this. Because chat shows talk about the subject of obesity and self-esteem fairly often, whether in terms of losing weight or living with weight, they actually give it a profile. Because they talk about it as a problem to be dealt with, they draw attention to its 'problem-ness'. They confirm it as a problem; they confirm ideological positions about fat is not OK, especially for women. This is a double bind because the problem and issues need to be talked about, yet the act of talking about them confirms the dominant ideology which one might wish to oppose. But, I repeat, this is not just any old talk: this is the language and discourses of television; this is the reinforcement of genre.

> In what ways does news as a genre confirm views of who is powerful or powerless in society?

Myths

Ideologies hide within cultural myths, and there is nothing so pertinent to genres as a good myth. These myths are cultural illusions – often in the way that people are represented – which stand for the wish fulfilments of that culture. They are also likely to stand for the interests of those who have different kinds of power in our society. So in that case we are indeed still with ideology.

As Figure 4.4 suggests, there is an overlapping relationship between concepts such as genre, myth and representation. They all contribute to understanding the ways that we look at the world, and to where these ways of looking may come from. They all contribute a definition of meanings, whether or not you believe that those meanings are in the text before they are in your head.

Myths in genres are meanings which can equally be approached through discourses. For example, there are ways of talking about masculinity. Genre material constructs myths about what 'proper men' are like. The masculine discourse uses languages in certain ways to reinforce the myth. An example of

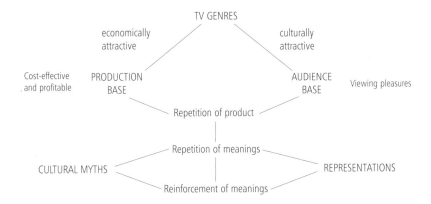

Television genres may promote cultural meanings through repetition and reinforcement: for example, about the innocence of childhood, the strength of family bonding in the past or the purity of nature. these meanings do not stand up to examination; they are idealised; they are myths.

4.4 Television genres and the reinforcement of cultural myths.

this on television in May 1991 was in the two-part crime drama called *Butterfly Collectors* (BBC1). One protagonist – the police detective – was played by Peter Postlethwaite. As represented, his character was interesting for the ways in which it endorsed and partly challenged myths of masculinities and the conventional representation of the detective hero. Essentially, ideas about masculinity equalling individualism, determination and separateness were maintained. There was also more than a touch of masculine ideas about aggression, physicality, intelligence. These are gender mythologies which both work in the interests of promoting the idea of male superiority, and are also part of the genre representation of male heroes, part of the conventions. The degree of challenge came in the emphasis of the piece on psychology and relationships, rather than on a process of detection with force on the side of law. The hero was flawed: he had a failed marriage and two children behind him; he was on medication to deal with his anxieties. Although it is true that such protagonists are often represented as failing in relationships – the loneness of the lone hero – in this case he was in another relationship and clearly had a self-critical and caring side. However, it has to be said that in the end the genre and its mythologies were endorsed by the denouement. In spite of bad behaviour and errors of judgement, he was shown to have been correct in assessing the scale and focus of the crime. He was right, and the rest were wrong.

To put this example in perspective, one also has to acknowledge all that other media material which constructs the myths and conventions, the ideas about masculinity and its 'rightful' dominance. It is also instructive to note the contrasts between film and television. For all the critical tone of my brief commentary on *Butterfly Collectors*, it was also an intelligent piece about demons in the soul, about relationships, about morality. It ran for for over 3 hours over two nights. The medium of television, its tradition of drama (not only genre drama), its experimentation with genres, its scheduling, all combined to produce something that certainly wasn't cliché. The contrast with most Hollywood product – full of action, effects and crudely drawn myths – is compelling. The movie machine has made this situation for itself: less product than television, bigger costs, a global audience for first screenings and a cultural position which positively wants to reproduce the myths.

These mythologies come out of genre collectively – that is, in a range of television output. Just as film stars are said to embody cultural myths, I would argue that television mythologizes cultural players such as Mother Teresa (sainted by the media for her undoubtedly good works), and it mythologizes its own people. An example of this was the murder in 1999 of the presenter Jill Dando. She had successfully fronted travel programmes, news and a crime investigation programme. Her persona had been that of the attractive, reliable big sister. The notion of the persona, of a public front, already implies a degree of mythmaking. She had also been fitted up by promotion for the 'blonde on the beach' and 'reliable dame'. Ironically, in the week when she was killed, the mythologizing of Jill Dando had taken another step with a full-page picture on the cover of the *Radio Times* listing magazine, trailing her forthcoming appearance in a new investigative show, and portraying her from low angle and clad in black leathers, sexy action-woman style. The range of female mythologies which she had occupied was being extended and reinforced. But finally the news eulogies completed the mythmaking process, in which her undoubted skills were subsumed within a story of talent lost, of a women who had become the nation's sweetheart, a confidante, an object of admiration, an object of safe desire. These are the mythologies of gender politics, of masculine desire contradicted by fear of female sexuality, of an able woman being contained within the mythologies of gender representation.

Television programmes engage us in several respects:

- they please us
- they are part of the rhythms of our everyday lives
- they offer us a grand buffet of information and entertainment from which to choose
- they are familiar in our conversations
- they are a point of reference in arguments
- they are interwoven with the meaning systems through which we understand the world and by which we run our lives.

5

Television, Narrative and Form

PREVIEW

This chapter deals with:

- Television flow as narrative
- narrative and realism
- mode of address and audience positioning
- different forms of narrative seen in television
- visual narrative
- narrative structures
- characteristics of television narratives.

TELEVISION OUTPUT AS SUPERNARRATIVE

If one takes on the idea of flow, television is a continuous narrative from the moment one cuts into it with the remote control and with one's consciousness. It also has a kind of narrative structure imposed by the schedulers. The voice-over trails provide a link to the next programme and across to the other narratives on shared commercial and BBC channels. This notion of television output as a kind of 'supernarrative' has the attraction of defining television narrative as something 'different'. One could equally argue that this is missing the point. Ideas about genre, like narrative, are applicable to many media. But this does not negate discussion of particular developments and treatments of genre on television. The same is true of narrative.

Output as narrative also begs the question whether this narrative is a construction of those who generate the output or of the audience who build a kind of narrative out of their selective viewing – zap the channels and make a story. James Hay in the Afterword to *Channels of Discourse Reassembled* criticizes a view of narrative in television which he sees as being tied to literary studies – the 'discrete narrative text' (Hay 1992). I would argue the other way around: that narrative only becomes meaningful as a term for the critic and as an experience for the audience when there is some kind of discreteness – in any medium.

This view does not, to pick up another issue raised by Hay, stop one debating narrative as another approach to the production of meaning. It does not stop one from seeing narrative as a way of realizing ideology. It does not stop one from recognizing that the text and its meaning may shift from one audience member to another. This situation may be further complicated by the cultural context of the audience, or by their 'narrative competence' in reading the text or the flow of output. But whether the meaning is produced by the audience or by the text on screen, still it has a coherence and a structure for each viewer which makes it more than a collection of sounds and images. In semiotic terms one has a code or interlocking codes, a meaningful organization of signs.

I am not saying that one cannot get any overall meanings at all from an evening of selective channel viewing. There may be ironic juxtapositions between adverts using idealized family lives, which appear within a drama that is about deception and adultery. But the notional supernarrative loses focus as soon as one looks for coherence of meaning, for moments of resolution, for more than something like a conceptual lucky dip. If one does dip into television output then, apart from the links, what one actually taps into are the programme narratives.

Still there is the question of what exactly television narrative is. In one respect I am defining it in the various sections of this chapter. In other respects I would define it as follows:

- the structure and meanings of events, relationships and ideas assumed by the viewer from watching a television programme
- the development of these structures and meanings, whether defined in terms of pace or of direction, or for example in Todorovian terms of equilibrium to disruption to resolution (and a new equilibrium)
- the programme itself as a consciously created narrative artefact
- ordered meanings which are built into the programme
- the means by which this order is brought about, either in the form and content of the programme or in the mind of the viewer
- that structure of sense which the viewer creates through interacting with the programme as text.

Narrative has been loosely referred to as 'the story'. One problem with this word is that it is sometimes tied to fiction. But all television programmes have narrative. Television has narratives because every programme has some degree of intention and structure behind it. As Sarah Kozloff (1992) puts it, 'in stories, events do not progress randomly'. How they progress is a function of textual organization and the audience working on the text. Our cultural experience not only knows about television narratives, but is driven to narrative anyway.

This drive comes from the earliest experiences – stories told to us about relatives, stories read to us from books, stories which we tell about our lives. Children play games which involve them making up stories about their lives and their toys. And then we should remember that television is also one of the early experiences of childhood. So a great range of cultural influences offer us narratives at an early age, and help define what narrative is. Television for children tells us stories from the screen, gives us animated stories, introduces us to ideas about establishing situation and conflict or about dramatic climax. I have watched children react to television narrative before they can read, responding to titles music signalling the start of the narrative experience, for example.

NARRATIVE AND REALISM

The idea that realism is a function of narrative – yet another aspect of telling the story – is perfectly reasonable. I have chosen to look separately at modes of realism in television in Chapter 7 because this is such a considerable area. However, the close relationship between the two concepts is unarguable. For example, the way that narrative devices position the viewer in relation to what appears to be going on with characters and events is very much bound up with the believability of that position.

David Graddol in *Media Texts* (Graddol and Boyd-Barratt, 1994) says directly that the 'dominant narrative technique for . . . storytelling is what is called realism'. This narrative realism is what I would define as mainstream narrative using a third-person address – what Graddol calls the 'infallible narrator'. When we are asked to take the view of characters within the story being unfolded by the narrator (a newsreader or documentary voice-over), he calls the devices which make this shift 'focalisers'. In television drama, the camera may take the part of the 'narrator's voice' by positioning itself as a neutral onlooker to the action. But sometimes it is also shifted within this overall third-person neutrality to take the part of a character. This is first-person narrative, described below (p. 104). In this case we understand the narrative for a while through that character's view, but we know that the omniscient narrator view is still there to go back to. Graddol would make the point that 'realist narrative encourages the reader to feel that they know more about this objective world (*i.e. that of the constructed story*) than any of the characters do'.

This point about a dominant mode of realism being part of a dominant mode of narrative is a useful one (see classic realist text, p. 112 below).

However, the rest of this chapter also illustrates the fact that narrative is rather more complicated than this – as indeed is realism. For example, to talk as Graddol does about the camera drawing us into the action in various ways suggests that there is a narrative action (a realism?!) existing out there. In fact it is that very camera which causes us to construct in our minds the idea of that action, which did not exist until we conceived of it. Similarly there is a danger that when talking about a privileged viewer position (as Graddol does) we may lose sight of the fact that this position is also 'a trick'. Because we see and understand more than any one of the characters, we are persuaded of the reality of the 'whole narrative', to which only we are privy. But the whole thing, narrative and realism, is a con job. We collude in this con, both using and being used by the text and its creators through the devices of the text. The 'story of' or the 'story about' doesn't really exist out there. We just choose to believe that it does for as long as we are engaging with that stream of images and sounds which we call a programme. This story, this reality, is not the same as the experiential reality that we inhabit in other parts of our lives. And yet the postmodernist fusion of these realities has been lurking for many years. In 1975 fans of the soap *Crossroads* turned up to the publicity-device wedding in Birmingham of characters Meg Richardson and Hugh Mortimer, treating it as if it were the real thing.

Fiske (1987) argues that realism dominates television narrative – 'realism imposes coherence and resolution upon a world that has neither'. He refers to Kuhn's (1985) summary of classic realist narrative, which may be paraphrased as:

- a linearity of plot, of cause and effect, relating to the setting up of an enigma which is in the end resolved
- a high degree of narrative closure
- fiction which is governed by the creation of a sense of consistency in time and place
- characters who are psychologically rounded, and who fit our sense of motivation/consistency.

Fiske also argues that the realism of television is an 'ideological practice'. That is to say, it is based on conventions which create the illusion that what is real in the programme works in the same way as for real-life experience. This of course is not the case. But by confusing the two, television realism persuades us, for example, that what is said about men and women is true for life. Men are actually not the attractive action heroes of some television series. Ideology, working through the narrative and the realism, is persuading us that they should be like this.

NARRATIVE AND MODE OF ADDRESS

The concept of mode of address has been explained in Chapter 2, as a way of understanding aspects of television form and the relationship set up between text and viewer.

It has a great deal to do with narrative in that our notion of this in any programme is produced through uses of form. For example, the significance of emotional reaction in a character from fiction is signalled through the use of a close-up. Or the significance of a goal scored in a football narrative is signalled through the use of an action replay.

If there is something called 'the narrative', as the 'meaning centre' of a programme, it is offered to us in certain ways and we choose to conceive of it in certain ways. So whether the narrative is a thing which is producer-driven or audience-made, still the way that it is set up for us is another function of mode of address. A docusoap such as *Airport* lays out a cast of 'characters' operating within story strands in which problems to be solved provide the 'movement' of the narrative – a sense of beginning to end. This is fictional narrative, whatever the use of real people with skilful editing to construct a dramatic narrative. The programme also uses the exdiegetic voice of a documentary-style narrator to underline the development of events, to dramatize crisis and conflict. This is what is done in the making of the material, which in turn creates something which we conceptualize as a television narrative.

The programme producers have an understanding of narrative and of conventions for building this (as well as other modes like realism). They use these conventions, these aspects of form, with the experience of audience response, the 'knowledge' of what they and the audience share in terms of making sense of television. They use the conventions in the text. The audience identifies and responds to these conventions in ways which may be more or less as the producers had expected. In this model, mode of address and reception of text incorporating that address are more or less the same as encoding and decoding the text (*see* Fig. 5.1).

NARRATORS AND AUDIENCE POSITIONING

This section might also be discussed under mode of address, because it may be read in terms of the relationship with addressee which the act of address sets up. In this case I want to draw attention to television's use of narrators, in their many guises. The positioning idea also assumes a text or narrative as a distinct thing, to which we as viewers may stand in some relationship. There is a neat contradiction which as viewers we ignore, but as critics we have to recognize. The text as conceptualized must be in our heads. So we – some kind

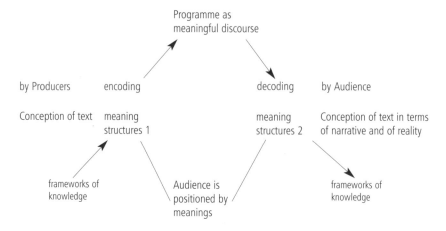

The producers and the audience are part of one process. But they encode and decode meanings on the basis of different structures/conceptions of what the text is. The audience also conceives of a narrative and a reality a part of 'text', which contributes to how they are positioned in relation to the text.

5.1 Encoding and decoding of meaning: positioning of audience.

of consciousness centre in the brain – are said to stand in a relationship to the text – another construction of the mind. We externalize the narrative as text as something called a programme, on the screen. But of course there is nothing fixed on the screen or in the transmission system which we can, as it were, put in a box and carry around. Even the electronic medium of broadcasting is transient, and in any case its 'existence' is a mental construct stimulated by watching and listening. This may seem to labour the point. But if one is to go on talking meaningfully about positioning in relation to the text, it needs to be understood that this positioning is entirely a conceptual operation. We build a sense of 'the narrative' as an entity, and then falsely separate ourselves from this entity, as if it were not within us.

Television narrators stimulate this operation, with different effects on how we believe that we relate to the text. This relationship could be in space or time, but it could also be in terms of, for example, how we feel about the validity of the text as record.

Narrators I take to be those who in general 'front' programmes – presenters. I describe them as narrators because they perform the same functions as storytellers, though they are not the only 'player' on screen. The newscaster tells the story of the news that day, bringing in others to contribute to that storytelling. The quiz compère controls the action in the studio, moving along the action of the games or the questions or the competition.

5.2 ITN newscaster Trevor McDonald is a trusted narrator of the news and a part of the news discourse which gives us meanings about the authority and reliability of the news machine.

They introduce and dismiss the 'characters'. Although television drama will sometimes involve a character who tells the story (seen or heard), in general this is not the case. So these remarks are directed towards the genres and modes of factual television.

Narrators may be seen on screen, as with Nick Ross of *Crimewatch UK*. They may be a voice-over – Kenneth Branagh behind the series *Walking with Dinosaurs*. If they are seen then they have more codes through which to position us. The voice of newscaster Moira Stewart has dignity and neutrality, but it is her appearance which affirms authority and reliability.

Narrators may create a **persona** through narrating, or have a previous persona which they bring to a programme. Either way, this persona may be part of the positioning process. Nowhere is this more true than with television ads. Richard Briars may be chosen to voice-over toilet rolls because his long comedy-career roles carry connotations of good humour with decency and reliability. The audience is positioned in terms of an emotional relationship with this material. They are prepared to listen and to show good will.

This idea of positioning works in terms of **role**, with all the nuances of that term: social roles, emotional roles, occupational roles, relationship roles and so on. The idea of narrator covers the gamut of presenters, compères, hosts, reporters and others who address us from the screen in vision and/or voice. Examples include Zoe Ball as 'best mate'; Jeremy Paxman as 'barrister for the people', David Attenborough as 'best loved uncle and nature expert'; Julian Clary as 'camp queen tease'; Trevor McDonald as the 'trusty newscaster'.

Whatever role summary one chooses and agrees, still the point is that that sense of role positions you, as a member of the audience, in relation to the personality and to the text of which they are a part. That 'positioning' includes an attitude towards the material, assumptions about how one is meant to read the personality and the text, and an orientation towards (an alignment with) the 'narrative as it is meant to be read'.

Positioning also creates kind of social relationship with the television narrator. When David Attenborough whispers his comments about the wildlife that his cameraperson is close to, he is drawing us into the situation, making believe that we are there with him, in some far-away location. We become co-conspirators in his adventure. Noel Edmonds has done the same thing on his *HouseParty* show, when he mugs to the camera and/or beckons us through it to come to the door with him, or to enter someone's home through a previously concealed camera. This sense of relationship, of closeness, of subjectivity, is strong on television. So often the face stares at us from the screen, addressing us, inviting us, sometimes challenging us.

Anne Robinson on *Watchdog* appears to talk to us through the camera (as much as to talk to the camera). This is the same illusion of presence which the expert newscaster creates by reading the autocue to us as if it weren't there. The relationship with the audience becomes personalized and individualized through technology and style of address. We are positioned into a false one-to-one relationship. Sometimes we are invited to write in or respond in some way. We go along with this positioning because it mirrors our social relationships and makes us feel comfortable.

Sometimes the positioned relationship is less one-to-one than 'join the group'. This is typified by the *Big Breakfast Show* in which we are meant to feel that the host and hostess are fronting a kind of party to which we have been invited. Our participation is guaranteed not only by frequent address to camera, but also by a camera which shows the cameras. This device of flattering to deceive, of authenticating the experience by showing the technology, is not a new one. But in this case the programme talks to the crew as well, invites their comments or action on air. We are drawn into the studio, and into the ambience in which this 'pseudo-party' is happening. We become a guest.

It is a kind of truism that the technology which transparently accompanies the narrator actually defines what we see and hear. It carries the images and the sounds. In the same way, the director controlling that technology from the gallery or the outside-broadcast van also has a narrating function. This is not to diminish or negate the function and effect of the narrator, as seen or heard. But it is to put their powers in a context. It is to suggest that the forces which position us as readers of television programmes are complex, and are a fusion of the changing possibilities of technology and of the collaborative intentions of those who make the programmes.

> Does audience positioning help us understand what a programme is about, or does it merely control us so that we stay watching the programme?

FORMS OF NARRATIVE IN PROGRAMMES

This section refers to varieties of narrative form in television programmes. These are not necessarily associated with genres. They have a great deal to do with the viewer's apparent relationship with the text, so comments made above about narrators are relevant as a preliminary to understanding them. The two basic forms are those which observe and those which involve: the objective and the subjective. These are ways of making narrative which are much older than television, and which have their evidence and origins in epic poetry and early novels.

Objective narrative

In this form the viewer appears to view the narrative as a made and real set of events and interactions. It is a form involving a degree of detachment. We, or rather the camera, look in on a scene from a drama as if peering through a window at life in a room. The metaphor has been explicitly used to describe television news – 'a window on the world' – with all its inaccurate connotations of an observed reality. Sometimes the spatial detachment is enlarged by means of exterior shots and view of action from a distance. Sometimes it is contracted: we may be taken into the room, but are still just standing watching what is going on. Television, given the confined scale of the screen, tight budgets and its location in the living room, is notoriously fond of the interior, as it is of the close-up. But these tendencies can be exaggerated – much sport, such as Grand Prix racing, takes place outside and on a large scale. Similarly, quite a few other programmes such as the successful *Time Team* archeology series also work outside, use long shots and employ objective narrative.

This form of narrative may be described in terms of its detached viewing position, but it is not necessarily about emotional detachment or lack of dramatic pitch. In any case, programmes will use this and subjective narrative form together. For example, the 999 dramatized reconstruction series has shown a boat in difficulties as if from another boat, and people drowning as if one is under water with them. Typically of television today, factuality is explained through some fictional devices.

Subjective narrative

This narrative form, where the viewer 'takes part in' the story, is further constructed by a camera which appears to take part in the action or to take the part of a 'player'. It is commonplace in fiction, where the use of a steadycam can cause the viewer to feel as if they are the prowler in the crime drama, peering through windows or walking through rooms. But even in documentary the camera-as-viewer-as-participant will be used. We are shown through a telephoto the lions which we have just seen the wildlife reporter looking at through binoculars. The docusoap *Airport* telephoto tracks along with the feet of two security officers, in a knowing reference to crime fiction and that shot of walking feet which conceals the identity of the walker(s).

A sophisticated version of this narrative form was used by Dennis Potter in his drama *Karaoke*. In this case the authorial persona was projected as an author on screen, eventually dying of cancer, and as an author-as-character seen taking part in episodes which the writer had apparently created. Generally we watched the writer, but sometimes observed, through that writer's eyes and comments on sound track, those episodes where the author as character was taking part in a story. This was a complex layer of realities and subjectivities. The viewer's ability to distinguish the story from the story-within-the-story is, I would argue, the effect of viewing experience, of having practiced shifts of reality and subjectivities. Such shifts challenge the viewer's ability to locate in space and time, all the while remembering that the whole thing is only a television text.

Events as narrative – plot

As one explores notions of what the word 'narrative' actually means in television programmes – story, if you like – it becomes clear that we are dealing with several things at the same time.

At one level, separate programme events can be read as meaning: you the viewer are meant to be there (place/spatiality); the time is meant to be this (temporality). This could apply to the drama which places you in Scotland in the evening or to *SM: TV Live* which places you in the studio, now. But then location and time can change. The drama can jump to another day. The Saturday-morning young people's programme can jump to an outside location. There are cues – in dialogue, announcements, captions, visual icons – which do this locating.

Then events are put in sequence, by writers, directors, editors, with the intention of making more complex meanings – about what is happening to characters, about what might happen next, about likely problems in the drama of relationships. These meanings come out of the ordering of events, the comparison of one event with another, the cumulative effect of events.

Narrative, development, motivation – impetus

We have a concept of narratives developing, usually in terms of

- the growth of an idea or theme
- movement towards some point of closure when propositions or events are resolved
- the development of relationship in some respect, perhaps from security to conflict to disintegration.

There is a sense in which we inevitably feel that television narrative develops because we spend a period of time with the television set and its programme, and because in our culture we conceptualize time as being about development: the birth, growth, decay model.

This sense of movement within time is of course reinforced by the creation of screentime in television as a medium. Screentime moves in and out of real time. We watch an interview with someone on a chat show in real time, and share a sense of the conversation moving forward, of the host bringing things out through questions, but also developing the conversation up to an inevitable moment of closure when he or she has to wind things up for the end of the programme (or the recording).

Equally, we can cope with screentime when fiction action (or edited documentary) switches between characters and locations, bringing together selected fragments of conversation. Again, we have a 'knowledge' of drive and control behind the visual narrative because we realize that this is not real time or real space.

This 'movement' dimension of narrative is not only conceptualized as a kind of progress in both events/action and drama/meanings. It is also understood in terms of driving force and of speed of movement. From this **psychological perspective** a great deal is invested in **motivation**. Again, it is common to talk about this in terms of why characters think and behave as they do in fiction. But in fact motivation also infuses factual material. News stories are about the motivations of two sides in a conflict. A documentary about social deprivation will in effect be much about the ways that deprivation motivates people who are deprived, and does or does not motivate those who interact with those deprived people.

So there is a view of narrative as movement, as development and as moving faster or slower largely as result of the motivations of people or institutions with which that narrative is concerned.

Relationship as narrative

Another perspective on the concept of narrative may construct it in terms of relationships: those between the players in the programme and the individual viewer, and those within the programme.

The text–audience relationship is partly explained in sections elsewhere in this book which deal with mode of address and with viewer positioning (Chapter 2). It also has something to do with each viewer's sense of relationship with those who appear in the programme. This raises the point that the concept of narrative should not be seen as a given object of viewing and understanding. The narrative is not just an object within the programme, waiting to be uncovered. Narrative is something which is dynamically created in the mind of the viewer as they interact with the television programme. The producers of the programme indeed may intend a certain kind of relationship, and even a certain kind of understanding of the narrative. They may use devices of television form to try and establish what they want. But they cannot absolutely control that relationship or that sense of narrative.

The sense of relationship concerned may be with any 'player' in any kind of programme. So, for example, the viewer's feelings of hostility or of empathy towards the presenter of a current-affairs programme or towards a character in a fiction drama will affect the definition of the narrative in their minds. The feelings will be a dimension of that narrative. Feelings about David Frost, fronting *Frost on Sunday*, will influence the kind of story or meaning that is built from viewing an interview which he conducts. Different kinds of attitude mean different kinds of attention to different kinds of feature in the interview. This difference may be interpreted as part of the making of different kinds of narrative.

More straightforward, as apparently being about content, are relationships within a programme. *Friends* becomes a story about how Ross gets on with Rachel, and so on. From this point of view, the stuff of relationships – their qualities, where they are going – becomes the stuff of narrative. But again, this covers material other than fiction. The relationship – and the public end to it – between Richard and Judy fronting *Good Morning Britain* is equally part of the story of the programme. They are both narrators and part of the narrative. They string together a set of stories through interviews, just as the newscaster strings together news stories. But they are part of a larger story which is the whole programme, including themselves. Although narrative is a complex term when examined closely, one can still acknowledge this relatively simple perspective of 'stories being about people', about how they relate to one another, about what appears to happen to those relationships.

> How may context and personal experience influence what the narrative is for the individual viewer?

VISUAL NARRATIVE

In this case one is referring specifically to the sequencing of pictures, as they make sense and make a story. This has a lot to do with continuity and with the so-called logic of an editing process which makes sense to the viewer in space and time. A simple example of this visual logic is made part of a comedy programme – *hale&pace@bbc*. The presenters get a member of the audience to dress up and act out lines read from cue cards. This set of performances is recorded, and then later spliced into a speech from a film made by a well-known actor. The editing produces cross-cutting from novice to actor, with continuities in set, and with a narrative logic to the exchange of dialogue. Cross-cutting a conversation is the most basic language of visual narrative. But it is a language that we have learned, like speaking.

Visual narrative as picture cutting is not in the end really a separate element from other narrative features. But it is underneath those features, because unless we can read picture sequences (and sound cues) we won't get any further into narrative. For this reason I would argue that though television may innovate to a degree, it is rarely if ever genuinely experimental in its narrative constructions. Even minority audiences for television are so large that producers can't risk alienating them with incomprehensible visual narrative. It is noticeable that much of what one would call experimental material on television actually comes from cinema – the Channel 4 'cinema shorts' seasons, or screenings of movies such as *Powaquaatsi* in which the montage of human activity around the globe is fascinating, but there is no narrative as plot.

Our feeling about how straightforward visual narrative is relates to what the titles and mode of address have set us up for. We expect a documentary about some ecological disaster to be pretty straightforward in the ways in which it sets up the background and explains what happened, in which the pictures illustrate the explanation on the voice-over or switch between presenter and interviewees. The visual narrative is part of a drive to make things clear. But a mystery thriller may be more complex in the composition of visual narrative precisely because it wants to make things less clear, more mysterious. In this case, there could be unexplained cutaways to places and people which make more sense later in the drama. There could be abrupt parallel editing from one set of actions (narrative strands) to another – again because we are meant to work on the visual narrative, try to make sense of it, wait until later on to see how the strands come together.

In the case of television news, however, we don't expect the picture editors or vision mixers to be playing games with us. We expect to know what we are looking at and why. We expect to view some location sequence and to understand what is happening, where, to whom and why. An example from 1999 would be a report on the Bosnian conflict in which we would understand that we are on the Kosovan border; that the unhappy-looking people are refugees coming out of Kosovo; that the aircraft belong to 'our side' (NATO) and are bombing Serbia; that the person interviewed is Macedonian and is talking about the problems of coping with the refugees. This kind of visual narrative may be explanatory to a didactic degree, including maps of the region to give us a sense of where the people in the pictures are located, where they are going to and from. And of course our sense of where we are, what is happening, why, is underpinned by the voice of the reporter on the spot. The pictures tell the story, but not all the story. The ability of the pictures to tell the story depends on how familiar we are with their content. So genre material can be more economical with pictures and continuity because we are more able to fill in the gaps, having seen this sort of thing before.

NARRATIVE STRUCTURES AND MEANINGS

What we call the structure, shape or organizing principles of a television programme may be described as a function of its narrative. These structures may themselves be described – linear or circular narrative, for example. But beyond this they can also give rise to understanding of how narrative works on our consciousness, of meanings that we make about narrative.

Series and serials

Television is a medium which nurtures these formats because of competition for audiences and the never-ending demand for product to fill 24 hours a day across many channels. Series and serials are about continuity, closure and open-endedness.

Closure describes that feature of narrative structures where the plot closes off at the end of the story. It is where resolution is achieved, for example to a conflict between characters and over principles which has been driving forward the narrative and holding the interest of the viewer. Series are closed to the extent that each episode is complete in itself, even though the genre and the characters remain the same from one episode to another. *Spin City* with Michael J. Fox would be a typical example of this structure. Serials such as soaps can only achieve a certain amount of closure because they have to preserve the illusion of life going on from day to day. So given narrative strands may be closed off, most obviously when a character dies.

In other respects soaps are serials of the most continuous order, and are therefore **open-ended**. Characters come and go. Quarrels are resolved. Even murders take place. But the narrative structure has an everlasting timeline which invokes a special sense of realism through parallels with life experience, because as in life there will always be another day (a slot) to be filled. Producers have the opportunity to defer closure of narrative strands in a way which is denied to those who deal with the 'one-off' programme.

Continuity describes those narrative features which link one programme to another. In the series structure, which may or may not be given the resonance of genre, those features have to do with character and environment. Sitcoms are a good example of this – same people, same place. But the storylines change: narratives are set up and resolved week by week.

The fact that one can say this points to a core feature of narrative, notwithstanding the complexity of the term. It suggests that it is centrally about what happens to whom, how and with what outcome. I would argue that however fiction-oriented this statement sounds it can be applied to any piece of television material. Examples of 'anti-narrative' or challenges to narrative – rare on television – actually reinforce this idea. Their challenge is to what is happening, to how, to consequences. Our sense of what narrative is, defined generally in these terms, is so strong that we work hard to sort out these core features. We will make suppositions on the most slender evidence. We enjoy the challenge of forming narrative in our heads.

Structures and genres

To raise expectations in viewers, structures must be repeated. They are, even in the unconsciousness of the viewer, predictable. Repetition and predictability are also features of genres. I have already debated what the term genre means, how useful it is as a descriptive term, and these arguments must qualify what follows. But certainly it is obvious the certain kinds of organization of narrative match certain kinds of programme.

The soap opera with its strands of parallel plots is an obvious example. The news has an episodic structure of self-contained stories strung together to make a whole programme narrative. *Blind Date* has what might be called a 'before-and-after' structure in which the main part of the programme has two elements: the competition to set up the date for the next couple balanced by the review of the success of the date enjoyed (or not!) by a previous couple. Chat shows are structured around the interplay between guest/interviewee and host, motivated by the expectation of revelations.

In the case of sitcoms, Goodwin and Whannel (1990) point to the simplistic narrative structure involving a problem which has to be resolved within a half-hour programme, threaded on a storyline which has a logical temporal sequence. They refer to the importance of characters in resolving the narrative. It is the very character traits that amuse us which also often lead to the problem and the solution. Goodwin and Whannel list three aspects of narrative which attract television audiences:

- form: 'the setting up of a mystery (*a problem*) which we know will be resolved'
- 'individuals we can identify or empathise with'
- ' "magical" endings'.

What they also suggest is that these elements of attraction, the repetitive structures which we expect and enjoy, are part of that naturalization process through which ideology masks itself from the viewer. In other words, familiarity stops us from thinking about how television is working on us, about what it may really be saying. It is rather like participating in a ritual whose meaning is obscured by the ceremony. We watch and laugh and wait for everything to be all right, and ignore the fact that we have been 'going along' with social inequalities which are not really funny at all.

There are also some programmes which are predicated on given narrative structures but not obviously tied to genre. One example is a comic romance, *Goodnight Sweetheart*, in which the male protagonist slips in time between the modern day and the 1940s. In this case there is a kind of parallel narrative, because we are made aware that events have continued in one time strand while he is in another. It is also a kind of mannered use of the flashback narrative in which the flash has become extended.

One can find other examples of structure as organization of events and of dramatic development in various television dramas. One fairly common example is the circular narrative, in which the beginning is the end, and the main part of the narrative is an extended flashback leading back up to the resolution.

It is clear that structure is indeed another feature of narrative, and that it provides a kind of conceptual framework within which events and interactions take place. It contributes to the meaning of those events and interactions. For example, in a circular narrative, if we know that the main story is a lead up to the opening/closing scene, then this gives us privileged knowledge of events to come behind that main part of the text. It imbues us with a special anticipation. It causes us to look for significance in actions. It allows the producers to play with the audience, knowing that it will look for that significance.

There is now a critical interest in what are described as **postmodernist texts**. One of the defining features of these may be a lack of 'conventional' narrative. Form, style, treatment become more important than structure. However, it has to be said that television programmes are not really inclined to postmodernism in this respect. For a start, audience responses suggest that people actually like plot lines and dramatic development. Then there is the structure of television programming, with its slots and advertising breaks, and the need to hold the attention of the audience. These facts influence narrative structure by requiring some kind of unresolved dramatic climax to occur just before a break. It is also the case that television does not in general have the budgets to give production values to form, to the way things are presented visually. In cinema, the sketchy plots of action films are invisible under a heavy gouache of stylistic tricks and ironies.

Of course, postmodernism is not to be defined simply in terms of a dichotomy between form and structure. But again, modernism in narrative is not defined simply in terms of the classic realist text, with its dramatic climaxes and narrative closure. Television has its postmodernist moments. There was critical excitement over *Twin Peaks* in the late 1980s, with its *mélange* of genres, its surrealism and its rambling multiple plots. But in the event it was an exceptional concept from a film maker. Some would argue it had a better postmodern predeccesor in the cult British paranoia series *The Prisoner*, in the 1960s. In this case nothing much happened structurally except that Patrick McGoohan was pursued endlessly (but grippingly) by ill-defined threats.

It could be argued that the audience take a postmodern attitude to narrative when they channel hop across programmes as if sampling party dips. But this does not mean that the programmes themselves don't have structure. Indeed one could argue that it is the immediate recognition of structures and other conventional features which causes the fickle finger of the controller to move on – 'been there, seen it'.

Television has the opportunity to break away from structures through its ability to put minicams in private places, and to broadcast live from many locations. Watch life as it happens and avoid the imposition of narrative structures (and the potential imposition of meanings upon the audience). But it isn't like that. A random glance at British television (on 21 May 1999) throws up examples. ITV is showing two fly-on-the-wall docusoaps successively: *For Better For Worse*, about a couple starting married life, and *Family Life*, following events in the lives of a family from Leeds. These programmes have qualities of naturalism and actuality which contrast with the contrived and structured situations of the sitcom *Only Fools and Horses*, repeated on BBC1 on the same evening. But they too have been edited and organized. They include dramatic climaxes, dramatic anticipation, problems and their resolution. *For Better For Worse* does have that postmodernist sense of intertextuality and fragmentation, borrowing as it does from soap operas. It dodges between the stories of eight different couples. It has to be understood in terms of its mixed genres. But still there is structure.

On the same evening, *Heartland FM* (BBC2) is described as an observational documentary series about a community radio station. It has something in common with the full-blown docusoap and like them develops a storyline out of its raw material. Perhaps the most postmodernist offering on this particular evening is one of the candid-camera category. *The World of the Secret Camera* (BBC1) looks at footage from many countries. This kind of television is all about the moment, the stunt, the denouement but little of the build-up. It is true that the programmes try to categorize their clips, to give some kind of narrative arrangement. But in essence one has only a presenter and a collection of video shorts. There is no plot to develop, there is no cast, disruption is fleeting. The video shorts could be played all day and it really wouldn't matter when the viewer cut into them.

> Is it possible to argue that most episodes of any sitcom follow the same structure?

Classic realist text: developmental plot structures, mainstream narrative

As with many media, the narratives of television programmes are dominated by what is variously called the classic realist text (in cinema) or mainstream narrative or conventional narrative.

In one respect this is marked by realist conventions which are located around a kind of naturalism – convincing the viewer that what one is watching is actually happening. But this material is also marked by a particular kind of structure that develops a 'story' starting from some established problem or conflict or disruption, and leading to an ending which resolves such conflict. This may be conceptualized as a kind of ascending line on a graph (*see* Fig. 5.3). It is what you might call the average storyline. It is not tricky to follow action and character in terms of where things are happening and of a progression through time. What is important is the kind of protagonists; how they deal with the problems which are set up for them; how the resolution or denouement is dealt with at the end. Television is full of this mainstream narrative, and not just in the obvious examples of fiction drama such as the murder mystery in which we are drawn into the lives of characters; a murder disrupts the social fabric; we are led through the enigma

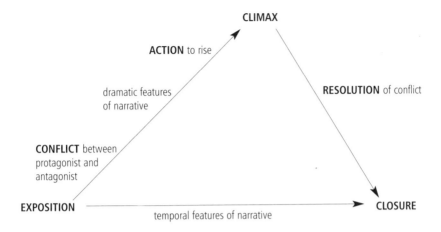

5.3 Mainstream narrative: the classic realist text.
Source: adapted from 'The Classical Paradigm' in Gianetti', 1993

of who commited the murder and why; and finally we are satisfied by a resolution which reveals the mystery and restores social order. A game show contains the same structural functions in principle. The participants are introduced to us, their lives are disrupted by their appearing in this game; we are led through the suspense of whether or not they will answer the questions correctly and win any prizes; the end of the game (or the show) resolves this question and restores order to a world in which the participants can safely go back to their ordinary lives.

Structuralism

This term describes a critical approach to media texts which which was first developed in the 1960s with the work of the anthropologist Claude Levi-Strauss, and was significantly extended in the 1970s through the writing of Louis Althusser. Althusser developed Marxist thinking about media and society and moved on to elaborate ideas about the power of discourses in organizing how we think about the world and about social relationships.

In this section I want to concentrate selectively and briefly on the core idea that texts can organize the understanding of the reader, and that these texts themselves are organized around some structural principles.

Vladmimir Propp (1968) carried out an exhaustive analysis of narrative patterns in European folk tales. His description of narrative produced six phases of a story. Described simply, these involve the villain committing some wrong which affects the hero, at least indirectly. The hero goes to sort things out, perhaps with help, and engages in conflict with the villain. The hero wins and returns to be acclaimed.

Todorov (1976) offers an example in which stories are seen as starting with a state of social harmony or equilibrium, progressing to another state of disharmony, then passing through a conflict between the two states to a conclusion in which equilibrium is restored.

Levi-Strauss (1968) looked at tribal cultural rituals and stories. In these he saw opposing ideas, characters and forces which represented social problems, cultural anxieties, perhaps moral issues, which the culture wanted to sort out. The stories dealt with these problems in a fictional form.

In each case the argument is that there are core structures to stories, whatever the culture, whatever the medium. One could describe it as a major modernist enterprise – trying to find order in the world. Two important ideas which come from Levi-Strauss and other structuralists are as follows.

Binary oppositions describe a pattern in which characters or words or behaviours are seen to be opposed to one another. The meaning of one gains strength from its opposedness to the other. The languages or codes of television speak in these oppositions as much as any other of the media. They reinforce how we think about the world. They cause us to think in terms of conflict and simple alternatives when dealing with arguments and issues. We actually have common phrases such as 'there are two sides to every argument', which are naturalized by repetition into standing for a kind of unarguable truth. But there could be five sides to a given argument.

Television is full of obvious examples of oppositions, such as the heroes and villains of drama or of the news. It describes politics in terms of the government and the opposition. Children's television 'leaks' suggestions that parents are opposed to kids. Sport trades on dramatization of national oppositions, even when football for example is full of premier-league players from all over the world. Television is not unique in this oppositional use of language and of ideas. But of course if it is argued that it has special influence as a medium because of its special place in the home in particular, then its use of binary oppositions shapes that influence. You may link this idea with Chapter 8, on representations, in which our sense of 'different' being opposed to 'normal' is also a kind of opposition.

So if narratives use oppositional language, if they use characters who stand for opposing ideas, then there is in effect an oppositional structure. We may be caused to think about kinds of people, moral issues, the exercise of power in relationships, all in terms of oppositions. In such ways television narratives have structures and structure the way in which we think about our culture and our social relationships. One may also say that this process is ideological because it frames off how we think about politics, power and social differences. We learn that criminals are opposed to the police or to 'law-abiding citizens'. We learn that breaking the law disempowers you, and should do so. We do not easily learn that 60 per cent of the British population have broken the law in one way or another. We are not invited to think about what this means in relation to a crude opposition between criminal and police. I am not saying that television programmes never attend to the complexity of defining criminal or to ideological contradictions. But I am arguing that the programmes with the biggest viewing figures do deal mainly in terms of sometimes simplistic oppositions.

Myths are ideas which are dealt with through these oppositional structures (see also p. 92, under genre). The original cultural research referred to above saw the stories as embodying myths, which were themselves about the deeply held beliefs of a given culture. On a simple level such a myth might be about 'our tribe is the best'. This kind of mythic meaning is very much alive in representations of sport and in the behaviour of fans. The opposition of male to female culture with reference to sport is also mythologized through television programmes. Coverage, as in the press, is dominated by images of male activity and celebration, interpreted by male commentators. This sense of opposition and mythic meanings is epitomized by the David Beckham–Posh Spice coverage. The one is a masculine icon celebrated for physical achievement, for scoring goals and making money. The other is celebrated for looking good, singing hit songs and producing a baby.

Myths work to naturalize oppositions, which are constructed differences – of gender, of class, of ethnicity. They define who is capable or incapable, who is villain or hero, and so on. If they do this they are pernicious, because these naturalized differences are false. But still their mythic qualities reside in the fact that they are so common, appear in so many stories and have done for so long.

> What cultural myths are perpetuated in soap operas by opposing certain characters, and certain ideas about those characters?

The hermeneutic code

This phrase, from critical writing on narrative by the semiotician Roland Barthes, draws attention to his version of narrative elements, their organization and the way in which interpretations of the narrative may be 'closed down'.

Barthes's idea was that the hermeneutic code organized key elements of the narrative. These elements comprise a question and a response to it, an enigma and its resolution. This is in effect much like talking about problems or conflicts and their solutions. Barthes also referred to narrative elements which would help set up and embellish the key question or enigma, and which might delay resolution. The code is about the elements in this view of narrative, and about how they are organized. In other words it is about rules.

Most television programmes can be described in terms of this code, in relation to the idea of enigma in particular: 'What will happen to the protagonist who has to resolve the problem of feelings which run counter to conscience?' or 'What will happen to these orphans who are the victims of civil war in this foreign country?' Soaps take the code in one direction, with a never-ending succession of enigmas and a never-complete solution (see closure, p. 108).

News moves in the other direction when it (frequently) describes 'events as facts' and not as leading to an enigma. There is no enigma about a government decision to allocate money to some area of the health service. And if a problem were to be identified (perhaps about the actual effects of this allocation) there could be no resolution because no one would know what would happen.

The concept of this code, this view of narrative, draws attention to audience pleasures in 'the mystery', and to the capacity of fiction narrative to 'control' all its elements. By contrast, it draws attention to narratives based on fact (other modes of realism) as being different because fact is verifiable information and because the viewer may possess other related facts. But while one cannot control the narrative (or the audience) for factual television in the same way as for drama, it is worth noting that documentaries can and do use the enigma model, withholding the key information as resolution until the end of the programme (see the orphans question above).

CHARACTERISTICS OF FICTIONAL TELEVISION NARRATIVES

The following list of such characteristics, with examples and some comments, draws heavily on the suggestions of Kozloff (1992), as applied to American television. These ideas are equally useful for British television. Some may be equally applicable to 'factual' television. It has already been argued that essential narrative structures are no different from those of fiction.

- **predictable, formulaic storylines**
  Genre material fits this model. Teen soaps such as the Australian *Heartbreak High* would be one among many examples.
- **multiple, interconnecting storylines**
  All soaps, such as the hybrid police drama *The Bill*, would fit this point.
- **individualized characters fitted into standardized roles**
  The eccentric protagonist is a case in point. This device goes back into the 1970s when Peter Falk played the one-eyed, limping detective Columbo in a crumpled raincoat. A contemporary example for the international market

is comedian Alan Davies playing the eponymous hero of *Jonathan Creek*, a magician solver of strange crimes.

- **evocative background and decor or simple, functional backgrounds**
  Sitcoms such as *Roseanne* provide strong examples of the cheap and simple set, contrasted with almost any period drama in which authentic interiors, locations and details absorb the audience nearly as much as the storylines.
- **voice-over (v/o) narration and direct address, perhaps used to naturalize the discourse**
  In this case one could easily invoke the example of news, in which these devices both naturalize and authenticate the discourse. Another example is the children's drama *The Mad House*, in which the girl addresses the camera/audience about the story and about her family.
- **interweaving of narrative level and voices**
  StarTrek is based on the narrative technique of the v/o and captain's log which recounts events that are happening or have happened. It is also common for the series to allow the voices of other leading players to take on a narrative function, just as the narrative action may slip between one person's view and another's, or between one time and another.
- **some omniscient narration**
  The documentary narrator is of course an omniscient narrator. So are sports commentators. They prove their power by allowing us to see the rerun of a touch down, or by talking us through a snooker frame when we know that no one in the live audience is allowed to talk. The camera also takes this role, especially in thrillers, and may either show us events denied to some characters or deny us shots which would explain what is going on.
- **emphasis on scene, and ellipsis between these scenes**
  Friends is very episodic, consisting of short scenes strung together, not least to allow for frequent commercial breaks on US channels. Ellipsis describes the jumps of time and place between such scenes, in which it is assumed that certain events have occurred without being shown to the viewer.
- **achronological order – previews and flashbacks**
  In one sense the preview scenes which link series/serials provide an example of this. But many dramas use this device: the award-winning *Looking for Jo Jo* used flashbacks to fill in details of the early life of the drug-dealing protagonist, played by Robert Carlyle.
- **emphasis on series and serials**
- **narrative cut to standard time slots**
- **permeable diegesis**
  Diegesis describes the enclosed, self-sufficent world of many films and novels. Television is much more 'leaky'. For example, the 'story' of GM food products presented on the news may also appear within a current-affairs debate programme, and perhaps as a theme within a drama. The actress Joanna Lumley might appear as a comic character in *Absolutely*

Fabulous and in the same week be featured in a documentary in which famous people are asked to survive alone in exotic conditions. She will make reference to her fictional character in the factual situation. The boundaries of television programmes are not firm.

An understanding of narrative in television is also about an understanding of how television material is organized to engage with us, which in turn is about how meanings are built into material and projected to the audience. Narrative organizes meanings and shapes the sense we make of television.

6

Television News

INTRODUCTION

Television news is a major genre. It has 24-hour channels devoted to it. It is a required segment of programming. It constitutes people's dominant medium of news information. It has huge resources devoted to it. It is at the cutting edge of new technology as used to access instant sound and images from around the world. It is indeed a cultural phenomenon. Because of this, it is also the object of considerable critical attention. It deserves this attention because it presents us with a particular view of the world which it sells to us as the only view worth taking seriously. This makes news an ideological operation, presenting as it does a selective view of politics, economics, society – in short, a view of power. It is about power as it is 'naturalized' to be, as it 'should be'. This chapter looks at range of critical ideas about the constructed nature of television news.

As McQuail says (1992), ' "news" is not simply facts, but a special form of knowledge which is inextricably compounded of information, myth, fable and morality" '.

Klaus Jensen (1995) takes a gratifications approach in summarizing four uses of news for the audience:

1 uses in context – e.g. news watching becoming part of domestic rituals, especially for males
2 informational uses – keeping up with what is going on in the world
3 legitimating uses – in which news viewing gives the audience some sense of control over events, and a sense of sharing some meanings about the world with other people
4 diversional uses – in which news becomes more like entertainment, in which for example the viewer enjoys keeping up with some 'story in progress'.

PICTURE POWER: SOUND IDEAS

It is a kind of truism that television news leads on pictures. The availability of videotape pictures and of their quality may determine whether or not a given item appears on the news. Picture power becomes a news value related to form or treatment. Pictures authenticate an item in terms of bringing the place and reporter to the viewer and making them real. By extension they validate the ideas being expressed by the newscaster and reporter about the event or issue. Authentication is one of the meanings of the discourse of news: a link to the power of believability.

But it is possible to overstate the importance of pictures. They are polysemic and so to a degree ambiguous. It is the utterances of the players in television news which anchor meanings, formulate issues, accumulate information. There are of course signs and codes and meanings offered variously by the camera, captions, non-verbal behaviour, diegetic sound effects, the whole narrative. But it is what is said that gives significant meanings. Television news is not a bald reporting of events. It may speculate on the causes of events. It offers alternative interpretations of events. It lays out possible consequences of events. It explains issues in its own way and is not neutral. But it is the words which provide us with the greatest amount of information and interpretation. The example of the reading of caption summaries as they appear on screen demonstrates the way in which television news, unlike some other fiction material, will give weight to the word.

Try listening to television news with your back to the screen, or watching it with the sound turned off, to appreciate the different effects and treatments of the two codes of communication.

NEWS AS GENRE

News is indeed a genre, with its formula of key elements bound by conventions (see Chapter 4). The idea of conventions links directly to looking at the material of news presentation, news values, newsworthiness. Key elements are the reporter or the expert as stock characters, politicians as heroes or villains, press conferences or war zones as stock situations. There are conventions about running major political or disaster stories first. The value (or newsworthiness) of recency may equally be seen as a generic convention.

It is the consequences of this genre-ness which are significant for a perspective on news selection and construction, for news as a maker of meanings.

Genre is about repetition and reinforcement of ideas, about anticipation and expectation on the part of the audience. Television news reinforces ideas about what news is by repeating the same sorts of topics treated in the same sorts of ways. News becomes defined as being about elite persons, just as their eliteness is reinforced by their repeatedly being the subject of news stories. The photo opportunity becomes an accepted component of stories involving politicians. If television news repeatedly represents certain social groups in certain ways, then this reinforces how we understand those groups. So if travellers are consistently represented as 'outsiders' or 'problematic', then this is how we come to see them. And of course one has to remember there is other television material which will reinforce these ideas.

The corollary of this process of textual production and audience construction of meaning is that the audience expects to see stories about natural disasters or political conflicts. They anticipate that stories involving Britain will take a largely approving line on British interests, British opinions, the views of British politicians. This anticipation relates to the fact that much television news is not new. We may to an extent predict what the news stories will be the next day, sometimes next week. The news machine predicts them partly by the resources it puts into covering some stories and not others, and through the news production process of building an agenda of stories early in the day. I am not suggesting that television news cannot respond to events, but it cannot respond that quickly and it doesn't start with a blank sheet every day. In particular, television news editors watch the press morning editions as keenly as newspaper editors watch early bulletins.

The **collusive nature of genre** – producer and audience have a mutual interest in keeping the formula together – draws attention to the fact that ideological conservatism in news is something that we the audience conspire to preserve, as much as something which is simply imposed on the viewer. It is an example of the workings of a hegemony in which dominant views are readily incorporated within the thinking of the television viewer when viewers wish to accept those views rather than to contest them.

Put rather simplistically, news as genre becomes the same stories told in the same ways to reinforce the same meanings about social power and social relations.

These ways of telling stories, as with any genre, are based on **production routines**. This refers to systematic and repetitive practices in making the material. There is a tightly scheduled pattern to the working day in a television news operation, dominated by the programme deadlines. There is a pattern to the choice of stories, driven by news values. There is a pattern to the presentation of the news, based on the running order and the central role of the newscaster. There is a regular trawling of standard sources for news. These routines produce economies of operation because the resources – staff, studio, equipment – are in use regularly by people who have familiar roles, working together in a regular way. This is cost-effective and useful in a medium where the technical practices involved in getting a programme together are complex. The significance of this routinization of television news is that it is concealed beneath the screen surface of smooth running, fused with a sense of immediacy and currency. When television talks about its news it emphasizes speed of reaction to a changing world. Indeed items may be added and changed close to transmission and on air. But most are not. It is, rather, the familiarity of presentation, of items on the agenda, which strikes one.

NEWS AS DRAMA

Television news may be dramatic because of the nature of a story, as when a volcano explodes and devastates communities. It may be dramatic because of the telling of the story: pictures of NATO bombing raids and soundbites of NATO ultimatums to the Serbs were used in 1999 to explain the hardline position of the allies towards possible conclusions to the conflict in former Yugoslavia.

If one talks of dramatization one suggests an intentional appeal to viewers and the choice of a treatment of the news material which departs from possibly more objective treatments. Drama and dramatization are also associated with fiction, reinforcing the idea that this mode of treatment opens up a debate about lack of objectivity in news.

The association of news with fiction undermines the dominant distinction in television programming between fact and fiction. It links with ideas about news and narrative. There is no fundamental difference between television news and television drama in respect of the producers' desire to attract an audience, and of the ways in which they construct a story. Both modes of television are scripted and made by a production team in a studio. Both are trailed and marketed. Both involve a regular cast of 'actors'.

NEWS NARRATIVES

Dramatization is also a feature of narrative (see Chapter 5). As with television fiction, news may dramatize through the intentional placing of pictures with emotional impact at a certain point within the narrative. News contrives dramatic moments and trails around commercial breaks, as do other programmes in a bid to hold the audience. News is distinctive, though not unique, in having **narrators on screen.** The newscaster is the master storyteller who introduces different elements in the news story and who hands over the storytelling for brief periods to the reporters. These are the people who are privileged to address us face-on through the camera. These people authenticate and interpret the story, convincing us of the validity of their version of events. They can set up a realist narrative convention by being the captain on the control deck in the studio, or by being the lieutenant in the field at the scene of action.

Storytellers have audiences. As the news audience, we are placed in a certain position by the news narrative which informs the news text. We may have a degree of freedom to construct the narrative and its meanings, but it would be absurd to suggest that news or any other television text is open to a wide variety of interpretations. The mode of presentation referred to above disposes us to a client or submissive relationship with the news and newsreaders. They talk, we listen. They explain, we accept. We have taken on board the conventions of the genre. Our unconscious acceptance of these disposes us to accept the view of the world proposed by our British news. In terms of semiotic analysis we read the newsdesk, the clothing, the face-to-camera shot as signs of power and of endorsement of the authority of news.

These very same signs may also be used in discourse analysis, when describing the language of news and its meanings. One arrives at meanings about authority and authenticity in news by another critical route.

News narratives, like others, have cues which direct their development. The most obvious examples are those such as verbal cues ('Our correspondent X is in Nairobi') or visual cues (the camera pulls in on the men of power greeting one another at the foot of the aircraft steps). There is the introductory review of main news items, which cues us up for the exciting bits of the story. There is the reporter's exit line – 'this is X outside the Kremlin' – which cues us up for the return to the studio.

The studio piece is itself an example of the episodic narrative structure of news in which the studio segments both introduce the next item and act as a kind of bridge between one item and the other. News narrative is like a string of short stories which contribute to an overall narrative picture. These do stand on their own, but collectively they build a picture of a particular kind of world. News structure is further defined by the running order which places a big story at the beginning (dramatic opening), saves a strong story for later (dramatic anticipation) and uses the tailpiece item (defusing drama).

News narrative may also be compared with that of soaps. There are multiple strands to the narrative, stories within the story. Closure is only partial in that if one story finishes there will always be another to take its place. Even individual stories – some international crisis, for instance – will be ongoing, and may not lead to the equilibrium/resolution of the classic realist text. Ellis (1992) would see this as being symptomatic of the flow of television product – the never-ending story.

> If television news is like other programmes in terms of its narrative and its genre qualities, in what respects is it different?

NEWS AGENDA AND SOCIAL REALITY

Television news sets an agenda by choosing news stories. In the first place, this agenda works on a short timeframe in respect of choosing specific stories (the death of a country's leader, perhaps, or a natural disaster) for a day or even a week. In the short term, news says that such events are important and significant. Those items which are not reported are off the agenda and cannot be important. But the concept of agenda also works in the longer term regarding the choice of news stories. This overlaps with newsworthiness and the idea of conventions. Disaster stories, events of great scale, are valued above others. It is a convention that they will be chosen. They are among the most newsworthy stories. They will be on an agenda which partly stands for assumptions about the way we see, or should see, the world and contributes to that thing we may call **social reality**: a set of assumed truths about social beliefs, social relationships, social differences, status and power. This reality, this agenda, is informed by news values such as cultural proximity, in which it is 'understood' that 'naturally' a flood in Britain which drowns a herd of cattle will get on the agenda when a flood in an Asian country which drowns a village will not. Our sense of reality may be shaped by the company merger which gets on the agenda while details of the social consequences of the merger do not.

By choosing to handle certain stories in certain ways, news presents a certain view of our society, not necessarily an accurate or full view. The agenda signals priorities. These priorities are part of that view. For example, employment statistics are often presented in terms of job losses and gains. When a company expands its workforce in one town or one region, what we are not usually told is what kinds of jobs are created, and for whom. The optimistic reality presented by the news may not match the other social reality of more jobs for older part-time women employees, but nothing to help the above-average unemployment of young males.

The agenda does indeed contribute to bias, which is discussed below. If one detects an emphasis on stories affecting London and the south of England, and an omission of stories about the north and Scotland, such an inflection of the agenda is simply another example of bias. One instance of this was when a story about a Scottish ferry being adrift for 6 hours in 1989 wasn't covered by the main news programmes, even though comparable examples taking place in the English Channel did make the agenda.

NEWS AND IDEOLOGY – SELECTION AND CONSTRUCTION – NEWS VALUES

Much of what is said in this chapter leads one quickly into notions of ideology. The news agenda, with its prioritization of stories and its perspectives on stories, is an example of this.

I have already said that ideology is about dominant views of the world and the dominant values behind those views. It refers to power relations. It refers to the naturalization of views and power relations. In many ways, this is all that news is about. News reporters often purport to speak for their viewers, to represent the public interest. But if they represent anyone, they represent a certain kind of public – people much like themselves with views which usually accord with the views and interests of those who run things. There are stories about the state of money markets or royal pronouncements or legal decisions which are not made relevant to the lives of those on low incomes or in far regions or living on estates.

I am not saying that news can be all things to all people. But I am saying that television news could be more things which are more relevant to more people. Its selective view of and presentation of the world is an ideological construction. News is 'an ideological construction of realities' (Allan, 1998).

The **selection and construction** performed through television news production is both inevitable and pervasive through the whole process of newsmaking. It is inevitable and unsurprising given the quantity of news material available and the confines of the time slots. It is pervasive in that decisions about what to cover and how affect every stage of newsmaking: news gathering, copytasting, news editing, news programme construction, news presentation. In this respect news is full of gatekeepers deciding what information is passed to whom and why. The arch decision-maker is the editor of the day. Decisions are made about sending out teams to cover a story, about what stories to buy from agencies or through the morning European news exchange. Decisions are made about the running order, about what goes on the agenda for a given programme. Decisions are made about what tape to use and how to cut it.

The very **sources of news** also inflect it. It is common to cover big institutional sources such as the police or major companies through press conferences and press releases. This is very much the case with government departments. In a sense the status of these sources spins off onto the news, just as the status of television news gives credibility to the sources. But this tapping of such sources is part of the routinized coverage of news. It should remind us that in some cases what the news says is happening is what the source says is happening, not necessarily what is really happening. News is not always as 'hard' and factual as it would like to be. Indeed, though television news is described as factual, it is as much 'made' as any other programme. In evaluating the significance of the news selection process one may ask questions such as

- What is left out of the running order and why?
- What other ways of interpreting events or telling the story might there be, and why weren't they used?
- Who makes the decisions about selection and on what basis?

Answers to these questions must have an ideological dimension. This dimension may be seen as part of an ideology of news specifically (see remarks on professionalism and on consensus below, p. 134). It may be seen in terms of ideology as a larger view of a naturalized world, into which news fits. But in both cases one is looking at a set of beliefs and values, at judgements based on certain ways of explaining events and social relations and of representing social groups and the exercise of power.

This is where one needs to reprise the idea of news values or newsworthiness. These values (*see* Fig. 6.1) are behind news selection and construction. They become a self-fulfilling prophecy as a means of justifying this selection. They are values of 'professional' news decision-making. They are the values which inform news ideology. But, I would suggest, it becomes difficult – next to impossible – in the end to disentangle them from those value judgements which are part of a larger ideology. For example, news values would say that fighting in the streets between supporters of football teams in a cup final has saliency as an event, which makes it likely to be chosen as a news item. But this choice is mixed up with ways that football supporters are represented. This representation, with its notions about violence, law and order and masculinity, is certainly ideological. The news item will have set up and reinforced ideas about the connection between football, males and violence, and about the need to use the force of law to keep these people in their place. The workings of ideology will have suppressed the information that most matches pass off non-violently, that the social cross-section of supporters is much more diverse than the common pictures of males aged 25 and under would suggest.

• frequency	the event must complete within the publication cycle of the news organization reporting it
• threshold	the event must pass a certain size threshold to qualify for sufficient importance to be newsworthy
• clarity	it must be relatively clear what has actually happened
• cultural proximity	it must be meaningful to the audience of the news organization in question
• consonance	the event must be in accordance with the framework of understanding which typifies the culture of the potential audience
• unexpectedness	within the framework of meaningfulness under cultural proximity and consonance, the event must be unexpected or rare
• continuity	if an event has already been in the news, there is a good chance it will stay there
• composition	coverage of events is partly dictated by the internal structure of news-gathering organizations
• actions of the elite	events involving elite people or organizations are more likely to be covered than those of unimportant people
• personification	events that can be seen in terms of individual people rather than abstractions
• negativity	bad events are more newsworthy than good ones

6.1 Newsworthiness/news values.
Source: adapted from Briggs and Cobley, 1998, after Galtung and Ruge, 1979

If news values are influential in shaping what the news is, then what the news is also conspires in a process of social reproduction. Values, ideological positions, social differences are reproduced and reinforced.

News speaks for the dominant ideology and is a potent carrier of its values because it speaks through the images of apparent factuality. It purports to represent the world as it is. Its very subject matter is central to defining social reality – economic events, political activity, wars, manifestations of social behaviour. So generally speaking the news confirms ideas such as the rule of law as endorsed by the police, the primacy of the family as a social unit, government definitions of enemies of the state. News does not challenge such ideas even if laws are demonstrably ineffective or unjust, even if a significant minority of households are not of a two-parent family unit, even if those 'enemies' (illegal immigrants, for example) are not hurting the state in any measurable way. In these ways **news functions as a normative influence on society.**

This is of a piece with Philo's argument (1990) that the research of the Glasgow University Media Group in the 1980s and 1990s shows that the 'social relations which structure the wider society were referred to implicitly and explicitly in news reporting'. The very key concepts of news operations as truthtelling – impartiality and objectivity – are themselves ideological. News presents itself as 'naturally' being objective – of course it is, it's news. But there is no 'of course' about it. Objectivity is an ideological invention which is supported by fallacies such as 'balance' and 'taking a detached view' and 'bringing you the news as it happens' and other such phrases.

> Would it matter if television news abandoned the idea of impartiality and openly produced different versions of news for different audiences on different channels?

NEWS REPRESENTATIONS, DEVIANCY AND MORAL PANICS

The ideas in this section have already been touched upon (as in the reference to travellers, p.121 above). Chapter 8 is about representations on television in general. But it is reasonable to draw attention to ways in which television news, with other news media, may contribute to creating a view of certain social groups as being deviant and others as fitting norms. The selection of certain words and pictures depicting and interpreting certain behaviours can accumulate to form a selective view of such a group. John Muncie (1987) describes a process through which the media misrepresent a minority, create a moral panic and bring about a reinforcement of ideological norms. In an adapted form it looks as follows:

- identify a 'subversive' minority
  e.g. football 'hooligans' or makers of 'violent' videos
- simplify the causes of their behaviour
  e.g. no moral standards or not enough state control
- stigmatize this minority
  e.g. through the use of emotional and critical language, verbal and visual
- campaign for action
  e.g. address the 'public' out there, calling for action

- there is a state reaction
  e.g. tougher punishments or forms of censorship.

This model is relevant to what is said in Chapter 9 about violence and effects, and in Chapter 10 about censorship.

Stan Cohen (1973) referred to 'manufactured news' when he investigated the coverage of the now mythical fights between Mods and Rockers back in the 1960s. Baldly, there was little fighting in fact, but a lot of news coverage which either invented conflicts or made a great deal of what little there was. This ties in with the 'conflict interpretation' of news events, and what Cohen called an 'institutionalized need to create news'. The creation of this representation of young males as violent was further complicated by evidence of the players being encouraged to perform for the news cameras.

All this may seem a long time ago – but it goes on happening. In 1978 Stuart Hall was writing about the representation of young blacks as muggers, and developing Cohen's ideas about '**moral panics**' generated through the media about a given issue or a supposed social problem. It is the news operations of the media which are particularly responsible for the creation of such panics. One can go on picking off examples – in the 1980s there was the representation of Labour councils as being a 'loony left'. Television news has never been part of the invention and invective of some newspapers, but by repeating some of the key phrases used in the press and by giving coverage to the panic topic (even in a more objective manner) it contributes to a distorted view in which muggers, teenage mums, Skinheads, football hooligans, are given an identity – as what Hall and others have described as '**deviants**'. There is an amplification of deviancy.

By the 1990s we had AIDS as the 'gay disease'. The panics die down when the media grow tired of them and run out of stories. But the effects of the representations linger on. There is an abiding cultural myth (not supported by statistics) of youth as violent or promiscuous. These moral panics and representations of deviancy serve ideology by implicitly defining the norms of social behaviour. In Marxist terms, Gramsci might see television news as part of the whole ideological apparatus of television. The 'branding through representation' of social groups and behaviours would be part of a process of social control through the promotion of consensual views.

It is also Gramsci who proposed that there is a struggle for hegemony, for the dominance of one set of ideas over another within society. The media, and television news in partiuclar, as a prime means of communication within society, would be a place where this struggle goes on. Moral panics have been seen as signs of the struggle.

Stuart Allan (1998) talks about a 'crisis of hegemony'. The equilibrium of consent by the masses to the dominant ideas of the few is disturbed. The reporting and discussion of something like AIDS is actually an unpheaval in which ideas are being rethought and a new balance is sought. Kirsten Drotner (1992) talks about media panics working on two levels:

1 a social level in which there is an attempt to reassert the status quo, quite often of the ideas of an older generation over the ideas of a new generation which is entering positions of social and cultural dominance
2 a cultural level in which there is a cultural struggle for the dominance of one set of ideas. The use of emotive language in discussing issues such as violence in the media or the behaviour of the young is a sure sign of anxiety and of its cultural significance.

NEWS BIAS (IMPARTIALITY AND DOMINANT IDEOLOGY)

Ideas about television news being unbiased, balanced and impartial are part of its ideology. They are at the heart of the professional credo of newsmakers. They are central to the rationale of codes of practice provided by the BBC and ITN for their newsworkers. They are written into the contractual and statutory documents which permit the BBC and commercial companies to operate and provide a news service. The possibility of aspiring to these states of grace, and the actuality of the performance of news operators, is not much questioned within news organizations. But it has been and is the subject of fierce criticism informed by academic research.

The idea of **balance** in the presentation of issues, points of view and conflicts is inherently flawed, drawing attention to the value placed on conflict as a way of making sense of stories. For a start, conflict may be proposed where there is none, but only disagreement. But then balance is understood in terms of two (opposing) points of view. The idea that there may be more than two points of view is excluded. In making sense of a political disagreement or in trying to understand the causes and consequences of a military conflict one can be left with a false choice.

If bias in news is a corollary of selection, then news must be inherently biased. If one looks at bias on a more relativist scale, there is the question of what benchmarks it is measured against – relative to what? One cannot cry bias simply because one does not agree with a point of view. I would suggest that bias in news is to do with **partiality** towards particular views and interpretations of events based on **selective use of information**. It involves the privileging of and emphasis on some information and views, and/or the denial of information and views. This privileging might include the privileging of information from or the views of authority sources, perhaps accessed via press conferences or interviews. It would include the screentime given to these views, and the editing in of utterances which tended to explain the issue in one way rather than another. Early treatment of the BSE crisis is an example of this, where the problem was initially played down.

Bias is unsurprizing – it is a cultural phenomenon. Cultures prefer to see the world from their point of view: they have been socialized into their set of values, their ideology. So bias in news is also in effect about ways in which the shape of our dominant ideology may be perceived beneath the sea of reporting that flows across our screens.

In the example of NATO attacks on Serbia in the 'Kosovan War' in 1999, the Serbs saw our news as biased, in spite of the screening of some reports from Belgrade about the effects of bombing and in spite of news screening of disagreements about strategies and effects of the campaign. The Serbs noted the privileging of views about a 'just war' and the predominance of pictures of industrial and military targets. They felt victimized within a general Balkan situation in which all ethnic groups have committed crimes against one another. Their view of the conflict was determined by a sense of cultural history in which struggle against invaders and the cause of maintaining national identity predominate.

In general, much of the material in this chapter could be used to illustrate the idea of bias. Prioritizing events onto the news agenda and prioritizing items up the running order both add up to a kind of bias in favour of one item rather than another. Just so, the absence of events and personalities from news programmes can stand for a kind of bias against them. News is biased in favour of its set of values, of its professional construction of the programmes. Value positions are part of ideologies, so ideology itself is a system of preference for one set of views rather than any others; in other words, it is itself a form of bias. Representations are entirely ideological, so they also contribute· to our understanding of bias where they appear in news programmes, or where they are notable through their absence.

A particular 'device' which contributes to bias is **nomination** or **exnomination**. These terms were coined by Roland Barthes to describe the power of naming and of not giving a name, especially with regard to sources of authority. In terms of news, the concept has been illustrated through labour disputes, in which the views of managers are exnominated. That is, they are given the power of apparent neutrality and objectivity by, for example, being expressed through a representative or a statement issued. The union side, on the other hand, may be diminished and exposed by being explained through named officials or leaders, who then become personally responsible for the disruption caused. This idea has been effectively explained by John Fiske (1987), who says 'that which is exnominated appears to have no alternative and is thus granted the status of the natural, the universal or that which cannot be challenged'.

If television news is biased in the ways described in this chapter, what new ways of handling news might remove this bias?

NEWS AS PROFESSIONAL PRACTICE

The ideology, the discourse and the values driving the production of television news are subsumed within a notion of professionalism. This term carries connotations of expertise, responsibility, reliability, knowledge and status. When newsmakers claim to be professionals, as they do, they invoke these connotations as an endorsement of their production practices. Professionalism, in all occupations, may become a shield to deflect criticism. Criticism may not reflect on the integrity of individuals, nor on the skills and complexities involved in getting material onto our screens. Still, professionalism is another discourse, a set of meanings, which works in the interests of those who claim it and which sometimes works against the interests of those who may question it or who experience the effects of professional work. If the news on screen is the result of professional work, then it is also founded on production routines, driven by news values and expressed through presentational practices or a certain mode of address. So the gathering and sampling of news from a range of sources against the pressure of deadlines is a professional practice. The choosing of an event as being newsworthy becomes part of professional experience and expertise. The reading of news scripts in a neutral yet authoritative manner becomes a professional skill. All this becomes a version of 'doing things the way they have been done for the reasons that have applied before'. It is what has become assimilated into our culture and is what makes the news audience feel comfortable.

Critical views would want to stand back from this naturalization of such professional practices and ask what these practices signify for what we understand news to be. They would want to ask about alternative ways of choosing and telling the news. News professionalism works for the continuity of getting the stuff on air every day, within a framework for understanding the world. Professionalism may work for coherence but it can work against self-criticism. It works with commercialism and against anything which might upset the audience, which is itself 'conservative' in its understanding of what news should be. So the removal of the managerial desk from presentation causes comment and a questioning of the reliability of the news (consider Channel 5). The proposal of views dominantly for or against joining the European currency is 'unthinkable'.

NEWS AS COMMODITY

The idea of commodification comes out of Marxist thinking about mass production, about ways in which social relations of power are driven by commercial interests, or economic determinism. The financial value of goods and of labour becomes mixed up with other ways of valuing these things – status and image value, for example. Equally, people's social value can become measured simply in terms of how much they get paid – Hollywood stars claim huge fees to bolster the idea that they are stars.

News is part of this confusion of value systems and of materialism. There is a price on news. It is a commodity because it is bought and sold via news agencies. Freelance journalists are paid for the news they bring to television. Television news is bought and sold by cable across Europe at 10.00 a.m. every morning.

In terms of news audiences, market information about social groups and their disposable incomes is bought and sold – there is a price on the economic relations between social groups. This information helps determine the advertising rates set around the news slots for commercial television. Commodification and the influence of the marketplace is pervasive.

The point here is to demystify news among media products. Businesses such as Reuters or VisNews make money out of news. People are paid to produce news, as with other programmes. Whatever the difference of news from other programming, it cannot be explained in a material sense. The material similiarity of news to other programmes is significant in light of its claims to objectivity. Where game shows celebrate materialism and entertainment, news exalts truthtelling and factuality. To look at the commodification of news is to raise questions about its provenance and its construction. Do items appear because they can be afforded? Or because they have ratings appeal? Perhaps not. But simply to ask the question changes established views of the 'quality' of television news.

NEWS AS DISCOURSE

> [N]ews comes to us as the pre-existing discourse of an impersonal social institution which is also an industry.
>
> John Hartley (*Understanding News*, 1982)

News has its own discourse in that there are meanings about what it is, which are generated by ways in which codes are used within it. It is the use of the signs of language – verbal and visual – which brings these meanings to life. News itself also contains and 'talks about' discourses of gender, technology, education and many more. The special place and influence of news is bound up with the fact that it includes so many discourses which range across all aspects of our society.

News 'has meaning only in relation to other institutions and discourses operating at the same time' (Hartley, 1982). When it uses these discourses it brings to life their meanings and reinforces them in people's minds. This is fundamentally the same as saying that news reinforces the dominant ideology. So when news uses the language of education – standards, achievements, exams – it reinforces the meaning of education or what education is understood to be about. The possible view that real education has nothing (and should have nothing) to do with exams never gets a look in.

It is the same for the discourse of news itself. This generates meanings that television news is an **authentic** view of the world, that it is **authoritative** in its knowledge of and presentation of world events and issues. It communicates these meanings through any number of uses of 'language'. Dress, posture, delivery and camera position for the newsreader have already been referred to. Such signs may equally be used to explain news presentation, news mode of address, news genre conventions. It all comes back to the same thing. We understand these elements to mean that the newsreader is a reliable source of truthtelling. Other signifiers of these meanings are reporters on the spot, experts with facts, interviews with people who are part of the real events reported, graphic presentation of statistics and so on.

News discourse promotes the idea of **conflict** as a way of explaining problems and issues. There is usually an opposition of views and values. But the British view, the dominant view, is right. Stuart Chibnall (*Law and Order News*) summarized an opposition of values which informs media thinking about the law and crime (*see* Fig. 6.2). This leads one to the dominant meaning of **consensus** within the news discourse, which deals with the conflict by being presented as naturally the answer to all such problems. The Glasgow University Media Group (1982) talks about 'an ideological perspective which is founded on the view of consensus, "one nation" and "the community" '. In a Reader of their work (Eldridge, 1995) they again refer to 'the unspoken and dominant ideology of our society – the liberal notion that there is a fundamental consensus'. Politicians and political news still take on this perspective even though it is contradicted by stories which reveal cultural differences and disagreements. Clearly Britain is not simply one nation when it has a Scottish parliament and a Welsh assembly.

Consensus also refers to the way in which television news tells stories about conflict and disagreement in terms of there being agreement about the solution to the conflict. Consensus is the desirable outcome. This consensus is itself based on the assumption that there are only two sides or two points of view, between which compromise needs to be reached. This meaning is signified by the space which is given to 'peace talks', 'negotiations', 'deals'. Those who obstruct negotiations are seen as being difficult (not as principled). They are holding up a deal (not holding out for a fairer solution). As part of the news discourse, consensus becomes an ideological position itself. Although it is often presented as being naturally desirable or socially more just, it is in the nature of ideology that it excludes other views. These would include the idea that a consensus outcome to some disputes is actually

POSITIVE LEGITIMATING VALUES	NEGATIVE ILLEGITIMATE VALUES
Legality	Illegality
Moderation	Extremism
Compromise	Dogmatism
Co-operation	Confrontation
Order	Chaos
Peacefulness	Violence
Tolerance	Intolerance
Constructiveness	Destructiveness
Openness	Secrecy
Honesty	Corruption
Realism	Ideology
Rationality	Irrationality
Impartiality	Bias
Responsibility	Irresponsibility
Fairness	Unfairness
Firmness	Weakness
Industriousness	Idleness
Freedom of choice	Monopoly/uniformity
Equality	Inequality

6.2 Binary oppositions: news values.
Source: adapted from Chibnall, 1977

immoral, unjust and solves nothing for those in dispute. Allan (1998) in effect talks about the influence of mode of address here when he refers to 'the fictive "we" '. This is news purporting to speak for us, making us complicit in a consensus about the world.

News and the public sphere

The notion of a 'public sphere' goes back to the writing of Jürgen Habermas. He was part of the Frankfurt school of thinking about the media – as creating mass culture, materialism, ideological subjugation, and as imposing on the audience. Not entirely accurately, it has to be said, he looked back to the eighteenth-century 'age of enlightenment'. In this period he saw the face-to-face political debate in tea and coffee houses, the explosion of political pamphlets, as creating a public sphere where citizens participated in a debate about their society, rather as the citizens of Athens might have debated politics in the agora in 300 BC. Habermas was guilty of a romantic view of such public debate, which did not include the majority of the working and illiterate population.

But the idea of a public sphere of debate, tied in with the notion of a free press – Edmund Burke's fourth estate – is still a seductive one. If the debate is indeed about society and politics, then news, of all media material, must be at the centre. The central issue is whether anything like a public sphere, as a forum for debate, actually exists any more. It is argued that the range of broadcast and print material creates the illusion that there is debate. But in fact any real discussion is closed down because the free press is not free any more. It is in the pockets of owners like Murdoch and corporations like United News and Media. Television reports events and stages studio discussions, but the views and comments are within an agenda defined by the media. Ordinary citizens are locked within a private sphere: the news is watched at home; its issues are not discussed in public.

I would suggest that jury is still out on this one. Politics can still be public – witness the very public demonstrations at the World Trade Organization meeting in Seattle in December 1999, which embarrassed the politicians present and brought about some changes of policy. Similarly, if one considers news on the Internet, first there are websites (run by existing news media) which function as broadcast sources and confine news to the private sphere of the home PC as receiver. But there are also hundreds of websites relating to political issues and debates across the world, through which people are communicating in a public sphere. From these comments it will be seen that the question of whether the news offers a public sphere of debate about issues is tied up with a discussion of interactivity, as well as of freedom of production and of expression.

> Does television news really bring public debate about political and social issues into the private sphere of the home – or does it stifle debate by presenting ts own cut-and-dried version of issues?

GENDERED NEWS

Television news incorporates inequalities of and issues relating to gender in a number of ways. These may be summarized in terms of:

- who controls and produces news
- who presents news

- what news is and how it is presented
- who watches news.

Information about the breakdown by gender of those running news operations in British television is difficult to come by. What information there is suggests that news managers are dominantly male, but that an increasing number of news personnel are female. Jon Dovey (1998) points out that more than half of journalist trainees are women, that the BBC is positively encouraging the participation of women in news departments, that in a local (Bristol) BBC news department at the time he was writing all three producers were women and under 28 years of age. Where there are gendered distinctions in management on a national level, this is likely to be seen in news material and through gendered differences in looking at the world, though one should also consider possible differences in management style. What evidence there is suggests that the most significant outcome for women working in news is that, rather than making any difference to the way news operates, they become assimilated into (male) news practices and news values. Liesbet Van Zoonen points out that the training women receive through news operations, their lack of presence in the technology of news production, the strength of institutionalized assumptions (see again professionalism, p. 132 above) about what news is, all conspire to keep news the way it is and to shut out something that might be described as a female agenda, a female perspective on the world.

What needs to be reflected upon is how far news practices, especially news items, do stand for male preferences. Lead stories about competition, conflict, the exercise of power, the status of public figures could, it may be argued, stem from a masculine discourse which emphasizes these factors. Female discourse is generally more about co-operating, not winning, or at least about emotional intelligence in the manner of winning. The relative status of, and conflicts surrounding, male political leaders are reported frequently. The effects of these conflicts on family life, the effects of the work of a male MP on his family, are not much reported. The opposite effect, but possibly from the same masculine impetus behind selection and construction, may be seen in the treatment of female MPs. There is a stereotypical inflection towards appearance as gender, symbolized by certain shots and phrases such as 'Blair's Babes'. Of course one has to be careful about just reconstructing another version of cliché attitudes – women's news is about health and fashion shows, men's news is about sport and 'fighting'. But, as I am suggesting, re-gendered news might be about different perspectives, as much as being about a revision of news topics.

One thing that a revised news might address is the false dichotomy between hard news and soft news. At the moment there is a definition of hard news stories as being the important ones because they are about 'major' issues, high-status people, matters of fact and very public events tied in with politics and economics. In short, hard news is masculine. By contrast, soft news is feminine. It is in effect about more general issues than about specific events. It is about human-interest stories, about 'more trivial' matters, of less status as news. There may indeed be different kinds of news, but to accord one as having more status than the other, by association with its gender qualities, is a false position. Perhaps the status, power and conflicts between, say, William Hague and Tony Blair are of less importance to our society and to our everyday lives than are the social and domestic consequences of government policies.

In terms of newscasters and reporters, the position has shifted enormously since the late 1970s, when female presenters were the exception rather than being familiar as they are now. Female newscasters present main news programmes and are commonly partnered by males in regional news, for example. It may be that some of the audience will see the male as more authoritative, but there is nothing that could be objectified about female performance and presentation to differentiate them adversely from the males. In terms of British performers one could not differentiate the delivery of Julia Sommerville from that of Michael Buerk. If their appearance, if signs of gender, cause them to be valued differently then I would argue that is about audiences reading texts as much as about institutions inflecting texts. This is relevant to the situation in Holland where the conscious placing of a majority of women in newscasting roles is also perceived by the audience as reassuring. These older women newscasters are seen as mother figures. The power of discourses is such that it is very hard to break away from stereotypes.

It is true that rather more males are seen in the role of reporter, but this varies from programme to programme. Its is also noticable that women are no longer assigned to supposedly 'female-interest' items, perhaps about healthcare or children. I have seen a male reporting on issues surrounding breast cancer. There are females reporting on politics and economics and from war zones.

News audiences appear to be gendered, according to evidence about the preference of male viewers for news (back to content again). This is linked to findings about men taking charge of what is viewed by hijacking the remote control.

ALTERNATIVE PRACTICES

Gender distinctions or kinds of bias surrounding television news lead one to reflect on possible alternative practices. The idea of different ways of handling news is as much hypothetical as actual – there aren't many examples about. For example, it wouldn't be possible to editorialize through broadcast television news (in the way that newspapers take explicit positions on issues)

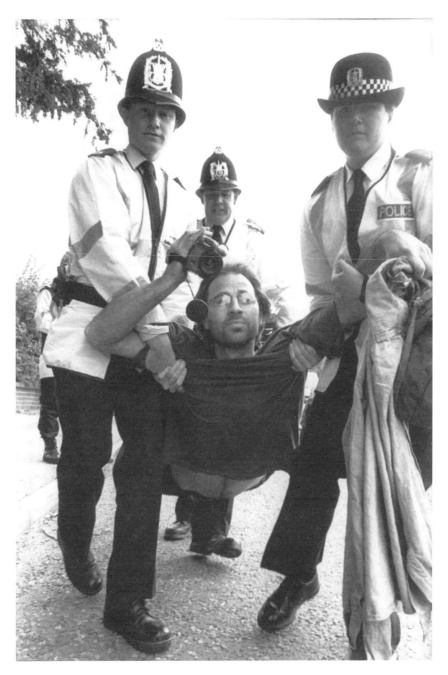

6.3 This image of a news photographer being carried away from his work by the police is from the alternative news organization Undercurrents. It may raise questions about libertarian models of the media, and it suggests comparisons with more conventional images of the police at work in the mainstream media.

because the contracts which allow one to broadcast also insist on impartiality. This may be a flawed and even redundant concept, but it is there. There are also the determinants of the marketplace. If you want to produce 'another kind of news', then someone has to pay for the production and distribution. In the ways that broadcasting is financed, no one is going to put up the money for an unproven version of newstelling which may not appeal to anybody. Audience is the other determinant. If the audience pays for the material, by one means or another, then 'other versions' of the news have to please the audience. But the audience is already acclimatized to a certain kind of news, a view of the world which is defined by what we have already got. People are also disinclined, as advertisers know well, to take on messages which are not framed within the values which they already hold. Hegemony means that we mainly believe in the dominant system of beliefs. At its most extreme it creates a closed and circular system. In fact cultural differences and social attitudes are sufficiently complex that one does not get monolithic, unchanging societies. However, hegemony does mean that it is very difficult to fund and present any alternative media practices.

One might ask the question, alternative to what? The answer must be to the dominant practices which are the object of my critique in the rest of this chapter. A summary of these practices might be:

- conventions of news presentation
- news selection and treatment based on news values
- the construction of a fairly predictable news agenda
- framing the news within a discourse that includes ideas about impartiality and conflict
- operating within predetermined programming slots.

Specific examples of resistance to these practices could be:

- not using a newsreader or a reporter in vision
- never using items about the royal family
- covering politics at a local rather than a national level
- avoiding conflict explanations of events
- presenting committed views on events and on issues relating to those events
- varying the time given to stories and to the programme as a whole.

A real example of a different practice is offered by the Undercurrents video organization. It distributes news items on video: the buyer helps pay for production, which is not driven by profit motives. This is not news with immediacy: the videos come out maybe a couple of times a year. It is news about British events and issues which are not normally covered or not covered from the given angle. It is news which is frankly partial. It is news which is pro ecology, pro minorities, pro those who are normally not heard. Its stories are, for example, about protest events, about social injustice, about ecology issues, about misuse of power. It uses voice-over comment rather than newsreaders or reporters as personalities. It uses personal testimony as evidence. One story specifically illustrated how alternative news journalists were being given a hard time by the police, even being detained and having videotape wiped. If the events illustrated in this 14-minute item had involved an ITN team it is likely that they would themselves have become a public issue and a news event.

So 'alternative' is not just about contesting choice of content, news values or style of presentation; it is also about contesting ideologies. It is about alternative ways of looking at social relations and the exercise of power. Alternative might be disturbing to established views of what news is and what kind of world it should represent. It might also be refreshing, thought-provoking and symbolic of democracy.

7

Television and Realism

PREVIEW

This chapter deals with:

- the illusion of reality created through television
- modes and categories of realism presented, such as docudrama, docusoap, documentary
- concepts which define realism in the viewing experience
- realism and ideology
- postmodernism
- a short history of documentary on British television.

INTRODUCTION

Realism in television can be seen as depending on two main areas of understanding:

1 the construction of television texts through various conventions
2 the deconstructions carried out by television audiences, persuaded not just by conventions but also by the nature of television as it is practised.

In any case, one has to take on the premise that television as a medium of communication is nothing but an artifice. It has no reality (or versions of realities) other than that which we believe it has. It is nothing but flickering cathode rays illuminating dots of phosphorous. We only see pictures because our optical electro-chemistry is slower than the operation of its technology. It may be no less than a sensory experience, as is our everyday living, our exchanges with friends and family. But it is not the same kind of sensory experience. It depends on two senses, not five. Its visual and auditory world has the limits of the definition of its technology. Its pictures exist only within the frame of the device that we call a television. In short, if we say that television has realism, that does not mean that it is real. The differences between viewing and living may seem to be merely mechanical, but they contribute to definitions of reality. In all these respects the seductive Baudrillardian position that the reality of television has become continuous with the reality of our lives is simply untenable. We do know the difference between embracing someone in life and watching an embrace on screen.

This is not the same thing as arguing that there is no connection between the two embraces. We may have ideas about embracing others, what it might feel like, from television viewing. Television viewing might encourage that superego position in which, while embracing in life, we partly feel ourselves watching that embrace – the camera's view, as it were. Our sense of what embracing means can be fed by viewing, by how it is 'told' within narratives.

Of course there is the particular issue of how we place within our consciousness the reality depicted by television that we have not (and perhaps cannot) experience in life. There is value in a postmodernist position on continuous realities – in recognizing that the viewing of a documentary on the Antarctic must be incorporated within our meanings about the 'real' world. Geographically, physically, we internalize a kind of reality about the locations. We have pictures in our minds. Documentary itself has conventions of realism that cause us to interpret those images differently to images from a drama.

Still, there are four aspects of realism which cause us to assign this 'reality experience' a certain value:

1 we know that we have not been to Antarctica, and so the pictures are not verifiable, even if probably valid within their technical limitations
2 we know that they are part of television and are therefore constructed – even if we don't stop at the time to reflect on camera angles or editing
3 we know that being in a place is different from being given a view of a place
4 we take on the premise that this is documentary and is therefore to be understood in certain ways.

This last point is of course the one that we could be fooled on because the cues that cause us to switch into understanding of documentary mode may all be manufactured. In a sense you have to make a best guess as to whether what you are watching is an elaborate hoax, rather as one calculates whether or not other people are telling the truth.

There is an important difference between realism as the physical authentication of place and realism as the metaphyical assertion of truths. So the Antarctica documentary is not just about giving us a physical sense of the place which becomes internalized as part of our reality view of the world. The programme will also give us meanings about such things as danger (from the environment) – science (experiments being carried out there) – ecology (the hole in the ozone layer). In other words, it has its discourses. 'Reality as the truth of ideas' is something else we have to take on – back to the truth of the experience of embracing, but without the privilege of having an embrace for ourselves. However, I would still argue that ideas about Antarctica (as opposed to ideas about what it is like to be there), are internalized on a conditional basis. We may take on ideas as being probably true, but they have a tag attached to them which identifies them as having been acquired via television. So again, I am not arguing that 'reality as truth' is not taken into our views of the world. I am not arguing against the power of discourses and their meanings. I am not arguing against the possibility of the classic 'false consciousness': realism equals ideological truths. But I am arguing that to say there is a continuum of reality in which viewing a television programme is no different from a conversation – 'It's all living, isn't it?' – shows a misunderstanding of what a television programme is and of how we watch television.

We might also recognize that at this point one is approaching a reductionist philosophical argument which might ask, how do you know that a conversation is real, either? What do I think, and therefore what am I? This is the premise of many a story – of the film *The Matrix*, for instance, in which the fabric of reality can be torn aside to reveal the 'real reality' beneath.

We may be seduced by the 'realisms' of television. We may take in different kinds of television in different ways. Some of the meanings of television may become (like other life experience) part of our realities, but not all of the meanings all of the time. Television is not life, though it is a part of our lives; and that distinction matters.

AUTHENTICITY AND INTIMACY

In spite of the huge range of material on television (some of it manifestly in fantasy mode and/or the result of electronic effects) there is much about television that creates an aura of giving us 'the real thing'. Film approaches this in some ways, and yet much of it is unreal because of the dominance of star/fiction/action material. Compared with most other media, television starts from a base of at least simulating reality to the degree afforded by the appearance of 'real' sound and of moving pictures. We know that it is really just a machine for delivering the illusion of pictures and sound, but at least the representations are iconic and not symbolic (as with books).

In any case, the cultural viewing environment favours reception in terms of believability and acceptance – a qualified reality, if you like. The box is in the private, domestic sphere. Its material is seen and discussed by the family. It acquires the status of 'family member', like the cat, simply because it is always there: it moves; it makes a noise. Indeed, television is simply switched on and left on in some households as part of a familiar environment. People expect

7.1 This studio shot from *The Big Breakfast* (C4) stands for a typically televisual mode of address which invites the audience at home into the show. Showing the studio guests and the technicians presents the illusion of enhanced realism which tries to deny the constructedness of the medium and to collapse the distance between production and reception.

to see it around, even at a glance through the living-room door. This intimacy with television becomes part of its realism. More than this, because it is in the home, television viewing can become an intimate experience, especially for those viewers living on their own, for those in the household who have their own television, for those who view on their own late at night when the rest of the family have gone to bed.

This sense of intimacy in context is reinforced by television's mode of address, and significantly by the device of **close-up**. There are the general close-ups, from whatever angle, which may be part of the visual rhetoric of a discussion programme or of a soap opera. They allow us to see the face or head in intimate detail. But then there is also the talking head. This is the face-to-camera close shot which addresses us from the screen. Television is full of this kind of engagement. There are comedy-show compères, reporters on the spot, quiz-show hosts, experts offering explanations to us on screen.

The dominance of this way of using and experiencing television gives the illusion of physical closeness, invokes those rules of social interaction which demand attention and which create some sense of social proximity. Audience research has produced accounts of people describing a kind of relationship with the figure on the screen, some even taking on the illusion that the face can see them.

Intimacy is also a product of intrusion. Television, especially with its minicams and undercover programmes, has the ability to intrude into others' lives and places where we may not. When the 'victim' on the show is caught unawares on the camera allowed there by a partner, especially in their own home, then their space has become part of our reality. Being in the space of others, caught perhaps on a collation of domestic video clips where silly things happen, rubs off onto our understanding of the medium, of its possibilities. Again, it contributes to a sense of television as a reality medium (even while, contradictorily, we do retain a sense of its artifice). The placing of the camera in a car (another private space) as part of a series on learning to drive (*Driving School*, BBC1, 1999), is another example of intimacy through technology and location of the camera. We shared in the frustrations of Margaret trying to pass her test for the umpteenth time: we were in the car with her.

This links to the idea that intimacy may be a product of declaration by those on camera. Television not only intrudes into private places, it also gets people to declare on private matters. There was a documentary about an Australian whose working life was selling sex to other women, with the knowledge of his wife. The man and the wife spoke to us on screen. We were privy to personal – even painful – secrets. Even the device of backlighting into shadow those who declare personal and sometimes dangerous secrets in documentaries actually increases our sense of the intimacy of the declaration. We become party to the declaration of this privileged information, even though the events of the interview have actually passed, and this is an edited version.

Private subjects, private locations, private devices are one thing. But then there is the feeling of the reality of television achieved through access to the world and through immediacy. So the declarations of politicians broadcast as they speak are also part of the quality of realism, of the reality aura of television. Real time is as potent as real space, and doubly so when the two are combined. Television is full of examples of this reality formation, through its news links and its outside broadcasting (OB). We can see sporting events as they happen and where they happen. The camera can even pull in on faces and moments of drama during the event. 'Events as they happen' are authenticated by the reporting of television. But also the act of reporting authenticates television itself as a reality medium.

Even where the technology is used as a kind of *tour de force* – flipping between real locations and events within a programme in a way that is only possible through this medium – still we accommodate the contradictions: the unreality of the moving around in space along with the realism of the places moved to. Authenticity as realism is a product of programme genres which collectively form a great deal of television output: sport, news, docusoaps, current affairs, documentaries, makeover programmes. All these programmes and more take us into real places and in some cases use viewers on screen, not performers. We retain an ability to discriminate between the conventions of the programmes, and to distinguish different handlings of realism. But there is a collective force of authentication which partly characterizes television as a medium, and which partly influences audience responses to it.

Why does the television industry want to distinguish between 'reality' and fiction?

MODES OF REALISM

Television has various modes of realism, which are defined in overlapping ways:

- generic by programming – e.g. the assumed differences between drama and sport
- generic by critical categories – e.g. the conventions of and differences between drama documentary and docusoap
- qualitative by descriptive terms – e.g. the differences between actuality and naturalism.

In every case, the distinctions are based on difference as much as similarity. They are defined through a particular combination of visual and sound cues – one might say signs – which distinguish one mode from another.

What is significant about all this is the urge to categorize on the part of industry and audience, and the increasing difficulty of distinguishing one mode of television presentation from another in this postmodernist age.

The television industry needs to categorize its product in order to market it both to the audience and to potential purchasers of programmes. Categorization is about understanding, about raising expectations and meeting them. This is indeed the genre argument revised under the heading of realism. So the industry may describe its product for various markets in terms which are defined by modes of realism:

- a hard hitting *documentary* which gets at the truth about . . .
- an unusual *drama* in which the heroes' fantasies come true
- a *docudrama* which reconstructs the experience of Restoration London through material from Pepys's diaries.

But the audience also needs to define the mode of realism that it is dealing with, in order to understand the material being watched. Viewers adjust their expectations and the way that they decode material, not least in relation to benchmarks of

- my life experience
- what I believe is others' life experience
- what I don't know, but think is a plausible life experience
- what I know already about the programme.

Social gossip, listings information, programme trails and the titles of programmes all contribute to this process of expectation and adjustment in terms of realism. As viewers we orientate ourselves towards television in terms of 'Is it true or not?', 'Did it really happen or not?', 'Do I believe it or not?'

This is not to say, as with genre and narrative, that the audience wants things handed on a plate. The challenge and pleasure of viewing lies partly in working out one's reality orientation. I would argue that orientation and understanding is a dynamic process, operating between producer and viewer, in which the rules of the game are continually changing, in which the pleasure lies in tension between recognition and puzzlement.

Because television consumes so much material it develops its language very fast. The various modes of realism in television are actually getting harder and harder to distinguish. Some people have a real ethical problem with a medium which is apparently playing games with the truth. I would argue that the benchmark here is intention. So documentary programmes makers who have been caught manufacturing material have quite rightly been disciplined and their companies fined. The lie is measured against the factuality of the information and the way in which it was presented – how the viewer was intended to take on the facts and indeed the value messages. But the handheld swift pan shots of *NYPD Blue*, resonant of single-camera documentary usage, while arresting on first viewing and while helping to shave the line between drama and documentary still closer, exist within an overall practice which signals drama and fiction.

Programming

So there is an expectation of and a treatment of realism in programmes which falls into categories defined by the institution. The validity of distinctions between types of realism is as much about a cultural understanding between audience and producers as about accurate description. There is an understanding that education will be about information and factuality. In this case there is realism as evidence and explanation. There are assumptions about the authenticity of and provenance of film as evidence used in programmes. Degrees of didacticism in style will underpin realism as truthtelling. Education deals in the currency of ideas and the truth about our world. We expect some talking heads or voice-over. Broadly, we expect the material to be allied to what we call a curriculum, or to subjects. This is a further guarantee of its difference and of its realism as television. The catch is that we are dealing here with discourses, with views of the world, with ideological positions – whether these be about geography, history, science or whatever. On this level, realism falls apart. **Reality as truth becomes a cultural production**. It becomes a set of meanings constructed through the language of television, through its codes.

Drama, on the other hand, operates on a cultural agreement that its material is evidently constructed. However authentic the sets and costumes of a historical drama, we know that these are performers, not 'real' people. We know that the interactions and the narrative are the invention and fancy of the drama's creators, not material from a film of actual lives and actions. We allow for the contrivance of coincidence and excitement. Drama may not be without realism, but this is always understood within the context, the supposed knowledge that it is simulated. So we are concerned about motivation for behaviour, we are concerned about the probability of events and actions. These become some benchmarks of realism. And yet still we approach the output of the drama department differently from our engagement with eduational material. It is based on (questionable) dichotomies between fact and fiction, truth and invention.

I leave you to create your own rationale for areas such as current affairs or religion. The point that I am making is that realism defined in these terms is both meaningful and meaningless. There are broad sets of ground rules for the use codes, for the provenance of materials in each case. But the more one looks at particular devices used to create a sense of realism, the less these seem to belong to any one area. There is also a crucial difference between realism based on the physical (real places, real people, real actions) and realism based on concepts (the truth, moral certainties).

Critical categories

So realism is defined in terms pretty much shared between producers and audience. These especially categorize material in terms of its relationship to our physical world. They judge implictly the provenance of that material – again the distinction between that which is recorded as it happens, where it happens and that which is constructed, probably in a studio. These categories are in effect ranged on an axis from the authenticated to the invented, from that which appears to be from life to that which bears no relation to life experience. This axis runs from documentary at one end to fantasy at the other.

Within documentary it might be argued that real time, or live broadcast, stands for the strongest kind of realism. Within fantasy it could be said that animation takes us furthest away from the mooring lines of physical and social reality. So live coverage of a sports event can be contrasted with *The Simpsons*. Within each of these categories one again acknowledges the imperfections of realism. Sports coverage contains action replays and selected camera angles. *The Simpsons* contains some very 'real' comments on gender differences and child development. But in spite of these qualifications, I would argue that the categorizing description does mean something. Mere fiction exists down the line from fantasy, offering realistic depictions in, say, a sitcom or a thriller, but still being an undisguised invention.

What is most interesting about the recent development of television is the appearance of different categories around documentary, describing shades of document and fiction. Documentary is worthy of a major section of this chapter (see p. 152, below), for the time being we can note that apart from the broad category of documentary itself, there is:

- **docudrama** – a mode of production which imports documentary conventions into a fiction base
- **docusoap,** which edits the lives of real people centred in one location and occupation into an imitation of a soap opera (see also Chapters 4 and 8): it grafts fiction onto document
- **dramadoc,** which dramatizes from a reality or document base: historical reconstruction would be an example here.

I call these various terms critical categories because they are in use by reviewers of television, even in colloquial use. What is significant is that they draw attention to the explosion of programmes of document on television, some generically defined other than by their realism – for example, the make-over programme. A combination of developing technology and economic pressures, as well as audience response, has combined to make television, at least on one level, increasingly the medium of reality programmes. More events are covered live – the Glastonbury music festival, for instance. More material is about real places and real people – consider the make-over programme *Changing Rooms*, which began running on BBC1 in 1998.

> In what respects is no television programme real?

Descriptive terms

The very words we use to describe the nature of the reality depicted and the quality of the realism created are themselves another definition of mode. But they don't necessarily belong exclusively to fiction or to document. In this respect the idea of modes of realism leads to interlocking sets of characteristics, each set having its own key phrase, its own kind of definition.

Naturalism refers to a kind of realism in television drama which achieves an unforced sense of being there with real people in real places. Devices such as real locations and 'real people' (non-actors) have been used to achieve this effect. *Brookside* is shot in real houses built for the job. Interior scenes force the camera into positions which make the viewer aware of walls and dooorways. Directors like Mike Leigh have also constructed naturalism through the use of improvised dialogue – a way of achieving colloquial rhythms of speech and exchange. Many drama documentaries work to achieve naturalism in order to subvert their fictional roots, to convince the audience of the 'truth' of the narrative.

Actuality refers to live, real-time footage, or to such footage reused. This sense of places actually existing and events actually happening or having happened, is an aspect of outside broadcast. Footage of real events is also likely in education mode or in historical documentary. But it is not impossible for it to be used in drama. This interpolation of one mode within another shades and redefines simple descriptors such as fiction.

Authenticity refers to that which is accurate and convincing, but which is not necessarily actual or true. Reconstructions, whether in drama or documentary, provide many examples. The locations are re-dressed to copy a period accurately. Physical details of sets and of dress are authentic to the place and the culture being recreated on screen. The scripted language is authentic to the usage of a particular time.

These three terms provide an account of ways in which realism is created in a television programme. It is worth mentioning that there are other terms which qualify our sense of realism without being comprehensive enough to constitute a discrete mode of realism.

- **probability** ties in with narrative and our sense of how likely it is that actions and events will occur
- **plausibility** is much the same idea, but is connected to the realities of the world created by the programme as opposed to realism in the world of our social experience
- **believability** may be qualified by the other two words, but its point of reference is what the individual believes could happen, what seems credible to any particular viewer. In this respect one could say that for some viewers *The X Files* is improbable but also believable given certain attitudes and convictions.

How might one argue that realism in television programmes is only a matter of conventions?

DEGREES OF DOCUMENTARY

The context for documentary realism has already been set above. Television has embraced forms of documentary and developed them to the point where they significantly characterize the medium and our sense of its realism. The modes of realism in the various forms of documentary are founded on our knowledge of (or beliefs about) the actuality of the source material as much as on its style of presentation. Whatever exactly documentary and its conventions are, they are allied to other factual forms of television such as news. Such factual forms both constitute a significant proportion of programming and contribute to what our overall sense of realism is. Our understanding of what documentary is therefore has something to do with viewing programmes such as *Gaytime TV* or *So You think You're a Good Driver*? Both of these use actuality source material and are a document of cultural experiences. But the former is framed as a magazine programme, the latter as a theme programme.

The fact that so many programmes do reconstitute material from actuality footage, from real-life sources, reinforces the point that television mediates cultural experience as well as being an experience in itself. If you like, television brings to the viewer images of real people, real places, real events, real opinions uttered – which otherwise those viewers would not have experienced. On the other hand, this document material is edited and shaped to particular modes of presentation. It is another reality moulded from the real. It has realism because of its evident origins in actuality. It even has credibility because of this. But it is not the original experience.

It is not hard to find examples of television programmes where orchestration of the actual calls into question the truth of the real. *The Jerry Springer Show* features real people in a studio. It could be set in real time but is in fact recorded. The situations of the people selected to appear on the show, however, and questions about the extent to which they have been primed, along with the evident manufacture of conflict on air by the host, combine to subvert actuality and manufacture drama. It's entertaining, it's rooted in document, but documentary it isn't.

Documentary is as ideological as any other category of television. Where it chooses to raise and examine issues, it is making an agenda as much as news is. How it chooses to represent social behaviour, especially if it examines some behaviours and not others, some social groups and not others, is as ideological as drama. Documentary is therefore both different from other television in form, as defined in terms of realism, and yet is the same as other television when looked at in terms of discourse, ideology and hegemony.

The strong showing of documentary/actuality/realist material on television both supports an uncritical view of television as providing a picture of the world, and reinforces a critical view of television as a means of drawing viewers into particular cultural positions and understandings. It may well also be a self-fulfilling process: the more people see of 'their world' on television, the more they will be convinced that it is a major function of television to bring the actual to the living room – to show police work in progress, for example. And then the more attractive such material will become to the viewer.

A production perspective on the rise and rise of actuality television also has a lot to do with the rise of independent producers. The charter for Channel 4, the quota system for terrestrial television, has forced what may be seen as competition. In other words, the 1980s and 1990s saw an explosion of independent production companies, which at the beginning of the twenty-first century produce up to 50 per cent of material. As a small independent outfit you can't afford the ruinous costs of mainstream drama. But you can afford the relatively cheap and portable technology which records and restructures material from life going on around us. People are interested in people.

Another institutional issue has been the rise of cable/satellite viewing, albeit that this still constitutes only a fraction of the audience for terrestrial television. Documentary has more exposure, but it has also been compartmentalized into different channels such as Discovery and the Nature Channel. New means of distributing television do not necessarily produce new ways of handling television. Indeed the cost of new investment tends to produce economies of approach, in a creative as much as in a financial sense.

Generally speaking, documentary on British television can be described in terms of a range of categories identified by content or by form.

Current affairs

These programmes, typified by *World in Action*, are 'issues-led' and deal with social, political, economic and environmental topics. To an extent, such programmes act as a support for matters raised through the news. They may challenge the status quo, but they still work within existing agendas. Realism is a consequence of the combination of interviews, expert opinions, authoritative narrators, actuality footage and the validation of issues by their appearance elsewhere in the news agenda.

They may also be described as investigative documentary insofar as they investigate the background to news events and the evidence surrounding issues of public debate. Those programmes concerned with consumer affairs – *Watchdog*, for instance – overlap with current affairs. In both cases the sense of realism is produced through technology used (perhaps secret cameras), through awareness of the actuality of the places and people investigated, and through the very process of investigation shown. This process positions the television makers on the 'side of the public' and as 'discoverers of the truth'.

Nature

These examples are dominated by the 'wonders of nature' category, in which technological devices such as timelapse photography are both unreal and yet reveal extraordinary facts about wildlife and about our natural environment. They take us into dimensions of reality, combining the realism of record with the authentication of devices such as the explanatory voice-over or the explorer on the spot. They may offer explanations of phenomena such as survival in apparently impossible conditions.

There are some programmes which introduce issues such as the destruction of habitat by conmmercial operations. But none of them really challenges the idea of 'nature'; they operate out of its discourse. Nature is to be managed and protected. Documentaries about nature are predicated on the notion that nature is apart from humans, that nature is exotic.

Science ✓

Science documentaries tend to combine explication of scientific developments with analysis of their social and economic consequences for our culture. The same devices shape the quality of realism in these programmes: our assumption that the processes described are 'true', is endorsed by actuality footage and the authority of status figures working in science. Of all discourses, science perhaps carries strongest connotations of being part of the world of the 'real' and the 'actual'. Television science documentaries are predicated on this image and reinforce it. But there are other ideas within the discourse which are themselves questionable. For example, the notions of 'science as progress' or 'medicine as rolling back disease', may appear to be forms of truthtelling but are highly questionable as ideas, not least on the evidence of science itself. So documentaries may employ devices of realism which help persuade us of the 'reality' of their information and the validity of their positions on that information. But that reality may itself be shaky.

Historical ✓

Much the same view may be taken of history as of documentary. History is a view of the facts (indeed of what facts are); it is meanings drawn from information; it is suppositions made about evidence. It is not the facts themselves. Documentaries in this area, whether they employ realist devices such as dramatic reconstruction, or depend on the realist evidence of a rostrum camera filming illustrations and text, or use experts testifying to camera, are still made up.

Mainstream

This term may be applied to those documentaries that are well established in their subject matter – social affairs, wildlife – and to those which are in the mainstream of devices of realism. Many of these devices have already been referred to. They include natural sound and lighting, long-held camera shots, location work, face-to-camera shots of people narrating or offering evidence. The devices are conventions for constructing a mode of realism that is distinguishable from others. It convinces us that the material is located in a physically authenticated world and in an ideal world of truth. I have already offered a critique of such realisms and realities. Documentary is more or less distinguishable from other television on the basis of form, but not on the basis of ideas and ideologies.

Fly-on-the-wall/vérité

This mode of documentary has been the specialism of film makers such as Roger Graef, who has produced series for television which went inside institutions such as the police and hospitals. As audio recorders and cameras become ever more lightweight, the technical achievement of getting inside rooms and private space to record 'life as it happens' seems less arresting. Nevertheless, the effect of authenticity achieved through watching evidently real people in real places living out their lives comes closest of all viewing experiences to looking through a window on the world. Long takes to suggest real time, mixed with other signifiers such as imperfect but 'natural' sound, enhance the feeling of watching true life as it happens. Whether the camera position makes us feel that we are inside the space as one of the participants, or whether it places us just the other side of that invisible window, still the effect is one of immediacy and involvement. This is realism on an intense level, even if it is still a set of devices. Viewer involvement is also likely to lead to viewer acceptance of the validity of what is shown and of what it may mean. It is easy to forget that still the material has been selected and edited, narrativized, shaped to the vision of the producers.

Dramadoc

This has been referred to above, and its devices for bringing dramatization into the conventions of documentary have been discussed. Dramadoc is distinguished from docudrama, which is a reversal of its practices: the grafting of documentary devices onto a fiction base. This distinction sounds easy, and generally works. But, given that realism is all an illusion anyway, there are examples where it is hard to be sure which base one is starting from and which set of conventions predominate.

A series about couples getting married (*Love Town*, January 1999) clearly started from a documentary base. There was no question of the authenticity of the couples, their pieces to camera, their exchanges caught on camera. But the series became dramadoc where it was evident that editing had selected out dramatic moments of anxiety and of conflict. It was forced to fit the framework of a classic realist text leading up to a moment of closure – the wedding.

On the other hand, reconstruction may fall either side of the line. There was a documentary in the *Timewatch* series on BBC 2 about the life of John Harrison, a seventeenth-century watchmaker, which used an actor and purported to show scenes which in fact could never have been filmed. But this was handled with reference to historical evidence. It was placed within a whole programme which also used voice-over and explanation. I would argue that this is still dramadoc, for all the invented source material. We should remind ourselves that these refinements of definition are not about categorizing for its own sake but relate to:

- understanding the nature of the relationship between the text and the audience
- recognizing the importance of realism as a value judgement for the audience
- understanding the distinction between realism as form, and reality as content and a state of belief
- recognizing the influence of different modes of realism on the meanings constructed out of the documentary, especially as they lead us into ideology.

Docusoap

These programmes have also been defined above as a kind of dramadoc whose fictional grafting is taken from soaps in particular. They represent a blurring of the reality line and a kind of postmodernist text in which intertextuality rules. As a hybrid genre they are marked by the following characteristics, common to both documentary and soaps:

- authentic locations and real people as the players
- handheld camera and natural sound and lighting
- people speaking to camera
- a group of people working in one location and dealing with the public
- these people (or players) being apparently chosen for, or filmed and edited to bring out, their differences

7.2 These images from *Airline* (ITV) and *Wish You Were Here* (ITV) refer to the evolution of genres and their interchangeable realism. Holiday programmes and docusoaps meet on the same visual ground.

- multi-stranded narrative created out of the document material
- ambivalence about narrative closure
- dramatic tensions and anticipation (narrative) created out of the material and the problems which the players face in their jobs: these, like soaps, often emphasize one or two 'characters' in a given week
- players who appear to be 'natural characters' being given more camera time: story strands built around them.

These programmes are trailed, like soaps, for the events, problems and characters to be seen next week. Their title sequences have the same mixture of location, character establishment and pace as some soaps and many dramas. Examples are:

Hotel: set in a large Liverpool hotel and leading on life behind the scenes. We see how the female general manager copes with sudden crises and how one of the male porters avoids getting the sack (for half the episodes!).

Lakesiders: set in an out-of-town shopping centre and mixing front-of-house interaction with some real characters from the public, with revelations of the players' personal lives.

Holiday Reps: set in various sunshine tourist locations and following the working and personal lives of the tour reps, mostly female. We see as much of their leisure and love lives as anything else.

Airport: set in a large airport complex, also exploiting tense situations in dealing with the public, contrasted with the backstage private lives of the players.

There are many more examples in which the formula is pulled one way or another. *Driving School* (see p. 146 above) had a more limited cast of characters. But the player named Margaret briefly became a media celebrity because viewers were absorbed by her long-running attempts to pass her driving test. As with soap operas, viewers empathized with a situation which many of them had gone through.

Driving School also exemplified the uneasy ethical position of material which purports to be real, if edited, but which is more manipulated than we may know. The scene where Margaret wakes up her husband to take her through the written test is of course a reconstruction. But it is not the only one in the genre. Andy Hamilton, in the 1998 Television Society Lecture, referred to 'ordinary people improvising around the theme of being themselves'. The docusoap has its own kind of contrivances, for all its protestations of actuality. People may not be paid, they may be doing what they would ordinarily do – but how are we seeing what they are doing? Has their reason for behaving as they do been subtly subverted? The relationship between people (performers) and life is plastic. Emma in *Lakesiders* might have seemed genuinely vulnerable when it emerged that her fiancé had two-timed her with her sister. But it also emerged later that she was hoping to get a recording contract on the back of her television exposure. And there was the notorious case in 1998 of Victoria Greetham, who for several months fooled C4 producers into filming her relationship with her father, for a programme on that theme – when it turned out that the man was in fact her boyfriend, 10 years her senior.

The fine line between devices of realism and the realities represented is also well exemplified by two cases. One example, a docusoap, was set on a cruise liner. The female singer/entertainer, Jane McDonald, performed on screen, and her career has bloomed. She has recording contracts, and is now working in entertainment away from the cruise liners. She has been reinvented by appearing on the docusoap. She has also appeared on television, singing, in her new persona. The second example links with *Holiday Reps*. Not long after this series was broadcast a fictional series about tour reps was screened, featuring the actress Michelle Collins as the main character. Michelle Collins had until 2 years earlier been a leading character in a soap opera – *EastEnders*. This fiction series – *Sunshine* – was itself more soap than anything, with more than a touch of the video travel promo. It was firmly located on Cyprus with a lot of location work. It was also multi-stranded and had a focused cast of characters – the reps working for a travel firm, plus some local characters.

The cross-referencing of textual details, genres and modes of realism is formidable. But it is the way that television is moving. Webs of references and shades of meaning are internal to the medium, and they link to other media. Television is the great accommodator. It is a showcase and a marketing tool for the pop-music industry. Sometimes it gives space to opera. More people watch films on television than in the cinema. The same is true of sport, where digital interactivity allows the viewer to choose camera positions on the match.

What docusoaps do reveal is the **transformational power** of the medium: the creation of personality, the manufacture of fame. This reflects on documentary itself, where in terms of realism one may say that the very act of filming a person and replaying that film to others makes the meaning of that person something more than it was. To see someone on the television screen makes them more and less than a real person. They are less because they lose their absolute reality, located in their everyday lives. They are more because they have, as Quentin Crisp put it, been 'sanctified' by television. Once you are a player in a docusoap you acquire by association the aura of 'television-ness'. You are on the same screen that has revealed the famous and the powerful from other spheres. In any case, the medium literally transforms the look and appearance of people. Lighting and the lens can erase blemishes, put on weight. Editing gives us the best bits, not the boring enactions of everyday living. The player inhabits screentime – that magic of selective compression into half an hour. And if you have distinctions in your performance then the screen frame, the close-up, the head shot will bring these out in a way that could not be seen by others in the rush of everyday working life. People become players: they may be drawn further into being performers. Appearance on screen makes them unreal. Docusoap treatment dramatizes them.

Docusoap illustrates television's love affair with an exploration of realism as a set of devices. It represents another way in which the medium sources its material in reality, in events as they happen, and then restructures all this into entertainment. It stands for a growing use of viewers to entertain the viewers – an approach familiar from the quiz-show genre and the use of studio audiences. It creates the illusion that television recognises its audience and works for its audience. I am not saying that viewers as players get nothing out of appearing on television. But we do need to remember that there are companies behind this hall of mirrors. Television is a business, however much of a populist front it puts on by incorporating its viewers and reflecting their opinions in various ways. Docusoaps are extending the 'viewer-as-player' approach because it makes economic sense. Players don't have to be paid. Setups and technology are cheaper than in full drama. Those who own the location are generally grateful for the publicity – no docusoap has ever reflected really badly on its place or its players.

Why are varieties of television documentary so popular with viewers?

CONCEALING AND REVEALING SOCIAL PRACTICES – REALISM AND IDEOLOGY

One thing this section can do is to confirm what is already evident throughout this chapter – that in many ways realism and reality are ideological constructs. At the point at which realism actually refers to truths about the world, then one has to remember that these truths are value judgements, ideological positions, interpretations of material (however objective we think our documentary 'evidence' is). We see things as being true which fit in with what we believe to be true. The naturalization of truths, of social practices, is bound up with realism and is part of the workings of hegemony. 'Common sense' is indeed itself an ideological position. This notion of 'social agreements' supported by their supposed basis in some natural (reality) process is founded only on our belief in those agreements. It is just another way of looking at the world. Devices of realism (conventions) become part of a mechanism for endorsing the common sense of that natural truth about how the world is and how it works. 'A documentary . . . will typically adopt a particular point of view on its topic and use rhetorical devices to persuade audiences to see things that way too' (Fairclough, 1995).

The phrase **social practices** may refer to that which is revealed and that which is concealed. Practices such as supporting your football team as part of legitimate social behaviour and popular culture are endorsed by hours of television showing that happening. But some practices are concealed – like what goes on in the football-club boardroom, which the fans are actually supporting. Only sometimes do they erupt into the public arena, as with the example in 1998 of sexist remarks made about female Newcastle supporters by the then chairman of the board.

When realism endorses certain social practices, and even particular ideological positions, it will also serve to naturalize them, to make them invisible. This is to say that when devices of realism make something real they also make it 'true'.

Television actually becomes part of social practices in examples such as gambling. Television screens show races in the betting office as well as in the home. The way in which the race is screened is designed to extract drama out of the event. This drama becomes part of the excitement of gambling. The qualities of, and backgrounds to, the horses and jockeys are discussed. This information is relevant to gambling calculations. If gambling is part of our culture and a social practice, then television is part of it, and endorses it through its representations. We are not just talking about pictures of races; we are talking about ways of understanding horse-racing. Television makes this understanding 'real'. It also conceals – more or less – other social practices which are part of horse-racing as an industry and are concerned with social status. So the wages and conditions of workers in the horse business – which are poor in some cases – are not part of the 'reality' of horse-racing as television constructs it. The fact that the business is underwritten by some very rich and powerful people for their pleasure, but not necessarily in the interests of other less powerful people, is not part of this sporting reality, as seen on television. I am not saying that such matters of background, with ideological implications, are never made available to the audience. But I am saying that they are largely concealed because they don't fit the version of reality that suits television institutions and those who run horse-racing.

A final and contentious example is fox-hunting. In this case the ideological conflict and contradictions are out in the open in television debate. There is a struggle for hegemony between two discourses of the countryside, one in which the social practice that includes chasing and killing foxes is naturalized, the other in which the opposite ideological position is taken. This is a classic Gramscian struggle for hegemony. It can also been seen terms of realism because each position stands for a different version of reality. Television has represented both positions, but it is not comfortable with the inconsistency and shows a leaning towards the anti-hunting camp. This is because there is a romanticized view of nature which cannot easily accommodate the idea of bloody death in the English countryside, and which dominates other television images such as *One Man and his Dog*. It does not want to reveal the violent practices which include industrialized production of animals and crops. Hunting as a reality is also a problem because, whatever the protestations of the hunting lobby, it is a manifestation of class and power. It could not survive without the acquiescence of those who control the land on which it takes place, and without the financial injections which pay for the expensive business of keeping horses and hounds. So hunting as a social practice is deeply ideological. It conceals other practices. Its representation on television through whatever kind of realism cannot but define realism in terms of ideology.

> In what ways may television documentaries give us a selective view of the world?

POSTMODERN IRONIES – INTERTEXTUALITIES

The fact that realism on television is bound up with its reworking and redefinition through intertextuality and hybrid genres has been exemplified in the comments on docusoaps above. If realism is a function of form, playing with and recombining conventions and devices, then these same examples show how postmodernist television has become.

It could be said that the modernist age of television was a more structured one, where distinctions between types of programmes were firmer and modes of realism were more clearly distinguished in terms of fiction and fact.

It might also be just possible to argue that there used to be a clearer distinction between watching television as a cultural activity and other 'lived' cultural activities in domestic and public spheres. Nowadays one can see a close interaction between television and 'life' – for example, representing social groups and social behaviours, marketing other leisure and cultural activities. This suggests that the television version of a concert or of unemployment becomes absorbed in some way within one's whole view and experience of the concert or of unemployment. How it is absorbed, what is absorbed, is contentious and unclear.

There is no sustainable argument that this interactivity, these potential effects, are a brand-new consequence of events of the late twentieth-century. Television in Britain achieved its millionth viewer at the time of Queen Elizabeth II's coronation in June 1953. Other potentially influential media with all their representations have been around for a hundred years. So I would argue that there has been no postmodernist revolution. Rather, there has been a process of change and development whose characteristics have crept up on us, not least through the agency of technology.

Some of the most postmodern programmes, in terms of their sense of irony, their intertextual reference and their ambiguous location in realism have been comedy programmes of a satirical or pastiche nature. *The Day Today* mimicked the conventions of news so well that I have watched viewers take it seriously for a couple of minutes, until some absurdity shattered the illusion. The game was almost serious in one episode where we watched the news-casters interview politicians into declaring war – very plausibly. *Alan Partridge* (Steve Coogan) parodied the excesses of chat shows with a straight face, so that their realism, their conventions, became part of the pleasure. But in both cases I would say that it was the exposure of pretensions to be real, to be more real than life, which gave the game away. If one is tempted to confuse art with life, such programmes remind us that television it may be, life it ain't.

Chris Morris's *Brass Eye* series took apart documentary modes of television in particular, imitating and exaggerating the realist conventions which had given them actuality and authenticity. Parody and satire merged as programmes pricked the realist intentions of some on-the-spot investigative journalism, for example. The ironic take of such programmes on their originals is postmodernist.

I am certainly not denying the development of interactivity between television and social action. *Crimewatch UK* is founded on the facts of crimes committed and actively engages the assistance of viewers to help solve them. Reconstructions are used as a kind of *aide-mémoire*. This interaction of realities is postmodernist – the original event, the recorded event, the reconstructed event, the retold event. But I would argue that it says more about the sophistication of the audience that can usually distinguish shades of realism than about the existence of a postmodernist society in which nothing and everything is real. If it is said that television is postmodernist because its form and style have become more important than substance and structure, this too is debatable. Insofar as this view is valid, it is also part of a whole cultural change. There are sections of young society for whom the wearing of certain clothes, the achievement of certain identities and lifestyles, is more important than having a regular job or money in the bank. You are what you appear to be, so the manufacture and flaunting of appearance becomes a priority. Television as a cultural tool, as an interface between artifice and livingness, shares in this. Style is not so much marketed through advertising as displayed through appearances in music shows, in children's television, in *Gaytime TV*, in holiday programmes, in fashion programmes. How you look, how you play, how you live – not how you work – dominates television. It is the stuff of the reality that television creates for us to absorb, it is the version of living that television proposes is 'out there'.

CASE STUDY: A SHORT HISTORY OF DOCUMENTARY ON TELEVISION

Although British television opened regular broadcasting in 1936, there was nothing like documentary on air. This was partly because portable sound and camera technology did not exist. There was no proper telecine, though a clumsy and poor-quality process of scanning film was used by Baird when his own camera system was obviously failing against the competition of the 'proper' Emitron cameras. There was no concept of documentary as we now understand it. Certainly there were nature and travel films in cinema. Film was used to document public events or exotic places, sometimes explorations or industries. Television actually broadcast part of a cricket test match in 1938. But the idea of filming real lives, or filming about social issues, was exceptional if not actually unthinkable. The working classes were in this respect invisible.

1950s

Things began to change after the Second World War, for six main reasons:

1 The development of technology through the war had produced portable wire and tape recorders (still big lumps with valves in) for sound, and relatively portable 16-mm Arrieflex cameras.

2 There was a strong tradition of newsreel documentary fuelled by the desire for pictures during the war period (e.g. Movietone News). The BBC produced its own 15-minute newsreels from 1948 to 1954.

3 There was a strong tradition of British cinema documentary, established under the inspiration of John Grierson at the GPO film unit in the 1930s and developed during the 1940s and the war, when many of the same people produced British propaganda films. These films did move into the recording of workers and towns (e.g. *Britain Can Take It*), not least because Grierson believed (in a paternalistic way) that film could encourage social change and progress.

4 Inspired by this tradition the 1950s threw up a new wave (Free Cinema) of young directors like Lindsay Anderson and Karel Reiz who positively wanted to get the camera into ordinary surroundings and capture life (e.g. *Covent Garden*).

5 The first videotape recording was developed in the 1958, eventually to replace the laborious telerecordings that put television images on film stock. At the same time as early telecine was converting film images into electronic ones. There was telerecording on film of the huge OB effort involved in covering Queen Elizabeth's Coronation in 1953.

6 The development of proper telecine from the mid-1950s onwards meant that filmed material could be broadcast on television with increasing ease and quality of image.

Also in 1953 the current-affairs programme *Panorama* first came on air. It is still running, and includes documentary background reports on the subjects under discussion. In 1954 *The War in the Air* was a series about airpower. In the same year *Zoo Quest*, fronted by David Attenborough, opened up a new variety of documentary and created an iconic personality for television. ITV came on air and Desmond Morris's career took off with *Zoo Time* (Granada, 1956–68). Indeed, wildlife proved a very successful variety of documentay. Other series followed the flag bearers, including Anglia's *Survival* in 1961. The Arts programme *Monitor* started in 1958, studio-based but with documentaries on its topics. These films varied from more straight documentation – *The Miners' Picnic*, on a brass band festival – to reconstructive biography such as Ken Russell's *Elgar* in 1962.

So within a decade, and under the stimulus of competition for viewers between the BBC and ITV, documentary established itself in the schedules and rapidly developed the modes and subjects with which we are familiar today. It is interesting that the 'father' of the British 1930s documentary movement, John Grierson, himself fronted a series called *This Wonderful World* (1958–65). This ranged across different places, but was centrally concerned with people, their jobs, their lives.

1960s

This decade not only brought further development of documentary form, but also saw some brilliant first films in the drama-documentary mode. Peter Watkin's *Culloden* (1964) is still gripping and convincing. It is a historical reconstruction of the battle of Culloden between the Scots and the English, and of the circumstances around it. There is no avoiding the painful actuality of scenes shot on real moors, where actors and extras were marched for hours without filming until they looked genuinely exhausted. Watkin's *The War Game* (1965) was so convincing in its reconstruction of a nuclear strike on Britain that it wasn't allowed to be shown for 20 years. Factual evidence of the unpreparedness of British authorities and tacit concealment of the real effects of nuclear strike might also have had something to do with this. Examples of realist docudrama using documentary conventions and looking at the lives of ordinary people were *Up the Junction* (1965) and *The Lump* (1967). The former was about the lives of ordinary women, the latter about working men in the building trade. These dramas, more than documentaries, were making visible working-class lives, class issues, gender issues and social practices which represented manifest injustice. The influence of documentary style on fiction was wider than might be realized. *Z Cars* started in the 1960s, using locations and copying the naturalism of everyday behaviour and speech. *Front Page Story* (ATV, 1965) adapted equipment to enable the production to be shot easily on the streets, without taking time for set-ups.

In terms of documentary and social comment there was the notable series *World in Action*, which started in 1963 (Granada) and specialised in investigating background to news events and issues and in examining social issues. There was also *Man Alive*, running from 1965 to 1982, which was social-issue/social-problem orientated, for example tackling the subject of child abuse. *Whicker's World* (1959–88) came out of short reports in the first evening magazine programme, *Tonight*. It was quirky and amusing as much as socially incisive. Spin-off series by Alan Whicker, exploring people and events in all parts of the world, were immensely popular. Whicker could ask awkward and revealing questions of his subjects, and in 1969 made a notable programme for Yorkshire television about the then dictator of Haiti, Papa Doc Duvalier. He was good at getting people to talk, at letting exposure to the medium make people interesting, from the Australian outback to Spain.

Dennis Mitchell was an outstanding documentary maker who favoured the approach of letting the subject speak for itself. He would produce impressionistic pieces of people and areas, dubbing music and effects onto mute film footage, as in *Morning in the Streets* (BBC, 1959). He was effective in pointing the camera and getting people to talk, making film in the 1960s about subjects as diverse as a Yorkshire mining village and African countries in the struggle for independence. His position of not wanting to come between the subject and the film was inherently contradictory, but the fact is that the films are absorbing and represent a so-called 'neutral' mode of documentary.

The BBC *Horizon* science documentary series started in 1964 and is still running. The documentary that examined culture and history took off in 1964 with Sir Kenneth Clarke in *Great Temples of the World*. He also fronted the blockbuster documentary *Civilisation* (1969), which looked at the civilizations of Greece and Rome and how they informed the subsequent development of Western civilization to the present day. This was documentary as big-budget film, on a grand scale, shot in 13 countries. It makes it clear that, through television at least, there is a huge audience for documentary material. While cinema took the fiction road and largely abandoned its equally documentary origins, television is the soil in which documentary has flourished mightily. The success of Clarke as presenter – like that of the Dimbleby family in the second half of the twentieth century – exemplifies the power of television to make personalities within the field of documentary as much as in lighter forms of entertainment. It is also interesting to note how this kind of high-culture, didactic approach continues a successful a tradition that goes back to the Reithian years of BBC radio in the 1930s and to those travel documentaries about other peoples, other places, other histories which were a strong strand of film making in the early years of the century. The more anthropological *The Ascent of Man* (1973), fronted by Jacob Bronowski, did a similar job in the science sphere. What is significant about this production is that it signalled the emergence of global television. It was a co-production with Time-Life and made a lot of world-wide syndication money for the relatively new channel BBC2. The history/archaeology documentary series *Chronicle*, starting in 1966, involved co-production with organizations such as the National Geographic Society. The series has been enormously successful, not least in terms of sales. Big series were often co-productions because the programmes looked at subjects abroad and could easily be sold to other countries. This strand of documentary by subject remains popular, not least in the example of what has been a 'hit' in documentary terms – *The Time Team* (Channel 4, 1997 onwards).

1970s

Established types of documentary remained strong, helped by ever more flexible and portable equipment. *Life on Earth* (1979) was a blockbuster nature series which came out of the highly successful *World about Us* (1967). These BBC series are all part of the astonishing career of David Attenborough, which, interspersed with periods in senior BBC management, has continued to build his iconic status, right through to a series in the 1990s, *Life in The Freezer* (1997). People like Dennis Mitchell continued to produce documentaries in their own style: *Seven Men* (1971) included a study of Quentin Crisp, talking freely in his flat about his lifestyle, his attitudes and his history. What is interesting about this example is that it can be contrasted with the fictional *The Naked Civil Servant* (Thames, 1975) in which John Hurt played Crisp in a dramatized but essentially true version of his life. This piece was autobiographical, was introduced by Crisp himself, and centred on the experience of being homosexual in the 1930s to 1950s. Mitchell's film contained little that was explicit about this side of Crisp's life, though this is not to say that it wasn't 'true' as a study of his lifestyle and attitudes. The two programmes were two different ways of representing 'the truth'. They stood for an acceptance that television could speak about previously taboo areas of our culture.

Mitchell's approach to documentary would have seemed vindicated in 1979 when a series about Fred Dibnah, a Lancastrian steeple-jack and steam traction engine fan and owner hit the screen. Dibnah is what is called a 'natural'. He talks with humour and absolute engagement about his enthusiams and his views on life. He has been revisited in one or two series since and is now an acknowledged 'personality', in great demand for opening events such as steam rallies, even 20 years on.

The appeal of the history documentary, and our cultural preoccupation with the Second World War, were illustrated in the success of Thames's detailed and comprehensive look at the causes, conduct and consequences of that war, *The World at War* (1973).

But in terms of the development of documentary perhaps the most significant single series was *The Family* (1974), which burst onto the screens with a fly-on-the-wall study of the Wilkins family. Paul Watson and his crew spent most of every day for weeks with the family. Footage was edited down to produce drama as well as naturalism, with a smack of soap opera. The innovative appeal of the series wasn't the individual film and sound techniques themselves: they had been used before. It was the intensity of the way they were combined. This programme initiated television viewers' love affair with really intrusive documentary and laid the ground for the explosion of video diary and docusoap modes of the 1990s. The same intensity and fly-on-the-wall techniques were used in Roger Graef's series *The Police* (1982), which looked at the work of the Thames Valley Police, giving the viewer long real-time takes and an intimate sense of police work. One programme, *A Complaint of Rape*, exposed the force to considerable criticism about their interviewing of a rape victim and generated a debate which led to revision of the procedures for dealing with victims of such crimes. Realism may in one sense be nothing but a set of conventions, but the impact of feeling 'the actual' within the framework of documentary modes has an impact which is as intense as, if different from, that of fiction.

Equally significant in 1979 was the screening of John Pilger's investigative documentary on Cambodia, on the killings carried out during the civil war, on the Khmer Rouge and on the adverse effects of the power politics of Western governments: *Year Zero – the Silent Death of Cambodia*. There was nothing new about the actuality footage, the evidence on screen, including documents or someone speaking to camera. What was different was the ideological position, which makes one realize how 'safe' much of television and documentary is. This is not to diminish the importance of a number of other hard-hitting documentaries over the years. *Panorama* upset the Tory government in the mid-1980s by examining how they had managed the media in the then recent Falklands war. But Pilger's occasional reports are marked by a bitterness in criticism whose effect is enhanced by a realization that he must have his facts right if he hasn't been prosecuted for slander. A later programme on the East Timor situation (*Death of a Nation: The Timor Conspiracy*, 1998) not only had the impact of secret film showing a massacre being conducted by the Indonesian authorities, but also revealed the indirect collusion of the British government through the sale of arms and aircraft which were quite evidently going to be used by the Indonesian government. Ironically, this programme was reprised and updated in 1999, when Indonesian oppression in the region was taken up by Western politicians, leading to a bloody independence for the country. This kind of documentary represents a breaking down of consensus, of assumed social agreements and social values which television usually prefers to preserve. Pilger had cut his teeth on *The Pilger Reports* (1974 onwards), which were briefer examinations of political situations and issues around the world.

It is perhaps no accident that the highly naturalistic drama series *Days of Hope*, set around the period of the First World War and taking a leftwing view of society, the war and the general strike of 1927, was also broadcast in 1975. This series and Pilger provoked enormous debate about their positions on events and about 'what should be shown on television'.

1980s

Safer, but excellent examples of their kind, were documentaries of the 1980s such as *Hollywood* (Thames, 1980), on the silent era of cinema, or *Ireland: a Television History* (BBC2, 1981). *Crimewatch UK*, to which I have already referred, started in 1984 (BBC). The same year saw *The Living Planet*, Attenborough's nature blockbuster for the decade. There was the interesting and culturally aware series *Equinox* (Channel 4, 1986) which looked at aspects of science and technology. Excellent as much of the work was in the 1980s, in review there is a sense that it consolidated styles and approaches that had already been established.

1990s

In the 1990s the subject-/content-based documentaries continued to engage and excite audiences in respect of science, wildlife and social issues. But it was the playing with technology and with conventions that proved most innovative. The arrival of minicams and Betacams, the relaxation of attitudes towards 'broadcast quality' of picture, meant that in some cases the public were given cameras so that they could produce documentary by themselves. *Video Nation* gave us short face-to-camera disquisitions on anything the viewer wanted to talk about. *Video Diaries* (1991–) has given us longer accounts of people's interests and activities as filmed by themselves. We have been with the police on real night-time raids to catch criminals. Docusoaps have put viewers on camera and have recombined conventions so that the lines between fact and fiction, viewer and viewed, are much less clear.

John Corner (1996) describes three developments in documentary relying on new camera and sound technology:

1 the emergency services type, e.g. *999* (1992 onwards) or *Blues and Twos* (1994)
2 the do-it-yourself type, e.g. *Video Diaries* or *The Real Holiday Show* (1995)
3 the hidden-camera format, e.g. *Undercover Britain* (1994).

In all these cases one can see the pull of two apparently opposing tendencies. One is towards enhanced realism: gaining access to life as it happens, drawing on real people and events. The other is about reconstruction and dramatization: a pull towards infotainment. This approach, with its relative economies of cost and its fascination with 'real life', continues to be attractive to producers and audiences alike. For example, *Mackintyre Undercover* (1999) is exciting, immediate and allied to investigative journalism. Indeed Mackintyre proclaims himself to be a journalist.

Typically of television in general, documentary is not only developing new forms by interbreeding what is there already, it is also crossing over with fiction. The old distinction between fact and fiction no longer holds true in this postmodernist world. The 'traditional' documentary providing a survey of some aspect of science or politics or society, still exists. But it no longer defines the form. 'Documentary has become a central element in broadcasting's performance of its public informational and critical roles as well as a general source of knowledge and pleasure' (Corner, 1996).

8

Television and Representations

PREVIEW

This chapter deals with:
- the meaning of the term representation
- stereotypes
- key words connected with representations – identity, naturalization and difference
- connections with ideology and discourse
- reading images
- representations by gender (including treatment in soap operas), race and youth
- representations of crime and the police.

INTRODUCTION – THE IDEA OF REPRESENTATIONS

The idea of social groupings refers to almost any way of categorizing large numbers of people as a set. Children are as much a category as, say, athletes. But since television manufactures versions of everyone and anything about our society and culture, the term representation can also cover institutions. So it has images of and ideas about teachers as well as education (*Hope and Glory*, BBC1), or soldiers as well as the army (*Soldier, Soldier*, BBC1) or nurses as well as hospitals (*Casualty, BBC1*).

Then there is the important distinction between representation in terms of appearance and of meanings. What was represented on the drama series *Queer as Folk* (C4), or through *Gaytime TV*, is that it is partly the appearance and behaviour of gay people which is used to define them. But more importantly, such programmes represent *ideas* about gay people, how the audience is meant to understand them. This is why the concept of representations is so important. It is about understandings in our heads.

In a broad sense all communication constructs representations. Even in conversation about people by groups we will use and reinforce ideas which already exist. However, television has to be looked at differently from conversation, for reasons which are mainly to do with its reach into the population at large. Even among the media it is special in its sheer availability. And there is something even more special about those television programmes which are directly tied to the representation of a social group. Programmes like *Acetate* (BBC2), about dance music culture, or *Hollyoaks* (C4), a young persons' soap opera, are both about and aimed at 'youth groups'. Whether they are watched completely or fleetingly, that experience will contribute something to the watcher's notions of 'youth' or 'young people'. To an extent, that viewing will build a physical representation which is about **appearance** – dress, hair, etc. To an extent it will be about **behaviour** – the dancing and romancing. But most fundamentally the representation will be about the *idea of young people*, what their beliefs, values and preoccupations are understood to be.

That understanding is created at the intersection of the programme with the existing set of perceptions and judgements which already exist in the mind of the viewer. Any one representation is also a complex of other contributing representations. A representation of maleness may also be part of, for example, 'husband' or of 'Bangladeshi'. It may be that in a given programme, one feature of gender or occupation predominates to fix the character in the minds of the audience. But even sitcoms with broadly drawn characters create them through a combination of elements which refer to different dimensions of representation. The characters in *ER* (ITV) may be representations of doctors, nurses, consultants, but the fusion of these with gender representation is crucial to the success of the hospital drama. Clearly there is an assumption behind all this that representations come, partly at least, from the experience of television viewing. Whatever is understood through television interacts with other sources of representations. But then there are basic questions to be asked:

- What kinds of understanding do we in fact get from television representations?
- Do different viewers understand the same representation in different ways?
- Who gains or loses what by these representations, especially in terms of relationships of power?

'Representations in media texts may be said to function ideologically in so far as they contribute to reproducing social relations of domination and exploitation' (Fairclough 1995).

It is worth reminding ourselves that there are two main kinds of critical position on the media in terms of:

- why they might construct kinds of representation

- how media product in general gets constructed
- the relatiohship between media producers and audience.

Determinism (Marxism) would suggest that, albeit unconsciously, the producers construct representations whose meanings work in favour of those who control society and often against the interests of those who are controlled and are represented. The media construct our idea of reality because they construct their words and images which become at least part of that reality. **Functionalism** would suggest that the media reflect public attitudes and give the audience what they want. If representations change over a period of time then this in itself is a reflection of changes in public attitudes.

STEREOTYPES

It is a misunderstanding to assume that representations are the same as stereotypes. Certainly television is full of stereotypical representations: those images, behaviours and meanings which have been rendered down to simple details, even clichés. Adverts and sitcoms both use stereotypes because they want a quick call to the audience's attention and understanding. They may want to exploit the stereotype to make fun of the character, or they may even want to work against it, having set the audience up.

In any case stereotypes are themselves distinguished by degrees of cultural intensity and accessibility. So genre material is full of stock characters who are familiar through repetition but are marked more or less clearly in their characteristics. **Types**, such as the barman in thrillers or Westerns, are recognizable but not very distinctive in appearance or function. **Stereotypes** exist at another level of intensity, with a wider and more familiar repertoire of characteristics: Rowan Atkinson as Mr Bean the bumbling nerd, or Barbara Windsor as the *EastEnders* matriarch, still the blonde and the barmaid.

Archetypes have a wide cultural reference, and pivot on characteristics which don't necessarily require familiarity with a particular genre. An example would be the working-class, opiniated, racist, sexist character of Alf Garnett from the old series *Till Death Us Do Part* (BBC1). In this case, the concept of the show was sold and successfully transposed to countries such as the USA and Germany. The character was archetypal. However, when NBC took up an option on *Prime Suspect* (BBC1), with Helen Mirren playing the lead character, a female crimebuster who is both a stereotypical loner cop and a complex personality, they eventually realized that the role wasn't archetypal enough to work, simply by sticking an American actress in the part.

This example also shows that one can have a stereotypical character at the core of a part, and yet make it more than a cliché through the quality of writing and of acting. The term stereotype does not automatically have to be one of critical abuse. What stereotypes are is part of the process of recycling and reinforcing representations by social groups. Their familiarity makes them intertextual. If you have invoked one example of a stereotype you have invoked all the others that this particular example is trading off, along with all the ideas around the stereotype. Victor Meldrew in *One Foot in the Grave* (BBC1) is referenced with Compo in *Last of the Summer Wine* (BBC1) and with Uncle in *Only Fools and Horses* (BBC1), and so on. These are all old codgers, sometimes crusty, talking too much about the past, but always game for something. It isn't their appearance which unites them, as is sometimes assumed where stereotypes are concerned. There are actually interesting class distinctions and markers here. But they are united as being cussed old males, somewhat like the old timer in the Western. It is the meaning of age combined with masculinity which is represented.

So while stereotypes may be the most recognizable face of representations, representations are about more than stereotypes.

IDENTITY

Representations construct identities for the group concerned. The identity is our 'understanding' of the group represented – an understanding of who they are, how they are valued, how they are seen by others. There may be negative as well as positive features. The understanding may be generally shared by members of that group and by others outside it. Nevertheless, a full understanding of the identity of a group by its members is likely to be different to the view constructed by those outside the group. So there might be a general understanding that family bonding is a strong feature of the representation of Jewish people. Within this understanding, representations of the Jewish mother may also have general currency, which can be exploited in drama or in comedy. There is a kind of identity here. But the non-Jewish viewer of the drama cannot share the sense of identity experienced by the Jewish viewer.

So identity is a slippery concept, meaning different things to different people, especially those within and without the group concerned – and yet also having some meaning in common. Identity is something that exists within consciousness, is articulated in communication, and is also lived out in a cultural context. Our racial and ethnic identities are in our heads, in the heads of others, in the articulations of television programmes, in the living out of our daily lives (which includes the watching of television programmes).

There is also a sense in which our identities are about what we are not, as much as what we believe we are. They may be defined in terms of oppositions. So television may feed a sense of being 'not rich' or of being 'male as opposed to being female'. (*See* Fig. 8.1.)

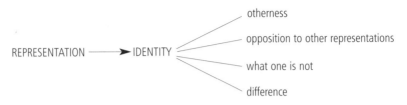

8.1 Representation and identity.

DIFFERENCE

This leads one straight into the idea of 'difference': that if one has an identity which is capable of being represented and which is meaningful, then by definition it makes those who *are* represented different from those who are not.

Partly this difference is about the distinctiveness of social groups, one as opposed to another. Distinctiveness may be marked by appearance and behaviour, as with the treatment of gay males in comedy material – the use of make-up, high voices and exaggerated gestures. But the appearance is symbolic of the real difference: lack of maleness, lack of masculinity, lack of what it takes to be a real man. Performers such as Julian Clary (in, for example, *All Rise for Julian Clary*) exploit this appearance of difference, and so reinforce its substance.

Difference is also about social norms. Representations draw attention to social difference in the ways that they do in order to reinforce norms of behaviour and to coalesce values around one kind of representation understood to be 'normal'. Thus homosexuality becomes different from heterosexuality. The differences of homosexuality are handled in negative ways. Therefore by contrast heterosexuality is understood to be normal.

There is also the use of a phrase – 'the other' – to define difference. The negative representation is other than the positive one. The person represented is the other. What you are is what you are not. A recurrent issue around television screening of Wimbledon tennis is about the relative lack of prize money for female competitors. In the arguments one hears positions such as – 'women are different from men' (not the other way around) – 'women don't play as many sets as men' – 'women don't hit the ball as hard as men' – 'women don't rate as highly as men in audience responses'. Such positions add up to the idea that women are other than men, that women are defined by being not men.

> In what ways may depictions of children in television adverts define them as being 'not adults'?

NATURALIZATION

Representations endorse a so-called natural order of things. They support dominant ideological positions.

Stuart Hall (1997) describes naturalization as a 'representational strategy designed to *fix* "difference", and thus *secure it forever*'. He is referring to the treatment of black people and to the intellectual conditions described in the television drama *A Respectable Trade* (BBC1), which assign black people the position of being 'children of nature', born to servitude in the 'natural' order of things.

Naturalization becomes an endorsement of certain views of social order as social relations, of certain power relations. Indeed, it serves to endorse inequalities of power in any subject of representation, including gender and class. Men are no more naturally incapable of caring for children or managing a household than black people are naturally better at activities such as sport or dancing.

IDEOLOGY

So it is that we are once more looking at ideology. Althusser (1969) might say that ideologies are systems of representation: the one defines the other. The meanings behind representations are the same meanings or value positions which are behind ideology, not least the dominant ideology in our culture. In projecting representations, television projects the ideology.

The act of representation becomes an embodiment of power relations in our society. Representation is 'a "vehicle" for transmitting ideologies in the service of maintaining/extending power relations' (Briggs and Cobley, 1998). The meanings of representations are about:

- who has power and who does not
- how power is exercised
- the values which dominate the ways that we think about society and social relations.

Stuart Hall (1995) comments that 'ideologies are not the product of individual consciousness'. In other words, they develop out of the attitudes of certain social groups and they work in the interests of those groups. So it isn't individuals who invent the notion of 'Islamic extremism' which is on the television news and current affairs agenda. Ask yourself where the idea may come from: in whose interests it might be to promote such an idea.

DISCOURSE

It follows, because ideologies are full of discourses, that representations may also be seen as being linked with discourses. These discourses work under the surfaces of representations to produce those same meanings that we have already talked about. For example, the discourse of femaleness works within television dramas, its meanings being understood in terms of the difference from and opposition to the meanings of the discourse of maleness. But the female discourse is mixed up with others – science, in respect of which women are supposed to be not 'naturally' capable (who fixes the car?), or health, in which women are supposed to have more problems than men.

As with all discourses, such notions have a history. Foucault's examination of discourses in relation to women and insanity in the nineteenth century makes it clear that there is a long history to a view of female mental instability or weakness. Even now television productions of Jane Eyre don't seem to excite much comment on the implications of Mr Rochester's mad and largely invisible wife. We don't know why she is mad. We don't even know what is meant by 'mad'. It is just 'naturally' factored into the story by the female author. The idea of the hysterical female remains with us, but we don't have a corresponding notion of the emotionally retarded male, measured against female normality. The discourses involved support differences of power and ideas about:

- women being more emotional than men
- emotion being opposed to logic (men are of course logical)
- an excess of emotion being undesirable (excess being measured against the normal behaviour of men)
- emotion as a sign of weakness.

Discourses battle for predominance in defining our understanding of the world. Conflict between gender discourses goes on. (*See* Fig. 8.2.)

LOOKING AT THE IMAGE

The process of looking at television images which comprises representations is a complex one. What does looking mean? It isn't just a visual activity. The act of looking is only part of perception, in that one has to make sense of what is looked upon (back to meanings again). There is the matter of the cultural experience that one brings to bear on this looking/perceiving. There is the question of who is doing the looking.

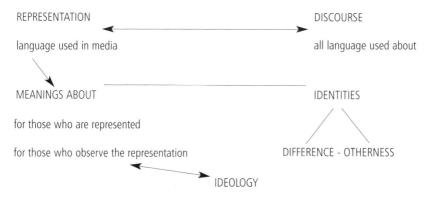

8.2 Representation related to other key terms.

Looking as critical point of view

In terms of representation, Stuart Hall (1997) describes three 'points of view', using the phrase partly in terms of viewer position but mainly in terms of its critical connotations – 'having a position on', 'the location of a position on'. The three points of view are:

1 **reflective** – the view of, the meaning of, the representation which is a kind of social and cultural view that is 'out there' in our social reality
2 **intentional** – the view of the creator/producer of the representation: the meaning as they intended it and conceived it
3 **constructionist** – the view that is made through the text and by the reader: the view that depends on uses of languages or codes – the visual and verbal codes, the technical codes, the dress codes, and so on, which television presents to the eye and the ear.

These views of representation raise questions about:

- where the meaning as representation is located
- how meaning varies according to who is generating it
- how the producer may inscribe meanings in the text
- how the text may construct meanings for the television watcher
- how the television watcher may construct meanings for him/herself
- the kinds of meanings that exist out there in our culture prior to production or to watching
- the relationship between the producer and the watcher as makers of meanings.

Looking as spatial or temporal positioning

In this case I suggest that point of view is taken more literally, in terms of image reading. With regard to time, for example, one is aware as a viewer whether what is happening on the screen is meant to be:

- contemporary or current time
- set back in time or history
- set back in time relative to the present time of the narrative (the flashback)
- happening at the same time as other events in the present, which we the viewer know about because the parallel narrative structure has operated to privilege this knowledge.

This has to do with the **temporal position** of the television text.

As far as place or space is concerned, one may refer to the **spatial position** cued to the viewer by the placing of the camera and by the use of sound. Sound is tricky because we tend not to notice logical impossibilities such as hearing conversations which take place many yards way. But a consistent, diagetic example would be the sound of a closing door off screen, before someone walks into camera shot. We are thus placed within the space on screen, experiencing it as if we were indeed there, listening.

The camera may also include logical impossibilities, such as the helicopter shot swooping over the landscape, or the shot through the back of the fridge from which someone is taking food. Television tends not to include the more extravagant shot positions of cinema – elaborate crane shoots – simply because they are expensive, not least in respect of the implied scale and control of the set or location involved.

The camera position becomes our position. It may be subjective or objective. We might be placed as the observer through a doorway, either as one of the characters in a drama or simply as some omnipotent onlooker to the events on screen. Camera angle and proximity place us in special relationships to the subject, and may affect the meaning of the representation. One shot in a BBC2 costume drama (*The Aristocrats*, June 1999) managed to represent passion and sexuality in a marriage with a sense of the discretion that marked the manners of the time. The point of view positioned us as if looking down the lower half of the wife's body, including the adoring husband caressing her foot and removing the bands of her silk stockings. It was an intimate position that was logically impossible. Its complex connotations would have been impossible if the camera/spectator had been placed 15 feet away from the actors, looking at them in profile – more detached, perhaps more voyeuristic because the view would have been possible within the space of the scene.

GENDER, WOMEN AND TELEVISION – SOAPS

The dominant argument about representations of women is that they are in varying degrees negative and socially repressive. They offer role models which encourage the submission of women in a male world, and which discourage self-esteem and proactive behaviour in young women. A typical talking point might be the images of girl groups in the mid-1990s – for example, the Spice Girls and the All Saints. They have an admiring female following whose approving comments usually centre round the phrase 'girl power'. What this power actually is, is more open to question. The types offered by such girl groups as B'Witched on *Top of the Pops* still focus on sexuality and sex appeal. It might be said that the female viewer looks at them and imagines that they themselves are being looked at. The group is an acknowledged marketing construct. Their occupation is exotic – singing and dancing – and may be said to have nothing to do with the real world inhabited by their fans. So as representations they are both powerful and powerless.

At the same time, it is important not to fall into a trap of describing all representations of females as disempowering or demeaning. There is a feminist point of view which suggests that women should not have to sacrifice their sexuality in order to achieve respect or social justice. There are a number of examples in television – not least soaps – which are positive in varying degrees. For example, the popular genre of chat shows is dominantly if not exclusively the province of female presenters, female participants and subjects which have been identified as female interest: relationships, emotions, self-image. Whatever the extravagances of the *Ricki Lake Show*, it deals positively with the importance of supporting self-esteem, talking about feelings and evaluating relationships. There are also tougher positive role models in some fiction – for example, Inspector Jane Tennyson (Helen Mirren) in the crime series *Prime Suspect*. Indeed there is a vein of crime fiction empowering female roles: Jill Gascoine playing boss in a police station (*The Gentle Touch*, ITV) in the 1980s; Amanda Burton playing the forensic expert (*Silent Witness*, BBC1) in the 1990s. As with all representations one also has to recognize that the categories and the meanings do overlap and intermingle.

There is a negative overlap between femaleness and oldness in that many cultures demonize old women as 'bags', 'hags' and 'witches'. Older female characters in drama may be bossy or plain frightening – for instance, the character Hyacinth Bouquet in *Keeping Up Appearances* (BBC1). It is suggested that such characters symbolize the desexualizing of the older female. She can no longer be 'placed' in terms of her sexuality, even disempowered by it. She 'knows' that she has nothing to offer men and so no longer fears them. Freed of childbearing and the demands of young family life, she has time in which to assert herself. She becomes proactive.

On the other hand, there are positive examples which work the other way

– female newscasters and reporters of mature years to match assumptions about male competence. Think of Kate Adie or Anna Ford. There are older fictional female characters who demonstrate the capacity for wisdom, affection and decision-making. Victor's wife Margaret in *One Foot in the Grave* is definitely not a stereotype.

Constructions

Ideas about female gender obtained through television are very much a construction and it is possible to identify specific aspects of these constructs.

Appearance is crucial to cueing up notions of femaleness or of femininity – the hair, the make-up, the dress. These are the essential ingredients for inviting the audience into assumptions about a female position when a male entertainer makes a success of a character such as Lily Savage (*Blankety Blank*, BBC1) – the strong woman, the brassy Liverpudlian with a voice like an ashtray. They 'entitle' the performer to assume a female point of view, to make remarks about women. In this case, they are cleverly pitched to avoid any hint of pantomime-dame exaggeration and yet still allow us to be complicit in a knowledge of the masculine inhabiting a female sphere. Looks are very much bound up with projecting sexuality, to a degree which is not true of the male. Television is part of an enormous cultural apparatus which socializes young females into prioritizing appearance and into measuring their self-identity and self-worth in terms of how they look. Television itself has an enormous range of programmes which explictly (in the case of, say, fashion programmes and advertisements) and more implicitly confirm that appearance is everything. Many of them project the simplistic notion that appearance means social value and personal self-esteem, without ever explaining how that connection is made, nor how it will work in the real world. *Heartbreak High* (BBC2) has plots to ensure that the right girl gets the guy. The girls are pretty. The guys are hunky or maybe just goodlooking and decent. But our lives are not plotted by benign script writers. (*See* Fig. 8.3.)

Behaviour is another aspect of construction: the notion that what you do is what you are. Some behaviours are represented as being more appropriate to femaleness than others. These behaviours may be broadly tied to:

- role – women as committed to domestic activity or to caring professions
- notions of femininity – women demonstrating emotion
- definition in relation to men – deferral behaviour in the company of males.

In this respect another feature of construction is about defining the female in relation to assumptions about the male. The female becomes the 'other'. Masculinity becomes a reference point for constructing the female. For

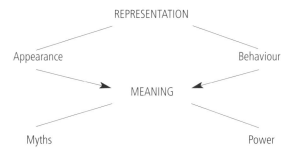

The surface of the representation of people by groups or categories is in the appearance and behaviour depicted. Making sense of this surface leads one deeper into representation, to meanings about the representation. Dominant areas of meaning have to do with cultural myths [women are naturally gentle] and with the positions of groups in terms of power [women earn on average less than men].

8.3 Representation: appearance linked to meanings.

example, many romantic narratives (loosely described as a woman's genre), are driven by notions of attracting the male, waiting for the male's attention, regretting loss of the male – Andrea Newman, who became famous with *Bouquet of Barbed Wire* (ITV, 1976), is very good at writing sophisticated versions of this for television drama. The heroine's motivation and emotional landscape are often defined as much by what the male wants and what they stand for as by her own needs and principles.

Females are constructed in terms of an **emotional reading**. In their various representations they are expected to be bitchy, passionate, jealous, vindictive, affectionate, and so on. A generous palette of emotional colours is ascribed to females, attached to stereotypes and tied to a simplistic notion that women are, simply, emotional (that is, again, more than men!). The fact that they may be more sensitive to emotions or that the reception and display of emotion may be a healthy thing is more or less written out of the agenda.

Values are part of the female construct, but always in the context of positioning women socially and ideologically. So, representations often privilege women as valuing beliefs and behaviours to do with motherhood, protectiveness, family. But it may be said that it is very convenient to construct such values as 'belonging to' women, if this confirms their domestic role, denies them economic power, and generally affirms a subordinate position in the social hierarchy. Dramas such as *Butterflies* (from the 1970s, BBC2) have amusingly but sadly tried to explore the velvet trap of middle-class domesticity for the wife and mother. The heroine's problem is still being explored more than twenty years on. She has no status without economic independence. She would still be vilified for either running off with her lover or for being seen to love him (something which the original series carefully skirted around in its version of courtly love).

Occupational roles are often part of a female construct. It is true that some jobs are seen as being women's jobs – nursing and primary teaching, for example, are dominated by women. The social construction of femaleness is entangled with the media construction. There was a British programme (*Ground Force*, 1998 onwards, BBC1) about families having a surprise 'make-over' of their garden by a television team of experts. This team was led by a male, the expert trade tasks were performed by another two males, and the single female (a capable gardener) was notable in her representation for the following features:

- she was often shown as being sent shopping for plants
- she was shown as standing around laughing, or sometimes carrying an object, or sometimes dibbing in a few plants
- camera shots dwelt on her figure as much as on her face, including the media reported bra-less frontage
- on a *Radio Times* cover she was shown naked but concealed, as in a 'fertility goddess of plenty' pose (*see* Fig 8.4).

She has become a 'personality', but is recognized for her appearance as much as for her skills.

Female domains are part of the construction of women – places which seem to 'belong to' women. Again, without ignoring the selective and exaggerated aspect of stereotypical media constructs, it is possible to move between media reality and social reality in pursuit of the domain. The home is seen as being a female domain, so also the bathroom, the kitchen, the bedroom (but not the garage or the workshop!). Just as in life one has heard a woman bewailing a husband's unemployment because 'he gets under my feet in the kitchen', so also television soaps, dramas and sitcoms reproduce assumptions about women (not men) deciding on the decor for their domain.

> In what ways do the social realities of women's roles conflict (or not) with the realities constructed for women on television?

Stereotypes of women

Stereotypes are not necessarily negative. The notion of women as mother, as protector and provider, may be perfectly constructive. One may debate this in respect of soap operas, against the view that these mothers are still trapped in the domestic sphere. There are examples throughout television of strong women who offer constructive role models. There is Madeleine Allbright, the

American politician, who is shown in the news as an active, decisive, older woman. There are the young female presenters for a British magazine television show – *The Late Lunch* (C4) – who are capable and humorous – or Kirsty Wark ably presenting news and current affairs programmes (*Newsnight*, BBC2).

On the other hand, television also harbours, for example, its blondes – its decorative blondes, its blonde goddesses, its blonde bimbos, its blonde assistants, especially in quiz shows. Sometimes they are typed into an active role. Anneke Rice fronted a programme about worthy projects being achieved against the clock: *Challenge Anneke* (C4, 1994–6). She would swing from helicopters, run through locations, chivy people along. But sometimes the role is much more passive, as with the compère's assistant Kelly Brock on the *Big Breakfast Show* (C4).

Television comedy has long been a home to degrees of female stereotyping. The seaside-postcard saucy comedy of the *Benny Hill Show* (ITV, 1969–89) has passed into history, with its innuendo and representation of women as girls, or rather as a set of sexual features. On the other hand, the battle-axe of a mother-in-law that Les Dawson impersonated in the 1980s is still with us in various forms: the forceful, snobbish, husband-bullying Hyacynth Bouquet; the unsmiling unromantic Nora Batty of *Last of the Summer Wine*. Perhaps there is something more knowing and ironic about Doreen in *Birds of a Feather* (BBC1). She is an ageing tart, and her tartiness and pretensions are made fun of, and she knows it.

Female unreality

Erving Goffman (1979) brings out a point about how we read gender and appearance. This has to do with the way that we read the representation of the male 'business person' seriously, but not the female. With the male, the clothes, however we may 'know' they are dressed on a model, still refer to a role. The image is plausible: we refer to social reality. In the case of the female, Goffman argues that we see the woman as if she is play-acting. She is only a model. We do not project her into a social reality.

It is in this sense that one may use a phrase such as female unreality to describe that mental positioning which sees the female in the advertisement as being apart from the real world. The very word 'model' has connotations of constructedness, of artifice. It conjures up women, not men. Men inhabit a more material world in our social construction of reality. Male models in advertisements may, for example, be crossovers from a more active reality – as with David Ginola from football. Supermodels are defined as being female. They are living wish-fulfilments. Interestingly, they rarely appear on television, except as part of a programme about fashion. Andy McDowell

8.4 Television creates and consumes personalities. In this case two *Radio Times* cover shots of Charlie Dimmock from *Ground Force* (BBC1) represent her as a goddess of plenty and as a classy dame. These images go to the heart of myths in representations of women. They also stand for that myth-making process through which the gardener from Hampshire becomes a television star. This kind of artificial democratization – television for the people, about the people and by the people.

79p 23–29 October 1999 www.radiotimes.com

LONDON

RadioTimes

Charlie Dimmock

The woman who likes to say YES

may be seen for L'Oreal. Claudia Schiffer has famously promoted Renault cars. Of course the high fashion industry has its niche-market magazines. But there is also a sense in which the familiarization of the screen in the home would spoil the myth of the supermodel if they did appear.

Van Zoonen and Meijer (1998) would agree that images of women are often 'unreal'. Indeed in discussing poster images of Pamela Anderson (who is also famous for her blonde beach-babe image in *Baywatch*, ITV) they point out that even Anderson the person is unreal and a construction in terms of having had plastic surgery to enhance her media appearance. More importantly, they pinpoint the difference between men and women looking at such images as the difference between identification and possession. The representation changes in the mind according to the gender of the viewer: 'an asymmetrical organization of looking, in which women are invited to identify whereas men are invited to possess: women can desire to *be* that image while men desire to *have* that image'.

Institutional power affecting representation

The issue here is whether or not the ways in which women are represented in television is related to their lack of power in its upper echelons. Women are not programmers or controllers for the major channels or companies. They are among successful television producers – Verity Lambert (ex Thames and now of the independent, Cinema Verity) – but they are in a minority. The same is true of technical posts. There are equal opportunities policies intended to change this position, but there is no evidence of significant change as yet. It is arguable that among other reasons for this situation are the high-pressure unsocial hours which exist in all media institutions. Such conditions work against women with family responsibilities. In any case there is the problem of changing the culture of the institution. Indirect discrimination is exemplified in ITN's cutbacks and greater demands on staff in the early 1990s, with the effect that in 1992 only 17 per cent of staff were women.

Jeremy Tunstall (1993) discusses the position of female producers. On the one hand he points to the stimulus of C4 in giving opportunities to female independent producers, as well as to an increase in the number of women employed by the BBC as a result of conscious promotion policies in 1989. On the other hand, he reports that in 1991 the percentage of women employed ranged from 25 per cent of the more senior executive producers to 38 per cent of the (less well paid) researchers.

Gaye Tuchman (1979) is sceptical about what women could or would do within institutions. She refers to the numbers of female journalists who appear to become institutionalized and simply to absorb a male agenda. However, it is not that she denies a connection between social reality and media representations. She refers to Gerbner's (1972) writing when saying 'representation in the media signifies social existence . . . – under-represent-ation and trivialisation . . . indicate *symbolic annihilation*' (my emphasis).

Liesbet Van Zoonen (1994) also reaches rather pessimistic conclusions about a correlation between women achieving institutional power of some kind and positive representations of women in the media in general.

For a start, her survey of research into women in the media evidences a situation in which few women in few countries hold positions of real power. Female workers may be marginalized, specialized or simply absorbed into male attitudes and practices. She points out that the organization and its practices may be entrenched and resistant to attempts by male or female workers to change these. She even challenges the assumption that there exist gender-distinctive attitudes which might or might not influence representations in media material. There is a widespread view that 'female communicators have a certain perspective, approach, preference or style that distinguishes them collectively from their male colleagues'. But if gender is not 'a fixed property of individuals', then one cannot expect that 'female communicators will have enough in common to produce a radically different type of media output'.

Women and soaps

Soap operas have a special place in critiques of female representation because it is acknowledged that they centre around powerful female roles and that they hold a special attraction for female viewers.

There are contradictions involved in arguing that female characters in soaps provide positive values and role models for female viewers:

- On the one hand soap narratives are dominated by powerful female characters; on the other hand female roles are still dominated by the domestic sphere and their occupations are generally inferior in economic terms.
- On the one hand soaps give pleasure by privileging reflection on the nature of relationships and of feelings; on the other hand, the reflections and insights don't necessarily lead to better judgements or decisions by the characters about relationships and how to resolve problems.
- On the one hand soaps place some emphasis on 'female issues' – lesbian love or the merits of home birth; on the other hand, over-emphasis leads to the danger of creating a ghetto of female issues, an introspective world that sidesteps another world in which women could be engaging with public not domestic power.

Yet again, it would be improper to argue for the privileging of one kind of

8.5 The characters Pat Evans (Pam St Clair) and Peggy Butcher (Barbara Windsor), from *EastEnders* (BBC1), are typical representations of the strong older woman seen in soap operas.

power in representation of women, and perhaps to denigrate the quality of women within traditional roles.

Geraghty, (1996) talks about a view of soaps which argues that there is 'in the relationship created between Soap Operas and their female audiences the potentiality for women to defy dominant understandings of femininity'. The idea is that even if women are seen to be in subordinated roles, this can be recognized and thought through, rather than passively accepted. It is argued that soaps come from women's experiences, out of popular culture, and are not a media form which is simply imposed on the audience. The nature of these experiences can be reflected on and discussed, and perhaps something can be learned for 'next time'.

SOAPS AND REALISM

The mode of realism of British soaps – naturalism and social realism – also contributes to the distinctiveness of the genre and its representations. The long-running *Coronation Street* (ITV) came out of the same era of northern working-class realism which also produced successful novels, plays and films such as *Saturday Night and Sunday Morning*. It has informed sitcom series such as *When the Boat Comes In* (BBC1, 1976–7 and 1981), and successful drama series of the 1990s such as *Our Friends in the North* (1998).

In redefining realism this new tradition also put working-class women on the agenda: indeed it celebrated their toughness and strength to the point of creating a new mythology which symbolically traps such women in the community, in the family. Their roles often demand strength as sacrifice, and deny self-development.

Vera Glaessner (1990) describes realism as 'a trap for its female characters'. She refers to the domestic focus of *Brookside* (the trap of the Close itself). On the other hand, it can be argued that the social issues – e.g. abuse of wives – raised by *Brookside* make it somewhat different from the more nostalgic *Coronation Street* (1960 to date) or *EastEnders*, which represent a close-knit community that in fact hardly exists any more, either in Manchester or in London's East End.

In a sense, the closed world of soaps, which rarely refer to headline events, and which in general remain located within their well-defined boundaries, is what enables them 'safely' to deal with provocative issues. Many of these issues, from unemployment to wayward children, also affect women from all backgrounds – hence the viewer interest and identification.

So the representations of female characters in soaps are founded in devices of naturalism, confined by the supposed social realism of the context, yet engage with the actuality of issues which are part of women's experience.

Female discourse – binary oppositions

If the representations of women are constructed within certain assumptions, encompass certain meanings and are decoded in terms of saying things about the difference of women, then they must also operate within a discourse of female gender. This may tie in with other discourses – perhaps age, or motherhood. But still, representations cannot help expressing discourses, in terms of both language functions and circumscribed meanings. So news reports 'cannot help' referring to females (even politicians sometimes) in terms of their clothes, their attractiveness, their children.

The structure of discourses can be seen to work in oppositions, none more so than gender. So in this example we would not expect to read of a male politician described in these terms: 'the government's representative, Mr Jimmy Smith, was wearing a mid-grey suit set off by an understated pale lilac shirt. He was accompanied at the ceremony by his children, Katie and Paul. He is married to Victoria Makepeace, of the Makepeace Chemical Group'.

Women and gaze

The notion of the **voyeuristic male gaze** at a woman – the sexualized representation of a woman – is well established.

More complicated is the question of **how women look at women**. If the representation is sexualized, does the female spectator see herself in that woman, being looked at by men? This would be a kind of narcissism – to love the idea of being looked at – but still 'on male terms'.

Van Zoonen (1994) points out that there may be a problem with accepting a 'dichotomous definition of gender as either masculine and active, or feminine and passive'; binary oppositions become unhelpful. Psycho-analytic interptetations offer the possibility that women too feel desire in gazing at women. More than this, one does not have to see the female gaze in terms of attraction or of sexual self-reflection. The gaze does not have to focus on appearance, but may attend to behaviour and interaction. It is possible to argue that a woman's gaze is more objective but still about identification. It recognizes that the image is a representation, not a real person, but it is also interested in the fictitious situation of that woman and how she deals with her situation.

There may also be recognition of the lesbian voyeuristic gaze. *Gaytime TV* has discussed the attractions of the women in the docudrama series set in a women's prison, *Bad Girls* (BBC1).

In spite of these points, it can be argued that:

- images of women to be desired are more prevalent than comparable ones of men
- women are represented as being looked at (i.e. men are shown to be looking)
- women talk about their social awareness of being the object of attention, of gaze
- women are the nominated audience for many images of women.

So questions remain about how women look at representations of themselves, and about how that look helps define how they make sense of their genderedness.

> What are different ways in which different representations of women on television may be looked at?

YOUTH TELEVISION

Representations of youth on television beg questions about the term 'youth'. It has been used rather condescendingly to identify 'Yoof television' as something which Janet Street-Porter had a lot to do with inventing in the 1980s through brasher, pop-culture oriented programmes such as *The Tube* (C4, 1988) or *The Word* (C4, 1990). Even the term 'youth' is rather curiously used to refer to males only in a number of cases – 'a gang of youths', etc. Certainly youth on the news is treated very ambiguously. Males between 17 and 22 years of age oscillate between 'youth', 'young man' and 'man', often it seems depending on the nature and severity of some crime or form of social misbehaviour that they have committed. Females are 'girls' or 'young women', again depending on the context.

Collectively, youth still seems to fit Hebdige's famous 'youth as fun – youth as trouble' model (1979). The news spots trouble at football matches and in street demonstrations (see also moral panics, p. 129), though it may allow for fun at something like a pop festival. So far as programmes for youth are concerned, it is all about fun – music and fashion – because this is supposed to please the youth audience and massage the ratings.

Definitions and representations of youth are complicated in sociological terms by the fact that phenomena such as club culture and dance culture actually include many people in their twenties and some in their thirties. To this extent 'youth' is a state of consuming rather than a matter of age.

Historically, youth television is something which had its origins in clumsy BBC1 programmes like *Whole Scene Going On* (1960s), emerged through the rather earnest and stilted *Oxford Road Show* (1980s), but seems to have found a real definition only in the late 1980s and early 1990s when the production initiatives of Janet Street-Porter led to programmes like *Network Seven* (C4, 1987). This kind of television was marked by its style:

- wild, handheld camera work
- the insertion of lively graphics
- young and cool presenters
- fast cutting.

Street-Porter was rapidly head-hunted by the BBC and produced programmes like *The Rough Guide to Travel* (1988) and *Reportage* (1989) in which information becomes entertainment in bite-sized slots, fronted by presenters like Magenta de Vine. Meanwhile C4 continued developing the form. There was *Club X* (1990–1), full of performance artiness and wild behaviour, but rather self-regarding. *The Word* (1991–3) was more successful, incorporating music, as *The Tube* did, but also playing with outrageous behaviours and a good dash of sex. However, Street-Porter left for Live Television channel in 1995, and the youth television phase had run out of steam. Mainstream television had taken over many of its 'tricks', as in the *Big Breakfast Show*. *Rapido* (C4, 1991–5) and then *Eurotrash* (C4) catered for those with a taste of sex and humour. *TGIFriday* (C4) exploited the magazine aspect of youth television and there has been *Noel's House Party* (BBC1, 1995–9) or *Light Lunch* to turn to in the mainstream. The change in youth programming may be symbolized by the figure of Jools Holland, a young and hip presenter on *The Tube*, now still pretty cool but more sober in *Later with Jools Holland* (1998–). In truth there probably never was a significantly committed youth audience because definitions of youth are so hard to make.

Youth, as a figure in programmes or as an audience for programmes, doesn't fit comfortably on that supposed divide between adulthood and childhood. It may be that the problem has to do with social ambiguities. Education creates (more for some than others) an artificial stage between being a child and being an adult which is neither one nor the other – being partly controlled, not having economic independence. So for some, youth might be 'the student years' – *The Young Ones* (BBC2) exploited this in the 1980s, as did *Heartbreak High* in the 1990s. Yet it is tricky drawing a line, when some of the characters and situations in the school soap *Grange Hill*, (BBC1, 1978 to date) could also fit a definition of youth.

Unemployment and poverty stops some young people from being able to assume what most would see as an adult role. Some in any case resist the trappings of adulthood by declining to marry and have children in their twenties – they continue to party as well as to work. All this tends to a view that youth television as a programming concept is very problematic. Many young people watch supposedly adult soap operas, just as adults watch *Neighbours*. Some of the soaps screened in the early evening have an audience young enough to be described as children. In other words, audiences are relatively fluid in terms of age definition. Programmes do become a cult among the young – *South Park*, for instance – at the same time as appealing to an older age-group. *South Park* has a majority of viewers older than 20.

Even if one accepts that certain programmes are orientated towards a younger market, this still begs the question of how they represent those young people. In general they represent them as having a lot of leisure time, which is the focus of their lives. There is a marked absence of reference to paid employment or to personal obligations (such as education or family) which would interfere with the prosecution of romantic relationships or the pursuit of fun. In short, the representation is as much of a lifestyle as it is of types. As far as teensoaps do represent types within their genre, they are models for the adult dramas: young women as *femmes fatales*, as heartbreakers, even as proto-mothers carrying some family responsibility. Young men are sporty types, or attractive hunks, or best mates.

One might ask whether the hugely successful *Friends* (C4) is about representations of youth, even if the characters are supposed to be 20-somethings. Certainly it is watched by a young audience. But these preppy types are curious as models, offering no rebellion or even much individualism. They are pallid alongside the feisty appearances in the pop-culture magazine show *The Word*, also very successful in the early 1990s.

On the whole the notion of Youth television as distinctive programming seems to be something of a fantasy, even where music is concerned. Examination of current schedules shows there is actually little of anything one could call youth programmes. And representations of youth in programmes are uncertain where they are not stereotypical. In terms of the marketplace, all this makes sense because the evidence is that young people are uncertain viewers, hard to pin down. Television viewing falls among late teenagers because they are out enjoying other leisure activities. Where they do watch, it is a mixture of films, soaps, late-night material, and cult shows such as *Beavis and Butthead* (C4, 1994–7) – or programmes which are watched by others in the household anyway.

As represented through various television advertisements from the financial services sector in the 1990s, youth is cool, youth is well-dressed in hip-hop style, youth life centres around music-technology and the night out. Youth wants instant gratification – stick plastic in the machine and cash comes out. Iconic figures like Keanu Reeves sell 'One to One' mobile phones – cool youth, in charge of technology, in touch. But these representations are mythical. It is relevant that someone like Keanu Reeves is a presence and an appearance as much as an actor. The films he is in are strong on form, style, the moment, the image. When bands are interviewed on Saturday morning shows for children (rising youth?), presentation is in terms of gossip and of appearance. It is about the maintenance of a sub-culture. In whose interests this culture operates is another matter.

> How is it that television is not so much produced for youth as an audience, as concerned with youth as an object of representations in some programmes?

RACE AND TELEVISION

McRobbie (1994) refers to representation as a 'site of power and regulation as well as a source of identity'. Hall (1981) says that 'the media construct for us a definition of what race is; what meaning the imagery of race carries, and what the "problem of race" is understood to be. They help us classify the world in terms of race'. He also argues (1995) that 'inferential racism' is about a 'naturalised representation of events and situations relating to race'.

Many would argue that race on television is marked by its absence as much as by negative stereotypes. Stephen Bourne (1999) points out that thousands of black people were living in London in the late nineteenth century. He asks why the 1999 BBC production of *Great Expectations* did not cast a black person in the role of Estella. Elsewhere (1998) Bourne protests about the programme *Night with the Girls* (1997), a history of women on British television. He points to the absence of black actresses and other players, not least of Moira Stuart who is a national newsreader of many years' experience and instantly recognizable.

John Tulloch (1990) refers to the lack of employment of black people in the media, to educational disadvantages and to ignorance as affecting the presence of black people in various roles in television. He refers to the absence of black people in most soap operas – an issue which was raised with reference to *Coronation Street*, as far back as 1983. The absence of black people in this soap made and makes no sense in terms of the realities of living in Manchester. As he puts it, 'the objective . . . is for greater representation in broadcast fiction and news programmes with a range, not of black characters, but of characters who happen to be black'.

This is about the naturalization of black people in television roles, so that their presence becomes, simply, unremarkable. I would risk arguing that this has largely become the case for news on British television. The newscaster Trevor McDonald is an elder statesman of the genre. Phil Gayle on *The Big Breakfast* is another generation with a lighter touch. Both men are good at their job, and happen to be black. The presence of black and Asian reporters is indeed unremarkable and by no means exceptional.

The audience's assessment of representations will be influenced by factors such as where they live. This will affect whether or not the presence or absence of performers from ethnic minorities is seen as remarkable. Social and cultural experience makes a difference to what one sees as 'normal' or 'exceptional'. In other words, what are one's expectations about representations based on? It doesn't make much sense to assume that politically correct television has a proportion of people in *each programme* who match the proportion of ethnic groups in Britain. Yet it does seem significant if the overall proportions of those in television don't approximate to demographics.

Therese Daniels (1998) reports on quantitative research in 1971, 1972 and 1974 which found that in specific weeks the proportion of people of African and Asian descent appearing in television drama was less than their proportions in the population as a whole. Daniels points out that there is a lack of recent research into the representation by race on television in general, let alone into issues such as employment in television institutions. There has been research by the GUMG (1999) into the proportions of representation in television adverts. This concludes that in demographic terms they are what one would expect.

One is aware of the multi-racial commissioning policy of C4 from the 1980s onwards, and of the equal opportunities policies of television organizations intended to encourage recruitment of black and Asian staff. On the other hand, there isn't enough evidence of how issues of race and representation have been covered by documentary and current-affairs programmes in particular. One should not judge race representation simply in terms of fiction on television. Issues of race on television have been the subject of, for example, the *Open Door* access series (BBC2). The issues cannot be dealt with simply by arguing for or against the racism of television on the grounds of one or two programmes.

It is in this context that one takes only a cautiously positive view of former sitcom series such as *Desmond's* (1989), which centred on an Afro-Caribbean family and Desmond's barber shop in Peckham. The ethnic origins of the family were relevant to some of the humour, but it wasn't a sitcom about race. It was simply a sitcom crossed with a soap, and pivoted on the character played by Norman Beaton, a very experienced actor who appeared in many films and dramas of the 1970s and 1980s.

The Broadcasting Standards Council/ITC report *Include Me* (1999) comments on the lack of ethnic minorities in senior positions behind the screen, and on the on-screen depiction of minorities as being confined to problem situations or comedy shows. There may be 8.1 per cent of BBC staff who are of an ethnic origin, but none are on the board of management.

Race, identity and discourse

Representations are an expression of discourses which give meaning to the idea of race (and racism). Hegemony is about the struggle for ascendancy between these discourses, for the assumption of the power of one kind of representation over another. It may be argued that identity comes with a representation: the identity is part of the meanings generated by representing certain groups of people in certain ways. The representation comes from the ideology, from its way of conceiving the world and power relations.

Discourse analysis would shift the argument subtly but significantly, and would say that:

- representations make the discourses apparent
- ideology is bound up with discourses
- in effect, there are only discourses
- power operates within and between discourses: a struggle to achieve dominance of one view or one meaning over another. Black may equal trouble if it is young males on the street; it may equal good looking and cool if it is footballer Ian Wright presenting a television show.

It may be argued that whatever the view of the relationship between concepts of ideology, representation and discourse, the significance lies in meanings about race which are in people's heads.

Briggs and Cobley (1998) point out that our notions of race have nothing to do with objectifiable biology – they are just ideas about race. In terms of identity, they point out that race may refer to a number of elements:

- the person's own 'racial' identity (e.g. 'white')

- other 'racial' identities to which that person's 'racial' identity can be opposed in a power relationship (e.g. 'black' vs 'white')
- a discourse that asserts the centrality of race as a defining feature of a person's identity (e.g. racism)
- other (non-'racial') identities to which that person's 'racial' identity can be opposed/complemented in a power relationship (e.g. 'race' may be outweighed by 'gender').

Though there is widespread pessimism about the space for positive images of race, there are examples. Comedy television programmes such as *Goodness Gracious Me* (BBC2, 1999), written and performed by an Asian cast, have made it on prime time, sending up both Asian and British attitudes. And music represents an interesting point of intersection between races and race images. television programmes such as *Flava* (C4, 1999) are watched by white people as much as black people, not least because young people have very positive images of black performers.

Naturalization, difference and otherness

If representations imply in their construction of views that they are endorsed by nature, by a natural order of things, inherent in racist representations is the unspoken but emphatically understood view that whatever 'white' is, is normal. Negative connotations of 'blackness' are also held to be naturally true.

The black person becomes 'the other' – other than a white person. So, colour and race becomes an issue, a divider, a schism between people who are not in fact notably different from one another, least of all in a biological sense. But representation makes some feature notable so that difference has some meaning.

Difference may be tied to binary oppositions, to ways in which language is used. Black becomes opposed to white. In this point of view there is a sense of conflict because black is not merely an alternative to white. It brings out notions of a power struggle – a struggle for hegemony – in positioning someone as 'the other' (not white, not male, not British) as a way of asserting superiority.

In terms of looking at black people on television one might say that if one notices colour then difference matters; if one does not then difference is meaningless. Is Paul Ince just another footballer on the field?

Race and sport

There are strange resonances about the representation of black people in sport, not all of them negative. On the one hand there exist stereotypical assumptions about black people being naturally good at sport. On the other hand it may be argued that success in sport is good for the self-image of black people and promotes social integration. Television pictures of black people winning races and scoring goals are double-edged in their meanings so long as ideas of difference are still in our minds. These images stand for sporting success, and yet may confirm the illusion that this is what black people are good at.

Blain and Boyle (1998) draw attention to the fact that 'sport . . . becomes deeply incorporated into people's sense of who they are and what other people are like'. In this respect sport becomes a focal point for identity. It has a richness of representation in a very public context. They are also pessimistic about the negative meanings inscribed in representations of people in sport: 'Ideologies of gender and race seem so deeply rooted, and class positions so well entrenched that . . . sports mediation will continue to function as a producer and reproducer of relatively conservative views of the world.'

Fetishism and the body

There is a respect in which the meaning of race, of black people in this case, is tied up with the body and how it is shown. This is analogous to representations of women which reduce them to the sum of their body parts – breast comes to stand for female.

The idea of fetishism has two main areas of definition.

1 The Marxist notion of commodity culture. In this case, the commodities subsitute for labour – our lives become the goods we own. Material goods become symbols of status or something else, but they no longer mean 'labour'. People may become commodities themselves. In the case of slavery, the slave as servant became a fetishized object that stood for eighteenth-century chic and status.
2 Psycho-analysis, in which some object or part of the body becomes a fetish object standing for sexuality. Men may substitute an item of woman's clothing for her sexuality – because they fear her sex. In terms of race representation, it is argued that a similar substitution process occurs when descriptions, images, representations of black people focus on body (not on person). This argument would say that representations of black male entertainers or indeed sportsmen are such that they deflect attention from the real object of racial difference fascination – the penis, and sexual power.

It may also be argued that this displacement process is not peculiar to representations of black masculinity. Teenage girls' poster displays are full of male torsos. In this case it would be masculinity, not race, which is the focus of representation. The picture and its torso are fetish objects.

> What may one notice about representations by race in television advertisements?

Changes in representations of race

It is very difficult to be detached from cultural practices of which one is a part. Some would argue that the enveloping power of ideology is such that it is impossible to see the world except through its filters. But then there are arguments that people do sometimes make oppositional readings of media material, rather than preferred readings. They don't accept racist meanings unquestioningly, all the time. And the material itself changes over a period of time. Equally, it is not wise to subscribe to a potentially false notion that 'things are better now' because we are in the present. Sexism and racism as manifestations of ideology are still only too apparent. But at least one can argue that the intensity and nature of stereotypical representations has shifted. It would be unthinkable for an entertainment programme such as *The Black and White Minstrel Show* (which survived until 1978) to be broadcast now on television.

Bikhu Parekh on *The Black and White Media Show* (BBC2, 1987) appealed for a change, for a situation in which 'a community is presented in a manner which does justice to its history, to its sensitivities'. Alvarado et al. (1987) argue that there are four main categories of race representation in the media in general: **the exotic, the dangerous, the humorous and the pitied.** The last category has particular resonances for television because it draws attention to all that non-fiction material (e.g. *Live Aid*, 1985) which shows us images from Africa and Asia depicting famine, poverty, disease and various kinds of suffering. Ironically, the developing technological reach of television has made it more possible to construct this view. It is not that the material is untrue, but that the repetitious screening of such problems tends to define these people as always having problems, as being problems.

Drawing partly on Bourne (1998) one may comment that British television in the 1950s, 1960s and 1970s was not generous in its representation of black performers and black culture. One might point out that at least people like Lena Horne could have their own show (1964, 1965), which could not then happen on American television. But it was still the case that black people appeared dominantly as musicians and entertainers. Dramas like *Hot Summer Night* (1959), which actually confronted racist attitudes through the relationship of a white woman with a black man, were very much the exception. One episode of *Z Cars*, 'A Place of Safety' exposed racist attitudes of the police and how they dealt with a black person. A black nurse was written into the hugely popular hospital series *Emergency Ward 10* (1964).

Sarita Malik (1998) argues that British television contributed to the construction of black Britons as a problem: 'Black people . . . were regularly located as troubled social subjects on British television.' She points out that there was more material on (or creating?) issues of race in the 1950s than people might realize – e.g. *Special Enquiry: Has Britain a Colour Bar?* (1955) or *People in Trouble: Mixed Marriages* (1958) or *The Negro Next Door* (1965). Malik also argues that even an apparently positive production like *Asian Club* (1953–61), a magazine programme for an Asian audience, actually operated through a discourse in which the idea of difference was still paramount. These comments also draw attention to the importance of 'factual' programming in constructing views on race. When the rightwinger Enoch Powell made his notorious 'rivers of blood' speech about the dangers of immigration in 1968 it was widely discussed in news and current-affairs programmes. At about the same time the moral panic about young black muggers erupted in the media, to be reported and discussed on television. Even though television news took a more properly sceptical and critical view of the (false) idea that mugging by young blacks was suddenly prevalent, it gave the view some credibility by giving it any airtime at all. Were television editors to conclude that certain stories – such as that there is a problem with immigration – had no foundation and to refuse to run them, it would make a lot of difference.

Stuart Hall (1981) proposes that there are three kinds of representation of black people – the native, the entertainer and the social problem. Television, including factual television, has contributed to these images. A classic example might be the 1974 dramatization of *Robinson Crusoe* (ITV), in which the assumptions of racial superiority and inferiority went unchallenged. Arguably the frequency and nature of representations began to change at the end of the 1970s and in the 1980s. Protests by Asian and black community groups and the creation of access programmes had some effect. Malik refers to *Babylon* (LWT, 1979), a series aimed at young black Londoners. There was *Skin* (1979), a documentary series for black and Asian people dealing with points of discrimination and injustice. In the *Open Door* access slot the Campaign against Racism in the Media made a programme, *It Ain't Half Racist, Mum* (1979). The arrival of C4 in 1981 made a significant contribution to programmes for black viewers – e.g. *Black on Black* and *Eastern Eye* (1982–5). The school drama *Grange Hill* (1978 onwards) had a racial mix in its cast from the beginning. Also in 1978 the drama series *Empire Road*, about black and Asian communities, appeared. It was about the realities of the life of these communities, including (but not dominated by) issues of race. It avoided casting black people as deviants of some kind.

The series *Gangsters* (1976–8), by contrast, also set in Birmingham, concentrated on the criminal aspects of black culture. This, one might say, was analogous to television news representations of black people and the Bristol St Paul's riots, in 1981, when the impression was given of a criminalized community. In fact most of the inhabitants of the area had nothing to do with the riots or with any crime, and went about their daily business in spite of events that affected mainly three streets. The comedy series *It Ain't Half Hot, Mum* (1974–81) exemplified offensive representation and naturalized racist attitudes. The situation was that of a British army entertainments unit based in India in the late days of empire. Where Indian people appeared in the episodes fun might be made, for example, of their accents. The same thing was done in *Mind your Language* (ITV, 1977–9), which exploited stereotypical representations of students in a language school for learning English. To make the other person a figure of fun isn't much better than making them, say, a figure of fear. Even where racist attitudes are apparently sent up, there is a danger that it is the racist comments that will stick in people's minds. *Rising Damp* (ITV, 1974–8) is an example of this, with the character of the oleaginous landlord Rigsby. One of his tenants was black and deliberately represented as educated, well spoken and much more sophisticated than Rigsby. One could argue that this was a positive representation, though the sense of contrivance in this character's exaggeratedly well-bred speech, intended to contrast with Rigsby's casually prejudiced comments, is worrying.

Looking at the 1980s, it is possible to detect a move away from stereotypical representations, and some recognition of the realities of a multi-racial British society. *The Chinese Detective* (BBC1, 1981–2) was interesting for David Yip's portrayal of the hero as loner because of his leaving, but not simply rejecting, the tight-knit Chinese community of his upbringing. It was a series that could have been extended because there was intrinsic interest in the cultural issues raised through an unstereotypical representation of an ethnic minority, set of course against the excitement of the crime world. Much the same could be said of the series *Black Silk* (BBC2, 1985), about a black barrister. *Elphida* (C4, 1987) was a drama about a black woman who wants to take control of her life through education. The play represented her cultural and gender dilemma as she realized that she didn't want to be tied to a family role for the rest of her life.

Representations in terms of race are always contentious when it comes to cultural differences and expectations. *Death of a Princess* (ITV, 1980) was a drama documentary focusing on the execution of an Arab princess and her lover for having transgressed cultural rules. The representation of the character and indeed the plot line were pretty accurate factually. This was the problem. The Saudi royal family had actually lived out these events; for them it was a private matter and culturally correct. A huge diplomatic row ensued and Britain lost trade as a result. But ATV defended what was an apparently negative representation because it was not a misrepresentation. Similar issues surround series such as *Tenko* (BBC1, 1981–2, 1984) which was about female British prisoners captured by the Japanese in the second world war. The captors were not all represented stereotypically, but they were not shown overall in a positive light. Historical evidence is that many Japanese soldiers did treat British prisoners badly, so the series was both 'true', and yet possibly also responsible for keeping prejudice and parts of 'orientalism' alive.

Black on Black (C4/LWT, 1982–5) was a news, current affairs and arts programme produced and presented by black people for a black audience. It was a successful and interesting programme that represented black communities as having their own cultural interests as much as, say, the Scots or the Irish. *No Problem!* (C4/LWT, 1983–5) was a sitcom, commissioned under a policy of multi-racial programming, about a family whose parents had gone back to Jamaica, leaving them the run of the house in London. Alvarado et al. (1987) argue that it still perpetuated some stereotypes, with one character living 'close to nature' in the garden. Such doubts have their parallel in Lenny Henry's African tribal chief character in *OTT* (ITV, 1982), pulling faces and yelling Katanga. However, Lenny Henry also appeared in his own comedy show (1984–5, 1987–8), producing among others sketches which were based on take-offs of various types, the most absorbing of whom was the old Jamaican Deakus, reflecting on life and change in a whimsical manner. Henry was aware of racial issues, but they did not dominate his material, and the humour did not depend on privileged knowledge of another culture.

For all the qualifying remarks made above, one might say that television has to a fair extent matured in its representations. Even the spectacular dramas set in India in the days of the Raj – *The Far Pavillions* (C4) and *The Jewel in the Crown*, (ITV, 1984) – represented a range of Indian characters with dignity, but did not evade awareness of imperialism.

Without taking too complacent a view, least of all about the realities of continuing racism in British society, it is possible to argue that there has been an increasing and 'natural' presence of black and Asian players in television in the 1980s and 1990s. Craig Charles is now famous for his part as Lister in the comedy SciFi series *Red Dwarf* (BBC2, 1988 onwards). But in 1987 he was reviewing video releases for the ITV nightly magazine programme *Night Network*. *Def 2* (BBC2) started in 1988 – an early evening magazine programme for a young audience with segments for black musicians. It has used a variety of presenters of various ethnic origins, including Sankha Guha co-fronting a rough guide travel slot.

One may also take account of more positive if not frequent enough representations in cinema, funded by C4 and therefore having privileged screening on television. *My Beautiful Launderette* (1985) describes the relationship between two young men from white and Asian communities, refers to racism, but in the end says more about the Asian families involved and their position *vis-à-vis* British society as a whole. More recently, *Secrets and Lies* (1996) has been released for both cinema and television. It centres on a black woman who has been fostered and then discovers that her natural mother is white. In the same year a two-part television drama *The Final Passage* explores the experiences of a family moving in the 1950s from the Caribbean to Britain. There were also interesting documentaries on the representation and treatment of black people on television, such as *Black & White in Colour* (BBC2, 1992). More recently, there have been a number of C4 programmes on race in Britain, including *The Slave Trade* (1999).

One should also refer to American television material in the 1990s which represented black people in many roles on British television. There is the middle-class Huxtable family of the *Bill Cosby Show*. There is Oprah Winfrey as a strong woman and chat-show hostess. There is the very cool Will Smith and his screen family in the teen soap/sitcom *The Fresh Prince of Bel Air*. There has been criticism of such positive representations as denying the existence of racism or as ignoring the realities of poverty for many black people in the United States. Judging the implicit effects of such ethnic representations is complicated by many factors. Does one achieve balance by making a sitcom about black family in poverty? Would the increased representation of poverty and prejudice in the United States actually increase racism? Is the problem to do with the high ratings of certain programmes?

It is for example not true to say that there is no television about the realities of black cultures. Louis Theroux in a personal documentary series (*Weird Weekends*, 1999) took us into the black power movements in New York. There has been a documentary series on Channel 4 reflecting on the 1950s migration from the Caribbean to Britain, and the feelings of the people involved. The question might be who watches these programmes, as much as what is the nature of the representations, or what is their effect?

C4 regularly screens popular Indian films. Satellite channels targeted at ethnic communities offer attractive material. There is IDTV, a black entertainment channel, and Zee TV for Asian audiences. The cultural issue is whether this narrowcasting really makes positive representations generally available, or performs a service for particular cultures while not necessarily helping intercultural relations.

CRIME, THE POLICE AND TELEVISION

Television represents ideas about the nature of crime, the police as an institution and police officers as role players. A significant number of television programmes are about crime and the police, even down to *Police, Camera, Action* (ITV), using police video material of poor driving on the roads. Ostensibly this acts in the public-service warning model, though it is arguable that events mediated twice, through television and through the grainy video, are detached from reality and personal reflection in the minds of viewers.

We may address a number of questions about representations in this area:

- What kinds of crime are represented?
- How are we meant to understand these crimes?
- How are such crimes dealt with?
- What view of the police force in the social context is presented?
- What different types of police officers are represented?
- How do they operate within their insitution?
- How do they interact with the rest of society?
- What do the answers to all of the above questions signify, not least in relation to the ideas of discourse and ideology?

Sparks (1992) suggests that the representation of crime on television is partly a barometer of changing public concerns about the nature of crime and of policing, and is attractive as a genre because it appeals to those concerns. 'Crime fiction presupposes an inherent tension between anxiety and reassurance' – 'this constitutes a signficant source of its appeal to the viewer' – 'it is in the dialectical play between these terms that anything resembling a specific ideology of law and its enforcement is to be found in crime fiction'.

With reference to tensions, Sparks also describes a structure of oppositions within the narratives of many crime dramas:

known	vs	unknown
safety	vs	danger
indoors	vs	outdoors
private	vs	public

One might suggest that the tensions for the viewer produced within such a structure come out of kinds of anxiety. Crime on television at once creates, frames and taps anxieties such as:

- a concern about social order and how it is maintained
- a sense of uncertainty about how public and private spheres should mesh when it seems that crime in public is getting out of control and invades the security of the private sphere
- worries about what the political process should legitimize and allow in the cause of controlling crime.

Crime types

Crime in earlier police series like *Dixon of Dock Green* (BBC, 1955–76) is often represented as being local, personal, petty, if not trivial to the victims. We are talking about crimes such as shoplifting, which seem 'manageable'. When this series started there were a million television sets in Britain, the majority owned by the middle classes, who perhaps responded to these notions of localized petty crime solved by a friendly policeman. There was a notion that crime could be controlled. In the 1960s *Z Cars*, while still about community policing, introduced a more realistic attitude to the nature of crime, covering topics such as pornography. Crime was no longer just about the working classes being naughty and being led to see the error of their ways.

But as television developed series about various branches of the police it also developed a representation which was truer to the experiences of the increasing numbers of ordinary viewers. Crime did involve violence. Justice was not always done. Crime waves were reported. Crime seemed barely controllable: violence had to be met with violence. In the 1960s there was a change from representing crime as a problem on which there was a social agreement, to disagreements over how 'the authorities', police, dealt with crime. Crime now included the behaviour of some ethnic minorities, rightly dissatisfied with their treatment by the police. It included dealing with student dissidents, culminating in the huge demonstration in 1968 in London against the Vietnam war. Society was no longer at one with itself. Minorities were being criminalized. The state used the police to try and keep them in order. This is not to say that there are no genuine crimes committed by minorities. But the nature of crime and of the law-and-order debate has become redefined because of a social splintering. This 'problem' has not gone away. Travellers and hippies have been harrassed by the police; fictional and factual television has represented this. The idea that crime/corruption could inhabit the police themselves also surfaced, perhaps most dramatically in G.F. Newman's four-part series on aspects of policing, *Law and Order* (BBC2, 1978). The bent copper of one episode outraged the police and 'authority'. But the news had indeed reported on similar crimes. Crime was not just something the police dealt with on our behalf. It was sometimes something they committed against our interests. This strand of police crime, making our world less secure, is something which is now established, having surfaced in series such as *Between the Lines* (BBC1, 1992–5). This programme focuses on the investigation of police malpractice. But even the investigators have faults, and sometimes the police being investigated seem to be getting a raw deal. Crime has come back to haunt the police. The lines between police and criminal are blurred. Representations of the police and of crime have moved from idealistic distinction in the 1950s to cynical attitudes in the 1990s.

American action cop shows led the way for definitions of crime as violence, perhaps associated with drugs or gang wars. Certainly such approaches have depicted crime (and police work) as being exciting. The murder-mystery version of crime tends to concentrate on crimes of passion and perhaps the psychology of crime. There are 'specialist' crime series defined by the crime work: *Cracker* (ITV), which revolves around a psychologist working with the police, uncovering criminals by discovering their motivations, or *Silent Witness* which centres on the work of a female police pathologist. Most of all, the representation of crime either values it for its drama and impact (kinds of death and suffering, say) or it is valued for the human-interest story built around it (effects on the families of criminals or victims, for example). What one sees relatively little of is computer crime or kinds of fraud. These kinds of corporate crime are in fact fast growing and statistically significant. But they don't have the impact of bodies, blood and tears.

We are dealing with fiction here. Fiction's notion of crime, which it may well be argued affects public perceptions, is distorted. Three-quarters of crime by women and two-fifths of crime by men is about theft and handling stolen goods. About a tenth of all crime for both sexes involves violence – a tiny fraction of that is about murder. Even in the case of men, very little crime involves sexual offences. These are not the proportions of crimes represented in television fiction, or even in news reporting. The exceptional and the dramatic get a high profile.

Police types

The representation of types of police has both range and change across time as television interacts with social changes. The idealistic intimacy of community policing in the 1950s is symbolized by the protagonist in *Dixon of Dock Green* (1955–76). A paternalistic figure, George Dixon dealt with people who had 'gone wrong'. He straightened some out. He addressed us from the screen, especially at the end of each programme when his monologue summing up of the story provided moral closure and security for the audience.

The new realism of a bleaker urban-estate landscape is picked up by *Z Cars* in the 1960s. The coppers in this series are still local figures, but they have become more cynical and authoritarian, hoping for the best from human nature but not really expecting it. They patrol Newtown in cars, not on foot. They become angry, though perhaps not despairing, about the effects of social conditions, as well as about people's selfishness and about emerging crime problems such as drugs. The series *Softly, Softly* (BBC1, 1966–70), which spun out of *Z Cars*, worked on a regional level. Coppers like Barlow and Watt were harder, detached from immediate community concerns. They had the status of inspectors. They dealt with serious crimes, matters of strategy.

By the 1970s, Regan and Carter in *The Sweeney* (ITV, 1975–76, 1978)

8.6 Representations of the police are often active and involve the apprehension of wrongdoers (*see also* Fig. 6.3). They are dominated by ideas of the older and wiser male. This set of images shows scenes from *Cracker* (ITV), about a psychologist-turned-detective; *The Bill* (ITV), which focuses on working life at a particular police estation; *'Liverpool 1* (BBC1), which is about a team of detectives and their personal lives; and *Police, Camera, Action* (ITV), which is a factual show based on video footage of the police at work.

(selectively set in the serious crime squad) are downright alienated. They hardly even feel the American private eye/cop sense of social value. Says Regan, 'it's a dirty job but someone has to do it'; 'It's a job. It's a war on crime. You can't trust anyone'; 'I sometimes hate this bastard place. It's a bloody holiday camp for thieves and weirdoes . . . Try and protect the public and all they do is call you "fascist" ' (Clarke, 1992). It is arguable that this behaviour both represents the frustration of actual police officers with perceived liberalism and is a mythic fulfilment, a way of dealing with criminals. It is bound up with public perceptions at the time that crime was getting out of hand. The anxieties of some viewers would be assuaged by seeing criminals get a good pounding from tough officers. But again, some of the anxiety would be bound up with a realization that social agreements, the consent of all sections of society for a certain kind of policing, were falling apart.

It is interesting that in the 1990s the series *Heartbeat*, suffused wih nostalgia, recovered a 'Dixon' view of the police, returning within a soap format to small crimes in a small community. But it was set in the country, not the town. And its view of the rural community was idealistic in much the same way that Dixon's Dock Green had lost touch with urban brutalities by the 1970s.

One also needs to take account of various representations of policewomen over the years. In the first place, in the 1950s and 1960s, they are simply notable by their absence. In this case art does mirror life. When we did get Angie Dickinson in the American series *Policewoman* (1960s), she was not a great deal different in role to her male counterparts (other than when camera or verbal innuendo glanced at her sexuality). This was the kind of tough role (the woman has to prove herself as a good guy) played by Jamie Lee Curtis in the film *Blue Steel*. The really interesting American series was *Cagney and Lacey* (1970s). The female protagonists did have to deal with a range of crime, but they also had to deal with parents and husbands and with their own temperaments.

These programmes were as much about human frailty as about crime-solving. Certainly they were not all about pleasure in violent action, or the satisfaction of meting out moral retribution. In respect of their complexity, in their soap qualities, they led the way for series like *Hill Street Blues* (1980s–90s) in which what was happening in the lives of the precinct police officers was as important as what was happening out on the streets. Life was a struggle. The meaning of being a crime fighter was discussed. In Britain, female protagonist police series were *Juliet Bravo* (BBC1) and *The Gentle Touch* (ITV), both running in the early 1980s. The latter involved stories about one character, Forbes, being stretched between roles as detective inspector and wife and mother. It trod an uneasy line between condescension about traditional views of women's problems in holding down 'men's jobs' and a more liberated realistic view of continuing inequalities in the respective role expectations of men and women. Immediately after this series, the lead actress, Jill Gascoigne, starred in a more fantasy-and-action series about a special crime-busting group of women (*CATS Eyes*, ITV), run of course by a status male – rather like the American *Charley's Angels* before it.

Juliet Bravo was a more edgy account of police work and of the position of a policewoman running an all-male police station. The sub-plot of gender politics and personal angst, meanwhile, is what has made the *Prime Suspect* mini-series so successful. Helen Mirren as Amanda Tennyson is not aping a male role, though there is a lot of the genre loner in her part. This series involves 'modern' crimes such as serial killing and child abuse – unthinkable in the culture of Dixon. To this extent its representation does not have the quality of realism of the *The Bill*, which gives us more of day-to-day policing on the streets. And yet *Prime Suspect* does have a strong sense of the high-pressure interior world of high-profile CID work. It also represents the intersection of Tennyson's personal and professional lives in a way that *The Bill* deliberately avoids.

There is a very successful representation of the British policeman which owes a lot to the murder-mystery genre. Modern versions of Agatha Christie's Poirot stories were still attracting good viewing figures in the mid-1990s (10 and 11 million). Inheritors of this tradition are the *Midsomer Murders* (ITV), starring John Nettles, or the *Inspector Morse* series of the 1980s (ITV), starring John Thaw of Sweeney fame, which put a cultural spin on the genre with the protagonist's enjoyment of good wine and classical music. The Ruth Rendell mysteries on ITV have given us Inspector Wexford and Inspector Dalgleish, also spin-offs from successful novels. But these series in varying degrees represent the policemen as living in some nostalgic version of England, often rural, with stories involving vicars and batty elderly ladies. The coppers are middle-aged men, father figures, solid representatives of middle-class England, for all the occasional crisis of confidence or of personal angst. These are the versions of the police, of England, of crime, which can be most effectively marketed. What they also represent to a greater or lesser degree is a love affair with the eccentric and the individualist as opposed to the leader and team player. Morse especially is at odds with his own superiors. It is virtually a class metaphor, given his love of high culture and the contrast with his more plebian sidekick. Ideology and cultural myths run close to the surface here. These products are of course also immensely saleable to other countries with preconceptions about what England should be like. Even the late-1990s series *Dalziell and Pascoe* (BBC1), which involves the personal lives of the protagonists, still lapses into nostalgia about the blunt Yorkshireman and the inspirational rebel crime-solver.

Police behaviour and crime solving

Clarke (1992) says that 'the police series as a genre . . . can be reduced to a very simple story line consisting of the basic components of crime, chase and arrest'. But, he argues, in the 1970s, representations of police work moved from a procedural approach to the action approach epitomized by *Starsky and Hutch* and *The Sweeney*. This change had a lot to do with what developing television technology made possible, as well as with creative innovation.

It is not true to say that the procedural view has gone. It is still in there mixed up with soap characteristics and the psychology of crime drama (epitomized by the 1980s series *Cracker*, in which Robbie Coltrane played a psychologist solving crimes which of course mystified the conventional cops). But crime as action is now firmly established. Ironically, it runs completely counter to the duller realities of real police work, which is very procedural and routine and gets to solutions through the grinding of information as much as the moment of inspiration.

In *The Sweeney* the style of crime-solving, the brutal panache of Regan, the emphasis on the chase, the energy expended in outbursts of violence often directed at the criminal, all created a kind of new realism. It was in London, in the streets, there was gunplay, this was serious crime. The travelling shots and close-ups involved the viewer in the action. But of course it was just another representation, with strong postmodernist qualities of ironic humour and an emphasis on form. This series in particular illustrates Richard Sparks's assertion (1992) that 'crime stories return continually to the conditions under which the hero is or is not entitled to use force or to resort to extra legal methods'. When *Z Cars* appeared in the 1960s, it seemed to represent 'real' police behaviour and approaches to crime. The key to this mode was naturalism – the setting in a gritty northern town, the cops who were ordinary human beings and made mistakes, the details of local police work.

It is the contemporary series *The Bill* which is the inheritor of the *Z Cars* approach, where finally soaps and cop series cross over. It is like *Z Cars* in that it seeks a kind of naturalism, in this case by shooting with lightweight cameras in an authentically recreated police station, by using location shots and by rejecting the action drama of car-chase cop series. It is about dealing with crime, not the excitement of crime itself. The stories are about things the police know and experience, so that we are positioned with them. Crimes are only seen if the police see them. These police officers are not perfect human beings, but they are usually shown with understanding even when they make mistakes. They have private lives. They have to follow procdures. They become upset by the human disasters which they encounter. They want to make the world a better place, but don't assume that they always can. Realism in the representation of police work always has a kind of relativity to cultural expectations and to the ability of series to remake conventions. Even *Dixon*, which accurately referred to aspects of police procedure and the law, had a kind of realism. *The Bill* seems real because we are positioned as the police.

Factuality of content, probability of behaviour does matter (see Chapter 7), but still the realism of crime series is largely a matter of form. Our understanding of crime, of the police and of police work is constructed by and through the media. What we experience from television may seem real but is in fact only a value-laden representation.

The constructedness, the artifice, the selectivity, the ideological weight of views of crime on television applies equally to non-fictional programmes. News selects dramatic crime stories and says little about painstaking police work, even in murder stories. Programmes such as *Crimewatch UK* (BBC1) may be regarded as infotainment. As Schlesinger and Tumber (1996) indicate, this factually based programme raises issues around representation similar to those which may come out of fiction:

- the crime stories selected tend to the dramatic and do not represent the majority of police work
- the dramatized reconstruction of the stories raises questions about the nature of their realism, and about inflections designed to appeal to the audience
- there is a tension between the need to excite and involve the audience and the simultaneous need to reassure them.

In an ideological sense all crime stories, whatever their mode of realism, are probably operating within a model of social control. In the case of *Crimewatch* the public are asked actively to become part of that control, to participate in the assertion of norms. *Crimewatch* also raises the special problem of editorial control: who has final cut on the crime stories – the police who control the information or the BBC producers who reshape it? It appears that the answer to this one is fudged, through the mutual interest of police and programme makers in getting out a successful prime-time programme which sometimes also helps catch criminals. And, in the context of some negative representations, '*Crimewatch* offers a generally useful public relations context in which the police are portrayed in an unambiguously positive and sympathetic light' (Schlesinger and Tumber, 1996).

In what ways can television news (just as much as a crime fiction series) construct a view of crime?

9

Audiences, Meanings and Effects

PREVIEW

This chapter deals with:
- problems in defining television audiences
- the construction of audiences
- active audiences
- audience pleasures
- perspectives on effects
- effects research and the violence debate
- children and television
- audience access to television.

INTRODUCTION

Audiences are the *raison d'être* of television. Whether one takes a commercial/marketplace model or a public service/social responsibility model for television, those who make it want to reach some kind of audience. The BBC needs audiences to justify its licence fee. Commercial television needs audiences to persuade its advertisers to spend money. The people who make the programmes want to know that they are talking to someone; they want positive feedback; they want the approval of their audience and of their peers.

But the word 'audience' is problematic. It is as if the very idea of mass audience has been naturalized into a truth – which works in the interests of the media themselves, wanting to boast to the public about their popularity and to the advertisers about their commercial viability.

In spite of the overall volume of viewing, one cannot justify a classic Marxist perspective of mass audiences soaking up the ideology of the elite. Still, there is ideology present, and there are power groups dominating our society. But who is absorbing what ideas and with what effect is another matter. It is true that television programmes can still attract large audiences – 16 million for an episode of a popular soap opera, even 22 million for large cultural events such as royal weddings. But this is not the scale of audience for television in general. Achieving a description of 'audience' is further complicated by variables such as the fact that the composition of an audience changes from one soap episode to another. The expansion of channels and programmes has fragmented audiences in terms of numbers and possibly of shared characteristics. Specialized programming is described as narrow-casting. There are no mass audiences, only a shifting variety of viewers for a myriad of programmes. As Fiske puts it (1991), 'people watching television are best modelled according to a multitude of differences'.

Traditional assumptions about the effects of television are as untenable as the idea of mass audience. It cannot be seriously argued that television simply does things to people. There is as much interest in what people do with television. Indeed, it may be said that television viewing is just another form of social behaviour.

This is not to argue that television has no effect on its audiences. But one can say that we are not at all certain about the nature of effects, or about the process through which they may be produced. The assertiveness in talking about effects in some quarters – especially to do with violent (*sic*) material or viewing by children – is not supported by evidence. It says more about the anxieties and convictions of those who make the assertions. However, in the relative absence of certainty, nor should one dismiss all anxiety.

To argue for any kind of effect from the interaction of audiences with television material is to assume that this material means something to the viewer, that the meanings are incorporated in some way and to some degree within the viewers' value systems and reality systems. What is clear is that given programmes can mean both similar and different things to their viewers. People will agree on salient features of a programme yet still put a different emphasis on these features. This takes us into the area of text and reading. It could be said that television doesn't exist where meaning is concerned. What there is, is the programme being watched, the text, and the meanings that are produced from it by the audience/reader. The meaning of television is only in the mind of the viewer.

There is also a perspective on textual analysis in television criticism which in effect sees the audience as being produced by the text itself. The emphasis on the text as being the one thing you were sure about was fuelled in the 1970s and 1980s by the structural discipline of semiotics onto which was grafted kinds of psycho-analytic theory. The nature of the text defines the audience because this is what causes a viewer to make sense of the programme in a certain way and therefore be a certain kind of audience.

It would seem that definitions of audience, text and television itself are interdependent. Whatever television is, is located somewhere between its producers and their intentions, the texts and their features, and the audience and their readings. Roland Lorimer (1994) talks of 'audience members, audiences as groups, the media, and cultures in which they reside as meaning generating entities which affect one another'. In particular, this reminds one of the matter of context, which interests more recent audience studies and a cultural-studies approach, in trying to understand how audiences make sense of television.

Christine Geraghty (Geraghty and Lusted, 1998) comments that 'television watching makes sense within a variety of contexts which may link it to social arrangements . . . or to other entertainment and communication formats'. But again, looking at how people watch television is not the same thing as knowing what they think about it. And neither of these things is the same as knowing what effects this watching has on them.

CONSTRUCTED AUDIENCES

I have suggested that there is no such thing as 'the television audience', only a shifting variety of audiences. The audience only exists when it is watching. As Nightingale says (1996) 'audiences only exist at the point of interaction with the text – not as a group in existence waiting to respond'. The channel-hopping audience shifts like a hyperactive butterfly. If there ever was such a thing as a captive audience in the early days of BBC monopoly, there is no longer one. Audience as 'people who watch television' is a description so vague as to be useless. A theatre or a concert audience at least has the definition of being a finite number of people in one place (a public arena) at one time for a unique performance. The audience for a television programme is scattered all over Britain, in their homes, watching a duplicable performance, changing as people 'walk in and out' of the viewing process.

In terms of making the word audience meaningful, in terms of getting people in front of the television, audiences can be seen as a construct of the television industry. They only exist in front of the screen, and the industry seeks ways of getting them there and describing them once they are there. The descriptions used are qualitative and quantitative. As John Hartley puts it (1992), audiences 'are the invisible fictions that are produced institutionally in order for various institutions to take charge of the mechanisms of their own survival'. Hartley also argues that critiques of television invent an audience. Thus John Ellis (1992) assumes a 'normal citizen' in his discussion of how television is understood and Morley makes assumptions about class groups in his study of the nationwide audience (1980) or about family in *Family Television* (1986).

It is possible to argue for an account of audience by programme or by category. There is the audience for *Seinfeld*, or the audience for Sport.

Whatever it is that attracts people to watch the series or the category is constructing the audience (the programmes themselves also being constructs).

TVRs represent a common measurement of audience by the industry for the benefit of advertisers. TVR figures rate the percentage of a target audience thought to be viewing at the time when an advert is to be screened: the probable number of 'hits', if you like. The target audience itself is defined in terms of common features such as age, occupation, socio-economic grouping – for example, women aged 25 to 40 in family households and in the C socio-economic category (middle and supervisory management roles). These descriptors are themselves produced through market research conducted by companies such as National Consumer Surveys, who hold the information on databases and sell it to television organizations among others. Television itself also conducts research, mostly though its own research company BARB, which is constantly trawling viewer habits and preferences. So TVRs represent an amalgam of research which constructs a numerical value for the audience which is based on both quantitative and qualitative descriptors.

Reach relates to TVRs – the percentage of the audience which tunes in to a programme or a channel for at least some time.

Share, on the other hand, is the percentage of audience (averaged) that tunes in over a defined period of time.

Viewing time can be measured as an average for a programme or channel. So one can reach a lot of the television audience but not have a very big share of actual viewing time. Or one can have a big share of the audience for a popular programme without having a high average viewing time for that channel.

Lifestyles explain the viewer in terms of leisure habits, how they spend their main income, what consumer possessions they value, the size of their disposable income, what they enjoy doing, how they spend their time. This description of a way of life also involves degrees of generalization, the construction of cultural categories which are not untrue but are not entirely true either. They are a notional grouping of people in an attempt to achieve correlation between the programmes they watch and what they spend their money on. As an account of 'audience' all these constructs are in the interests of television institutions, not of other sections of society.

Psychographic profiles define people in terms of their sense of identity and of their values. Once more, the intention is to group people by significant features, to appeal to those features in (mainly) advertising. If this appeal is successful then the advertiser or the scheduler has generated an audience.

Programming by television channels is also an industry device for attracting audiences. Whether or not that programming attracts a certain kind of audience, constructs a coherent audience, is another matter. The evidence for channel loyalty is ambiguous. People watch Sky Sport because they are interested in sport and in some events to which that channel has broadcasting rights. People also stay with channels because of inertia, having been attracted by a given programme.

Scheduling devices such as hammocking cause viewers to stay with a programme placed between two others which attract them. People who enjoy adverts are likely to go to ITV1. People with minority interests are likely to go to BBC2 or to C4. But still relatively few people actually watch so much of one channel (as opposed to simply leaving it switched on), that they may be understood as a constructed audience for that channel. Television executives may like to talk as if this happens, but in general the audience is attracted by programmes, genres and the need to watch television as a diversion (in which case they will channel hop until something holds their attention).

ACTIVE AUDIENCES

The word 'audience' has connotations of passivity, of receptiveness, which are not borne out by the evidence of viewing habits. Similarly, the notion of the 'couch potato', while not entirely untrue, has also achieved unjustified proportions as a way of interpreting people in front of the television.

Television viewing is active in a variety of ways which give the lie to the persistent cliché of the braindead audience. There is evidence of active responses to material: sales of tie-in books; the social and charity activity associated with 'events' days such as Comic Relief; the appearance in the UK of American football clubs following screening of this sport on satellite television. There is research into viewing behaviours which shows clearly that people do a variety of things while the television is switched on, from domestic chores to playing a musical instrument (Collet and Lamb, 1986). There is interactive behaviour – comments on and discussion about the programme in progress – which contradicts another cliché about the deadening effect of television on family life.

Above all there is the active mental processing that the audience conducts while watching. Decoding television, reading the text, involves making sense of multiple codes in this polysemic medium. Sitting still is not the same as being inactive. **Uses and gratification theory** is often used to make sense of this kind of internalized activity. The audience uses television, not the other way around. It uses television to gratify inner needs to do with the social self and with self-image. These may be summed up as:

• the need for information – to maintain and enhance our picture of our geographical and social world (e.g. through news or through drama)
• the need for idenitity – to use television, especially personalities and enacted roles, in order to check out our sense of self and our social behaviours (e.g. through characters from fiction television)

- the need for social interaction – to experience interaction and relationships (e.g. through following lives in soap operas)
- the need for diversion – to use television for entertainment, as a form of play.

This view has been criticized on the grounds that needs, like all psychological constructs, are merely a notion. They are inferred from behaviours. By this argument all propositions about internal mechanisms of motivation and understanding would be suspect. Since the notion of needs actually seems to work as one interpretation of social interactions, it seems reasonable to accept it as a partial way of understanding audiences' interactions with television. Morley (1991) also argues for the limitations of this approach in respect of the emphasis on individual responses, ignoring the 'audience as group'. In fact, I would argue that the idea of needs being common to many people answers this objection. A view of audience as a collection of individuals with a mobile set of common responses is a fair one.

The notion of active audience engagement with television is one that has been taken on within cultural studies in particular. As described in 'pleasures' below, it is seen as a way of making meanings, of making culture, of taking control. Ideology is resisted or sidelined. Adorno's ideas about mass culture and the power of modern media (1991) are disregarded. Mike Wayne in (1994) talks of 'two contesting traditions' and concludes that

> Problems within the mass culture tradition are more than balanced by the blind spots of popular traditions which come through very strongly in audience studies. Here, there has been a tendency to conceive the popular as a realm of cultural self-making where 'the people' reconstruct their identities and their sense of place in the world at will. Thus questions of power and ideology are suppressed by methods which celebrate audience creativity and/or dissolve the text as an object with any effectivity.

However, I would suggest that it is now understood that one does not have to make choices about one tradition or the other. It is also understood that issues around power and ideology are not in fact irrelevant, and won't go away for being ignored. Television audiences may not be passive victims of the programme as text, but they do engage with material over whose production they have no control, and the features of which seem to be designed to produce and prefer certain kinds of understanding. In this case, Stuart Hall's writing on the notions of dominant, negotiated and oppositional readings of texts (referred to in Morley, 1980) still seems to be valid.

> In what ways may a passive model of television viewing be an ideological construct which relates to particular cultural attitudes and which stands for an attempt to assert power in our society?

CONSUMPTION AND PLEASURE

The notion of diversion is little removed from that of pleasure. The nature of pleasure for the television audience depends on what diverts you. Pleasures do not have to be passive. An active alternative to other occupations, not least work, can be pleasurable. The documentary is as valid as the game show in this respect. The idea of consumption, stemming from a critical Marxist position, may have undertones of passivity, of the audience as victim. It could be said that television is consumed much as milk pudding may be (and implicitly, with no more substance and just as much seductive sweetness). Television programmes are just so much more product. They are marketed. They are valued only for their attraction, consumption and profitability. Indeed, Horkheimer and Adorno (1972) rejected such pleasures: 'to be pleased means to say Yes. . . . Pleasure always means not to think about anything'.

But there is such a thing as consumer choice. People don't have to buy – and if they do buy they may choose someone else's product. Admittedly the metaphor invites critical rejoinders such as 'But what kind of choice, of what value?' But when one moves into consuming as a pleasure, I would argue that audience pleasures are not to be denigrated. A postmodernist position would see the underlying question – 'But what is this television stuff doing to you?' – as being irrelevant in respect of assumptions about consumption being bad for you because it is a function of capitalism. From a culturalist position, one would say that the evidence for audience activity invalidates arguments for audience as victim. The connection between institutional policy, textual construction, its influence on the audience and audience responses is so problematic and tenuous that macro theories about television having any large effect on its audience aren't worth bothering with. Let's understand the audience in its cultural context. Let's understand the pleasures that the audience may get from television. Indeed, let's celebrate what the audience does with television texts as a manifestation of popular culture. Let's see this as a subversion of the dominant ideology attempting to frame social behaviour and thinking. It is OK to enjoy television.

The nature of pleasure in relation to television product has been discussed in Chapter 4. What is worth bringing out here is that this is about the audience's engagement with the text. Pleasure is not something which the producers can control, or can circumscribe indelibly in the form and context of the programme. It is a meaning which the viewer produces for a variety of reasons. It may said that pleasure comes from gratifications of needs – perhaps for diversion from other stressful experiences. It is something obtained from genres in a tension between that which is familiar and that which is unexpected. In terms of a cultural analysis, even if one initially sees the programme as a commodity for consumption, the view that the audience wrests control from the producers by making meanings and pleasures for themselves means that it becomes part of a cultural economy. Just as cash circulates in a material economy, so ideas and pleasures circulate in this economy, produced by the audience.

The complicated layers of pleasure are exemplified by game shows. There is a studio audience directly involved and enjoying spectacle, challenge and the right to respond. There is a domestic audience taking pleasure at a distance. There is a pleasure in the ritual and control of game shows – control usually being mediated through the host. But then there is pleasure in the potential for anarchy in unscripted behaviours and those that are socially rule-breaking. In the view of people like Fiske (himself drawing on ideas from Bahktin about carnival, excess and 'bad' taste), this is television as class resistance to dominant ideologies. The audience is in control because it defines what it enjoys through its responses, and therefore defines what is likely to be produced. Fiske (1987) talks about 'a theory of pleasure that centers on the power to make meanings rather than on the meanings that are made'.

Bourdieu (1984) has argued against this kind of autonomy. He proposes the notion of 'habitus' in which people are predisposed to respond to experiences in certain ways because they have been culturalized. This sounds like structuralism by another name and takes us into an argument about who controls the meanings as pleasures. I would suggest that the argument is pointless. To an extent the audience is exploited and its pleasure responses sought in the cause of commercial gain. But this pleasure is not entirely predictable. Clearly television is the dominant popular-culture medium because of its sheer reach, its variety and its attraction of huge audiences from a range of backgrounds. It doesn't follow either that it is a force for malign control of society or that it is always approvable because popular culture must be approvable *per se*, coming from 'the people'. Morley (1991) draws from Judith Williamson (1978) when he talks of 'an uncritical perspective which simply endorses popular tastes because they are popular'.

Ethnographic research has been used in particular since the mid-1980s as a way of addressing the qualitative nature of audiences, of investigating viewing as a cultural activity and of taking account of cultural context in explaining the ways that people make sense of television. This approach includes conversational engagement with respondents rather than (prescriptive) questionnaires. The research takes place in the home. As Ien Ang says in *Desperately Seeking the Audience* (1991) 'the ethnographer . . . conceptualises media audience-hood as lived experience'.

Researchers such as Roger Silverstone (1994) and David Morley (1992) have found that viewing involves gender issues such as males controlling the television remote control or women having their viewing circumscribed by domestic tasks. Women are more inclined than men to talk while viewing. Women seem to prefer soap operas and dramas; men more than women like to watch news. Morley (1986) argues that 'changing patterns of television viewing can only be understood in the overall context of family leisure activity'. Silverstone (1994) refers to three factors of interest in his research:

- description of what is going on when viewing happens
- dynamics within the family affecting use of media, such as age or gender
- consequences of viewing and of context both for the individuals and for the family as a whole.

This kind of research goes back at least to Dorothy Hobson's work (1982) on women viewing the then early evening soap opera *Crossroads*. She too found that married women were trying to watch and prepare a meal and deal with children at the same time. Effects must be relative to the nature and the conditions of audience interaction with television. Similarly, Morley (1986) found evidence that men asserted the superior value of categories such as news, sport and documentary, imposing a benchmark of values about television within the home, the domestic cultural sphere. In such cases, it is argued, women's viewing of for example romantic drama is a kind of resistance to asserted masculine values. There may be a degree of pleasure in a kind of defiance.

In such cases one can see how audience study is approached on a level of detail which contrasts with the mass audience – mass effects scale of propositions. Even textual analysis has been sidelined in favour of textual engagement and the conditions of engagement.

> How may viewing of sport on television become a 'popular pleasure' and a social experience which involves the audience 'joining in'?

EFFECTS RESEARCH (THE VIOLENCE DEBATE)

This section is concerned with methodologies and their validity, especially in relation to research into the effects of 'violent' television on audience attitudes and behaviours. It is impossible within the space available to cover all effects areas – political influence and voting habits, for example. Trying to evaluate the effects of television viewing on the audience raises questions about a complex interaction of factors. The nature of this complexity is such that it substantially undermines the validity of any conclusions about the effects of television. Questions one might ask are:

- Who is the audience for the programme or programmes which may or may not affect them in some way?

- Is this audience coherent enough in character for one to generalize about effects?

  (For example, pronouncements are made freely about 'children' in relation to depictions of violence or of sexuality, but the definition of 'children' is so variable that it is hard to objectify effects.)

- How does the audience obtain meanings which may affect them in some way?

  (In other words, to talk about effects is to assume that particular meanings are obtained, assimilated and 'acted upon' by the audience; it is to raise subsidiary questions about whether these meanings are 'imposed' through the text and /or constructed by the audience.)

- How does one take account of the layers of cultural context within which those meanings are obtained?

  (For example, factors such as upbringing, conditions of viewing, cultural values, relationships, will all have some bearing on how every individual, audience member (let alone the audience collectively) makes sense of a programme – what they do with it inside their heads.)

I shall be saying more about the problems of measuring effects and validating pronouncements about effects of television viewing than I am able to say in terms of supported assertions describing effects (*see also* Fig. 9.1). There is no question that we believe that effects and influence exist. The censorship of television discussed in Chapter 10 is evidence of this. The problem is to prove it. Evidence may be partial or contradictory. For example, it is evident that families are brought together in talking about television programmes as much as they are fragmented by individual programme watching. However, it is negative perspectives on television which tend to prevail in popular mythology. It may also be relevant to point out that, for example, in 1997 the ITC intervened with licensees only seven times over issues relating to violence in programmes.

Certainly television has some effects. We know that popular programmes cause millions of people to switch to a given channel and watch them. We know that people give millions of pounds to the Children in Need charity every year because television spends most of a day asking them to give. We know that sales of given goods and services increase in response to a television advertising campaign. But we don't know that people vote for a given political party simply because of its electoral marketing campaign on television.

Gunter (1987) says of news and politics in particular that although 'television may indeed have some influence on political socialisation, this effect may be mediated by or dependent upon the nature of other factors concerning the individual's personal make-up and upbringing'. In *Television Form and Public Address* (1995) John Corner at one point looks at television in terms of its influence on democratic politics. He provides a useful summary

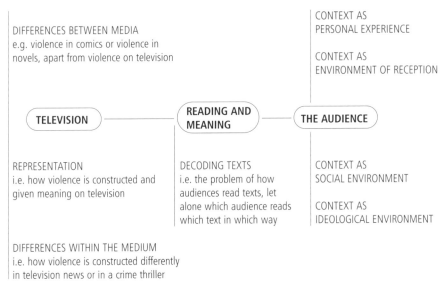

9.1 Problems with researching the effects of television violence.

of positions, both negative and positive, having acknowledged that research provides a framework but no firm conclusions about the influence of television on political activity and thinking.

1 Negatively, television has become a sphere of knowledge management in which information comes from dominant sources and is placed within an interpretative framework. Positively, television has 'massively increased the proportion of the population who have regular political information'.

2 Negatively, television has caused politics to be understood in terms of 'strategic personalisation': 'political issues and choices are projected within a theatricalised framework which emphasises the personality and personal qualities of key political actors'. Positively, television journalism exerts pressures on politicians which lead to some degree of accountability and the need to explain and justify policies.

3 Negatively, television is more taken up with creating the illusion of realism (through new technologies) than with real critical engagement with political issues and behaviours. Thus it conceals power relationships and the workings of ideology. Positively, television technology can operate so quickly and directly from source that it makes it difficult for political interests to manage and control events.

Barrie Gunter (1994) describes major issues which keep coming up in relation to research on media violence:

- How much violence is there in different media?
- What is the extent of exposure to violence for individuals?
- What are the effects of media violence?
- What does the public really think and feel about media violence?

Typologies of effects

These mainly come down to attitudes and behaviour. Behaviours are evident as actions, though the correlation between television performance and audience behaviour is usually impossible to make. Attitudes are even more tenuous to deal with because they are implicit, to be deduced from what people do and what they say. So even if half a million people give to Children in Need one can't make assumptions about their attitudes towards children or charities, for example. And one certainly can't make assumptions about generosity or caringness in respect of all those people as an audience in the collective sense, because they have no coherence as a group.

Gunter (1994) categorizes effects as **cognitive** (attitudes and beliefs), **affective** (emotions) or **behavioural**. His further distinctions of type of effect, and comments on research evidence, may be summarised as follows:

- **Catharsis:** the idea that violent television gets rid of violent feelings and attitudes. There is a lack of support for and of research on this view.
- **Arousal:** violent material arouses feelings, not necessarily focused for good or bad in the first place. Evidence is that the aroused mood quickly disappears.
- **Disinhibition:** violent television undermines social controls against the idea of violence. There is some research which evidences the development of anger and aggression towards women.
- **Imitation:** violent television induces imitation of its violent behaviours. There is no clear evidence for this view.
- **Desensitization:** watching violence causes the audience to become hardened to the idea of thinking violence or of being violent. There is no clear evidence for this view.

Short-term and long-term effects. Whatever we think we know about the effect of a television charity appeal at the time of its asking, we can't be sure of audience attitudes and behaviours one month or one year later. Ironically, although some simple short-term effects of television are easy to evidence (though not violent behaviour), it is long-term (and attitudinal) effects that now most interest researchers. In this case, it is supposed that the repetition of material, of meanings, over a period of time may influence attitudes and values. The obvious problem here is about agreement on the reading, the meaning. Even when one deals with agreed meanings about stereotypical role models – the disabled as villains or victims, the woman as sex object – it is still very difficult to measure audience attitudes, or the effects of these on their behaviour. Most of all, it is impossible to distinguish the influence of television in this respect from other media or from other social influences.

Cumulative effects represent a notion allied to the idea of long-term effects, in which it is argued that screen violence can only affect us over a period of time (see also desensitization, above).

General or specific effects speak for themselves as a kind of categorizing. Copycat killings might be cited as a very specific effect. But it has to be remembered that creating a typology of effects is not the same as demonstrating that they exist.

Functional and dysfunctional effects focus on the positive and the negative. Research may be inflected and reported either way. Meanwhile, there are generally deep-laid negative cultural attitudes towards television, certainly among those of the middle classes who are influential in setting agendas. Fundamentally, this stems from a frankly elitist, high-culture position that was loudly articulated in Britain in the 1950s and 1960s, and which still persists. This position stemmed to a great extent from the Leavisite literary tradition that only quality literature mattered (and that university teachers knew what good literature was). Television (like most film) was damned because it involved viewing not reading, because it was popular, because it was 'easy'. So a lot of what is said about television effects is about why it is in various ways 'bad' for you. Again, by any standards, this simply isn't true. Television dramas of the 'classics' have brought people to read those books, which should please the anxious teacher of literature. Television documentaries have generated public debates about matters of concern, such as the treatment of children in local-authority homes. Television programmes, from those for children such as *Sesame Street* to the Open University educational productions, have in every sense educated people. So the relative weight of effects research in areas such as violence is misplaced. The proportion of negative conclusions about violence and effects is unsustainable (see below). The degree of publicity given to negative conclusions about the influence of television, not least in respect of violence, is improper.

McQuail (1983) produced a useful model of media effects. This is dominated by two axes, of intention and of time. Something like advertising has a high degree of intentionality and aims to have an effect within a short time. It is interesting to see that long-term and non-deliberate effects include the exercise of social control over the audience, a process of socialization, and a defining of reality for the media user. This reality could refer to all dimensions of the world as we understand it: social, ideological and geographical (*see* Fig. 9.2). The problem with all these descriptors, or categories of effects, is that they do not of themselves demonstrate that an effect has taken place.

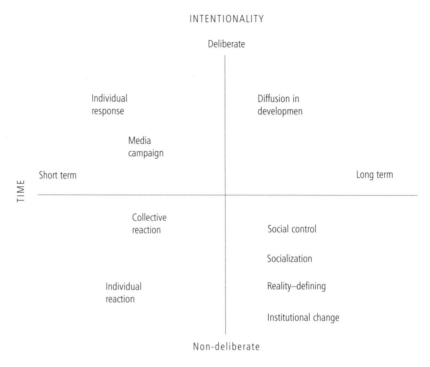

9.2 A typology of media effects.
Source: McQuail, 1983

Models of **the effects relationship** between television and audience exist alongside typologies of effects. The **hypodermic model** describes an early and persistent view underpinned by the assumption that the media do things to people. Television carries the force of the dominant ideology, as the Frankfurt School would have it. Television helps exert hegemony, brings about consensual control, as Gramsci (1971) would say. In fact, this early view that television could inject people with ideas which quickly led to undesirable behaviours was discredited many years ago. Joseph Klapper summarized effects research to this end as long ago as 1960: 'Mass communications ordinarily do not serve a necessary and sufficient cause of audience effects, but rather function among and through a nexus of mediating factors and influences'. Hence the development of ideas about long-term influence as opposed to short-term effects.

The **two-step flow theory** was another influential model produced as long ago as 1955 by Katz and Lazarfeld. In this case they identified the influence of the opinions of individuals important to audience members. Those who are personalities working in television – the trusted newscaster, for instance –

are seen as **opinion makers**. Those who are trusted members of one's social and work groups – the people one listens to – are described as **opinion leaders**. The process of influence is therefore one in which ideas are mediated by these two sets of people. The trouble is one still cannot be sure what the audience does with these ideas, whatever they are, once they have been so mediated.

The **uses and gratifications model** has already been explained. **Textual reading** has also been explained, along with the notion that reading may go along with the (supposed) intentions of those who made the text, or make sense of it in another unexpected way, or even positively resist those intentions.

Implicitly, all these are process models of one degree of complexity or another. They pick out the flow of ideas, the mediation of ideas, key points in the process, the complexity of contextualizing influences. None of this demonstrates cause and effect. Research has been most valuable in exposing problems and identifying factors which have to be taken into account. But it is not conclusive.

Research methodologies regarding effects are themselves problematic. Gunter (1994) summarizes these as laboratory experiments, field experiments, correlational surveys, natural experiments, intervention studies and longtitudinal panel studies.

Elsewhere (*More Than Meets the Eye*, 1997) I have pointed out problems with four methodologies in relation to research into violence.

- **Closed experiments** (e.g. in a laboratory) are culturally restrictive and ignore the importance of the social environment in which viewing actually takes place (see ethnographic research, p. 218).
- **Field studies** have to cope with a variety of problems relating to questions and respondents. For example, it has been shown that children may lie about violent videos they are supposed to have watched in order to gain attention or to maintain peer-group credibility.
- **Content analysis** is often flawed in terms of what it defines as violent acts. It also deals with the programmes and then simply assumes that there must be some effect on the audience if enough violent acts have been scored.
- **Correlation analysis** may suffer from making false or selective correlations.

David Gauntlett (1998) provides a hard-hitting critique of 'Ten Things Wrong with the Effects Model', with particular relation to violence and children.

- The effects model tackles social problems backwards – it does not start with the social violence which is the point of reference, and work towards media usage.
- The effects model treats children as inadequate. Largely as a result of

assumptions made from within theories of psychological development, it is assumed that children don't or can't 'cope' with media violence. Research that deals with children's responses suggests otherwise.

- Assumptions within the effects model are characterized by barely concealed conservative ideology. Most noise about media violence is made by commentators who demonstrably start from a conservative position on the potential of media for encouraging violence.
- The effects model inadequately defines its own objects of study. Definitions of what is anti-social or violent behaviour in media are sometimes partial and highly questionable.
- The effects model is often based on artificial studies. The methodology of study – e.g the artificiality of laboratory experiments – may undermine the conclusions.
- The effects model is often based on studies with misapplied methodology. Inconsistencies and false correlations are cited by Gauntlett as examples.
- The effects model is selective in its criticisms of media depictions of violence. Research is dominated by attention to fiction, rather than looking at news and violence, for example.
- The effects model assumes superiority to the masses. Just as people interviewed about media effects tend to deny this, so also researchers themselves take a superior detached attitude to effects on themselves and how this may influence their work.
- The effects model makes no attempt to understand meanings of the media. Assumptions about a clear message from the media as well as the detached ability of the researchers to identify that message ignore the complexity of meanings produced and adduced by media users.
- The effects model is not grounded in theory. Assumptions about effects are simplistic and too often founded on assertions. Contexts, reasons for media behaviour, and other questions about what is going on are largely ignored.

This last point about **contexts** is one to which we continually return. Ethnographic studies are about the viewing context. Ideological or discourse analysis is about a context of ideas. Television is not the only medium to represent violence. And of course a violent episode exists within a programme, which itself exists within the context of the whole mass of television and, indeed, writing about television. The complexity of contexts, the difficulty in demonstrating that television is a dominant influence among all these contexts, provides the most serious objection to making any assertions about the influence of television.

Attempts to use **textual analysis** as a precision tool – semiotic analysis in particular – are no more productive. In essence, studies show that large numbers of people read texts in different ways, and certainly don't agree about what is a violent act on television, or what kind of acts should be censored, or what kinds of act will affect which children in which way. Again, this is not an argument for moral anarchy. But it does suggest that the codes of practice operated by television organizations and regulatory authorities represent a consensus among those who run television, not a consensus of society at large. As such they will always be contested. As long ago as 1975 Grant Noble (*Children in Front of the Small Screen*) was writing somewhat wearily about the obsession with television violence as affecting children. He reviews the then dominant research and questions both its validity and its negative conclusions, mostly on the basis of the artificiality of research conditions. From his own work, he suggests that if one takes observation out of the laboratory there is even some indication that television aggression makes aggressive play more imaginative and less violent.

> How does television actually help in understanding discussions about violence in society?

The idea that concern about violence is as much a cultural phenomenon as an objectifed cultural debate is supported by ways in which the issue is dealt with. For example, the weight of research is on fictional representations but violent episodes also appear in factual television. In any case it has been demonstrated that most people, including children above the age of 8, deal with fiction as something separated from reality. Significantly, those who do appear likely to enact violence have, for various reasons, lost a firm sense of that division, as the film *Natural Born Killers* effectively and satirically demonstrates. Investigations are also much taken with physical acts of violence – shootings and stabbings – and pay little attention to psychological violence. The representation of conflict between parents in some drama may be quite as disturbing to a child as a physical wounding in a thriller.

Theories and propositions about the influence of television *vis-à-vis* violence and crime move in and out of fashion. Gerbner's **cultivation theory** (1986) was attractive for a number of years. It argued that the accumulative effects of violent material cultivated a fear of crime in the mind of the viewer. But research could not demonstrate that this cultivation took place. People acquire 'knowledge' about what crime is, and indeed about 'crime prevention'. What they do with that knowledge is something else.

Corner (1995) points to some interesting contradictions in the depiction and evaluation of violence on television. For example, there is criminal and non-criminal violence: violence by those in authority is condoned; violence by those deemed to be outside the law is condemned. Also, violent behaviour is condemned in everyday life, and yet we 'allow' a disproportionate representation of violence on the screen. We no longer condone public pleasures in violence (contrast popular attendance at Tyburn hangings in the eighteenth century) but we do 'condone' the pleasures of watching mediated violence on television. Corner also refers to Docherty's research for the Broadcasting Standards Council (1990) which opens up ideas about the culturally significant nature of violence as play. Then there is the idea that violence in the context of British-based realist drama creates more anxieties for the audience than violence in manifestly fictional US drama, which is by definition culturally distanced.

It could be said that all television material, including that which might be deemed violent, at least provides information for the viewer. What information is taken on, how it is used in the internal models which a viewer constructs about 'the world', is not clear.

More useful than research into effects is the kind of survey (e.g. Hargrave, 1993) which demonstrates reactions:

- people are concerned about the overall level of violence on television (including fiction)
- violence in factual television is more acceptable yet also more upsetting because it is 'real'
- dramatic techniques (e.g. reconstruction in a documentary) make the impact more upsetting
- news should have the most 'licence for violence'
- people should be warned about upsetting material to be screened
- female viewers feel especially vulnerable as a result of watching violent material.

Gunter (1987) says that factuality, memory and gender all matter in terms of impact. His research suggests that violent news items are remembered better than others, and better by men than by women.

Guy Cumberbatch (1989) points out that what the media say people think about violence and what people actually say in response to a detailed survey may be two different things. He acknowledges the existence of public concern, but also says that research claiming to prove that television causes violence is simply inadequate. Cecilia Von Feilitzen (1998), summarizing research into effects and violence, is similarly critical, saying that television and the media generally have at best a small part to play in bringing out violent and aggressive behaviour. Other factors are more significant, such as personality and environment. It seems that television may cause us to form views on which members of society are perpetrators and which are victims of violence. People who have been victims find television violence especially disturbing. Violence in American television relates to dominant cultural values, behaviours and what is tolerated generally in the USA. Again it seems that what is most useful about effects research is not that it proves effects, but that it demonstrates the importance of a wide variety of factors relating to context and to the reading of television.

Schlesinger et al. (1992) argue that women's anxiety about violence and how it may affect them ties in with how they conceive of themselves and their situation. They also suggest that anxiety may lead to selective viewing as much as viewing leading to anxiety. But the writers also assert that 'it is questionable whether any easily sustainable causal relationship can be drawn between exposure to television and public perceptions of crime'.

It is interesting to note the results of a content-analysis survey of violence on television carried out by the University of Sheffield in conjunction with the ITC. The survey covered all channels and 28 separate days between January and June 1996. In this period it was found that of the total broadcast hours, only 1.39 per cent contained acts of violence.

CHILDREN AND TELEVISION

Children as audience for television have always been regarded as a special case because of their assumed suggestibility and susceptibility to effects. Assumptions about effects are also implicit in the nature of programmes aimed at young audiences, including those which are explicitly educational. Kinds of censorship of television described in Chapter 10 are also particularly framed for children. But there are huge problems in discussing young people and the effects of television, not least when those with the strongest opinions are least willing to take account of our relative ignorance about how children view and what they make of television material. Children mature in different ways at different ages. There isn't a clear agreement about what 'maturing' means anyway. Children grow up in different environments which may or may not help them interpret television. Sub-cultural variations in environment are certainly important in this respect. What children may say about television and what may be suggested about effects on them operates in any case within the framework of what adults think about children. Adults have their own views about what children should be like, what childhood experiences should entail, and so of course about what the effects of television on children ought to be.

Stephen Wagg (1992) talks about 'the conceptualisation of the child as a passive receptacle, and the accompanying clamour for standards, decency, censorship and so on'. Shaun Moores (1993) refers to childhood as 'a socially constructed category'. I would add that ideas about children's supposed lack of discrimination where television is concerned are mixed up with this construction. Balzagette and Buckingham (1995) broadly concur with this. They refer to the idealization of childhood and of some supposed former age in which there was harmony between adults and children. They also identify false assumptions about how children make sense of the media.

All these factors skew what broadcasters feel they can and should offer to children, let alone what it is supposed the effects of television on children are. The ITC Code of Practice on Advertising defines children as being aged 15 years or under. It is concerned about the blurring of fantasy and reality in respect of selling toys and games, for example. It explicitly bans some persuasive tactics such as the association of status with a product. It bans until after 9.00 p.m. adverts showing children self-administering medicines. Advertisements for products such as alcoholic drinks, matches and vitamins may not be placed around programmes for children. Advertisements for 'expensive products' must include the price. Advertisements must take account of all kinds of safety issues. Children may not be displayed in a sexually provocative manner. Children should appear to be 'reasonably well-mannered and behaved'.

Some research does suggest that television in association with peer-group pressures may exert influence on children. One piece of research carried out in Wales used a healthy-diet video, employing persuasive techniques with a group of young children. The message was that by following the diet shown, the children could become 'Food Dudes'. It transpired that their eating habits were changed for the better, and that change seemed to persist even after the project had finished.

Gauntlett (1998) points out that effects research involving children is based on assumptions about the child state and child development, for example the idea of stages. Children are seen as 'not adults' and therefore ideas about 'adult' responses are less likely to be built into research. Children may be seen as 'not at a certain stage' (in the terms used by, for example, Erikson, 1950), which again may skew how the research is set up.

News represents an area of television where, Stuart Allan points out (1999), very little is known about how children react. There is an assumption, supported to an extent by audience research, that children and young people up until the age of 15 or so are disinclined to watch the news by choice. On the other hand, Allan refers to an study by Sheldon (1998) in Australia which indicated that 92 per cent of 1600 children aged 5 to 12 in the survey did watch television news. Children (and parents talking about their children) said that violence on the news was disturbing, mainly because it was understood to be real. Allan also refers to an ethnographic study of 14- to 18-year-old Punjabis in Southall, London (Gillespie, 1995), which showed that the young people watched the news in order to help translate it for their elders. They gained credibility and felt it as part of growing up.

Both the BBC and ITC codes of practice are keen on the idea of the watershed in programming – 9.00 p.m. – before which programmes and advertisements have to to take care of the young audience that is presumed to be watching. For example, usually no 15-rated film should start before this time. It is known, however, that many children watch 'adult' television (including on video recordings), regardless of the 9.00 p.m. watershed.

Effects and meanings

The debate about children and the effects of television is skewed by the same problems that affect understanding of adult audiences. If anything, the reactive/behaviourist assumptions about the effects of television on children are stronger. This is part of a view, an illusion, that children are miraculously non-violent and asexual. Alternative approaches, such as those followed by David Buckingham, would look at context and at what television means to children (rather than at active effects). Buckingham (1990) argues that children are much more discriminating and knowing viewers than adults give them credit for being. For instance, they are not easily taken in by advertisements. Television meanings should be evaluated in areas such as gender or race. It can be argued that the obsession with sex, violence and language is misplaced. People like Marie Winn (*Children without Childhood*, 1984) express recurrent anxieties with these factors, but the arguments are based on proposition and assertion as much as conclusive evidence about what meanings which kind of children make of what kind of programme, with what result for the children.

Interpretations of research into the effects of television on children sometimes seem to fall into the 'moral panic' category. The media pick up on some report and temporarily generate a climate of anxiety. Factors such as the inclination of more aggressive children to watch more violent television (Huesman and Eron, 1986) tend to get ignored. The question of variable effects on boys and girls, given the differentials in our social gender climate, is not raised. An example of such a panic surrounds the publication of the Newson Report (1994) on violence in the media generally, stimulated by the murder of a child by two other children. Its negative findings were widely reported in the media. The report itself made a number of assertions about effects, for which it actually produced no evidence (and could not). For instance, it was said that a great deal of research exists which links media violence, heavy viewing and violent and aggressive behaviour. This is not true. Research does not all suggest this. And it only suggests connections when there is a certain kind of home and social context for the child.

Patricia Palmer (1994) comments on considerable variations in viewing preferences for children, defined by age, gender and physical and social maturity. She argues that children are active viewers and that they organize their viewing as part of their whole domestic experience. Her argument is supported by reference to research which indicates a dynamic interaction between the child and the programme, relating to cognitive development. She argues against the criticisms of the medium made by Marie Winn, rejecting the passive-viewing model and pointing out that television is not merely a machine but a medium of human communication. Palmer is interested in viewing, not in effects as such. She emphasizes what children do with television viewing, which is at odds with descriptions of them as human sponges. This is what Silverstone (1994) refers to as 'the creative work engaged in by children in relation to the medium'.

Buckingham (1995), in a critique of the children's programme *Wacaday* (BBC1, 1993–5), comments on a 'pleasurable complicity, a membership of a club' created for the child viewer. I would draw attention to the effect of the style, the mode of address, the devices employed in this type of programme, in making the child viewer complicit, in defining an experience in which life is fun and is defined by its contrast with the adult world.

> What assumptions are made about children when it is said that television is a 'bad influence' on them?

TELEVISION AUDIENCES AND ACCESS

In spite of the rejection of the idea that institutions, their producers and their texts simply impose on a well-defined audience, it remains true that the relationship of viewers with television can feel like one-way traffic. The viewer chooses from and makes sense of what someone else has decided is to be available. Viewing figures, research results, letters, phone calls, viewers' panels, live audiences on shows all represent kinds of indirect feedback which do influence programming and programme treatment. But, notwithstanding the promises of electronic interaction, audiences don't have much access to television production. There is a useful chapter on the subject in *Television Times* (Corner and Harvey, 1996).

The issues involved are located within ideas about social democracy and the power (and therefore effects) of the medium. Arguments about allowing viewers to 'make' programmes come down to the issues of editorial control. No broadcaster will allow 'outsiders' to construct a programme as they please and have it sent out regardless. One question is whether reluctance to do this is based on a necessary sense of responsibility for the legality and taste of programme content, or on other less justifiable criteria. Related to this is the problem of needing to entertain audiences, who may not want a large diet of low-budget access programmes produced by their fellow citizens. Another question, related to running arguments about whether extreme rightwing political parties should have electoral airtime, is to do with who decides what people and their interests should be allowed any airtime at all. In other words, there are strong arguments for saying that there is not enough public access to television programme-making, but there are also arguments for placing boundaries on this access.

Access television began with BBC series such as *Open Door* (1970s) and *Brass Tacks* (1980s), both essentially documentary in format and broadcast out of peak time. The production unit involved would collaborate with some 'community group' to present a given issue and views on it. *Open Door* had, for example, programmes on the situation of Devon farmers, and one about bias on television news by the Campaign for Press and Broadcasting Freedom. The accessees were given a lot of scope to present their material and ideas, within the legal constraints on broadcasting. The broadcaster provided, as it were, the expertise to create something which was watchable at home. Such programmes put 'community' into broadcasting and raised issues with bite and with authenticity. But there were not and are not that many of them. It is true that there has been a relative expansion in the numbers of programmes about and for minority interests, including minority social groups. Channel 4 has done a lot in this respect. But I would suggest that there is an important distinction between programmes in which such interest groups genuinely initiate ideas and materials and have a lot of say in how these are handled, and programmes which are initiated and pretty much controlled by the broadcasters. Corner (1995) defines access as 'the avoiding or the correcting of imbalances in broadcasting's representation of politics and society by the articulation of a diversity of 'directly' stated views from different sections of the public and by the reflection, again 'directly', of the real diversity of cultural, social and economic circumstances'. Access programmes are needed because existing broadcasting is not truly representative of views and diversity. Programmes such as *Points of View* (BBC1) are not truly 'access' in giving airtime to viewers' opinions, because their agenda is set by the broadcasters, who also edit material.

New technology has moved forward the possibilities of access programming. *Video Diaries* (again BBC) realized this in the 1990s with, for example, *Ratcatcher*, by a former neo-Nazi group member turned exposer of such groups. The person involved was simply given a quality lightweight camcorder to make his film, in the editing of which he also had a say. *Video Nation* (BBC2) gives people a chance to speak directly to viewers for a short time on a subject of their choice – often a reflection on their personal situation and preoccupations.

In such cases the distance between private and public spheres has been closed. Television can provide access to the public sphere, the arena of public debate which it controls. The viewer as public has the opportunity to become part of political and social processes, not just an onlooker for information and debates which are staged and controlled by the institution. The explosion of digital channels makes it more possible for access programmes to be seen and heard. But still the issues around editorial control, funding and viewing figures won't go away. The achievement of more access programming on television is as much about changing the culture of television institutions as anything else.

> Why don't we have more access to television for the public?

10

British Television: Regulation, Censorship and Constraint

PREVIEW

This chapter deals with:

- use of the terms censorship or constraint
- facts about legal and regulatory constraints
- examples of censorship and the significance of these
- case studies of the Falklands and Gulf wars
- what is implied for the relationship between television and government.

INTRODUCTION

In the strict meaning of the term there is no censorship of British television. That is to say, there is no one regulatory body, least of all run as a government department, which can dictate programme content or treatment.

However, many programmes have in fact been changed or withdrawn over the years. Kinds of censorship can occur which aren't about re-editing or pulling programmes. There is no free-for-all in television. There is a variety of constraints – legal, political, financial. Arguably the operation of those constraints has sometimes been unnecessary and questionable. For example, in the late 1970s I was acquainted with a BBC documentary producer who described kinds of direct editorial interference with his work. He eventually resigned rather than acquiesce in the deletion of a particular shot from a film he made about Northern Ireland. The shot was that of a grave inscribed with, among other words, 'murdered by British soldiers'. The words exactly documented the beliefs and attitudes of one section of that Irish community. As it happens, legal events have since confirmed that some such murders did take place.

The example also demonstrates that there is self-regulation within television, as within the British media generally. But television, unusually among the media, is also regulated by the terms under which broadcasting is allowed at all, and by other mechanisms such as the ITC. So television is the most regulated of all the media. This returns one to earlier comments about its supposed power, to anxieties about its influence. One might also ask, who is that anxious about television? Certainly politicians are. The web of political control extends from political appointment of all the governors of the BBC to denial of the right to editorialize. This kind of regulation and constraint can be argued to be censorship before the fact of broadcasting: censorship by stealth. Areas of prime concern seem to be taste, bad language, depictions of violence and sexuality.

MECHANISMS AND PROCESSES OF CENSORSHIP OR CONSTRAINT

Censorship operates through the following processes:

- the law
- bodies constituted to oversee standards in television
- internal codes of practice operated by the contractors and by the BBC
- indirect influence.

The Law

First there are the **Broadcasting Acts** which allow and define terms of reference for broadcasting of television in Britain, including via cable and satellite. In effect these acts piggyback on top of one another, starting with the plain Wireless Telegraphy Acts (1904). The BBC was enabled by a royal charter in 1927. An Act of Parliament allowed commercial broadcasting to start in 1954. The principle of requiring a range of broadcasting, including factual and educational, and of maintaining standards of good taste within legal boundaries, applies in both cases. British governments have always been motivated by an antipathy towards the US free-for-all commercial model. They prefer to use the law plus regulatory bodies in the public sphere, in order to loosely define television output and to broadly control what goes on.

The **Law of Defamation of Character** applies to television through definitions of slander, which are established by precedent and case law. All television organizations maintain a legal section to vet problematic material.

The **Obscene Publications Act** (1959) can in theory be used against television broadcasters. Some MPs wanted to invoke this in 1986 when C4 broadcast Derek Jarman's film *Sebastiane* in a series of 'gay films'. This homo-erotic movie is set in Roman times and is fairly explicit. C4 was already (but temporarily) using a red triangle warning system to advise viewers of potentially offensive content in programmes. This device was in itself an attempt to head off possible censorship. These examples and the counter-reaction to them indicate that 'censorship' is relative to the mood of the times: that obscenity is a cultural notion.

The **Contempt of Court Act** (1981) forbids the publication of anything relating to a trial in progress which might prejudice its outcome. This is why news reports of major trials feature drawings rather than photographs of those involved in court.

The **Official Secrets Act** (1989), periodically modified, is a blanket device through which government may seek to prevent broadcasting of anything which it decides is 'not in the public interest'. This may actually mean 'not in the government's interest'.

In the 1980s there was the 'Arms for Iraq' affair in which it emerged through leaks that the British government was condoning secret arms sales to Iraq, which was then under an embargo from the West. The Act was initially one way of containing this information.

In relation to military matters in particular, the Act is invoked through a system now falling into disuse, known as the 'D Notice' system (a reference to one Colonel Danby during the Second World War). A 'D notice' is issued as, in effect, a threat to use this (draconian) act. In practice it has mostly been applied to the more independently minded press, rather than to television. In spite of the examples given below, I would argue that British television has always been more amenable to government wishes for secrecy than have the more persistent members of the press. In any case, there has been enough defiance of notices since about 1980 to cause recent governments to be careful of trying to throw their weight around through D notices.

The **Prevention of Terrorism Act** (1974) is mainly directed at control of information about and style of coverage of events in Northern Ireland. There is concern not to give encouragement to terrorism through documentaries or news. In general television producers have shared this concern, partly because evidence indicated that violence was sometimes staged for the benefit of the news cameras.

Some would argue that there has been too much control, voluntary or otherwise: that political views and issues uncomfortable to the British establishment have been suppressed. Many programmes about Northern Ireland have been modified or withdrawn.

An interesting and now rescinded (1995) modification of the act was when, for several years, the voices of Sinn Fein or IRA representatives could not be heard on television, for fear of giving encouragement to the Republican terrorist cause. After a while television producers began to use actors' voices as a way around this censorship.

Regulatory and advisory bodies

The **ITC** deals with **standards in advertising**. It works in conjunction with the contractors through the **Broadcaster Advertiser Clearance Centre**. It may disallow proposed adverts or ask for modifications. It is the ITC which maintains 'rules' such as the one that there may be no more than 7 minutes of advertisements in an hour (9 minutes for cable and satellite), or the ban on advertising by dating agencies. It allowed the 1986 government AIDS campaign to display condoms for the first time in the cause of safe sex (see also Chapter 4). It was the ITC which dealt with the 309 complaints about the use of *Viz* comic's characters the Fat Slags in an advertisement for Lucozade.

A specific **Control of Misleading Advertisements Act** (1988) is backed by the ITC codes of practice, which are mainly concerned that advertisements should not:

- be misleading
- encourage or condone harmful behaviours
- cause widespread or exceptional offence.

The ITC also deals with **programme regulation**. Its programme code mainly insists on the following:

- programmes should not include material which offends against good taste or decency, or which is likely to incite crime
- news must be accurate and impartial
- programmes dealing with controversial subject matter must be impartial and fair
- religious programmes must not misrepresent religous beliefs
- there must be no intrusion into privacy unless it serves the public interest
- commercial products or services must not be promoted within a programme
- technical devices may not be used to convey messages that the viewers may not be aware of (subliminal advertising).

The ITC Cable and Satellite Division regulates programmes in the same way.

The **Broadcasting Standards Council** became a statutory body under the 1990 Broadcasting Act. It is unusual in that it is the only relevant body to have been set up by government outside a media industry. The Council does not have the power to veto material. It is in principle an independent public body. But, typically within British political life, it is in fact a kind of quango, shaped by the power of political appointment. Therefore its pronouncements are listened to by television executives because it is listened to by politicians.

The Council's role is to 'consider' violence, sexual conduct and matters of taste and decency in broadcast material of all kinds. It examines complaints, and it publishes its findings in a monthly bulletin. The Council can order broadcasters at their own expense to publish findings either on air or in the press. The Council may make reports to the government on aspects of programmes falling within its remit. For example, in 1992 such a report caused the government to take action to ensure that a satellite porn channel, Red Hot Dutch, could not be accessed in Britain.

The **Independent Television Commission** is a public body set up by government (half the governors are appointed by the home secretary) in effect to regulate commercial television. It awards the contracts for broadcasting. If companies do not meet 'standards' such as a proportion of community and regional broadcasting for the contracting area, then these contracts are not automatically renewable. In the south of Britain, Southern television lost its contract in the last round: Meridian won the business.

The ITC also monitors advertisements through a vetting committee which has to see every advert (or script/proposal) to be put out on national network. The ITC discusses the main features of schedules a couple of times a year with the main producer/contractors such as Granada and Carlton. It has the power to disagree with proposals. The ITC requires that it be informed about potentially 'controversial' material. It may make rulings about such material, and expects the given company to respond to such 'advice'.

Although the transmission system has been privatized out of the hands of the ITC, it still has the power to veto transmission in the unlikely event of a contractor defying its wishes regarding some aspect of a programme. So the ITC is an important moderating influence on the commercial sector. It is a 'censor as regulator'.

Self-regulation, institutions and codes of practice

Editorial control is the most direct form of self-regulation. In this area the word censorship seems least appropriate, though it is true that heads of programme divisions can make decisions that others would describe as censorious. What is in operation here is a distillation of **institutional values**. The BBC in particular has always prided itself on its system of 'referral upwards' – if in doubt ask the next person up the line. It should be remembered that where politicians do put on indirect pressure to modify programmes, it is the senior producers who end up at the receiving end, perhaps acting as censors for those other interested parties.

Codes of practice are internal documents produced by the BBC and the ITC which refer to standards, content and treatment of programmes in terms of audience (children), of material (sexuality and violence), of values (balance and impartiality), and within programme areas such as documentary.

What should be remembered is that such self regulation is not as voluntary as it seems. The codes of practice are grounded in the terms of the Broadcasting Acts which allow television in Britain. They are steered by political debate and opinions offered by ministers, who have shown themselves willing and able to interfere in the affairs of television. Similarly, the nature of editorial control comes from these same influences – from both a legal framework and cultural influences that emanate from centres of power in Britain's social system. So television is shaped by the kinds of people who become MPs and the kinds of people who get top media jobs. On the shop floor of television this comes down to the probability (in terms of self-censorship) that journalists or producers, for example, are not going to put up material or views that they know won't get past their senior staff.

The ITC codes of practice cover the following areas (among many): language, sex, violence, exorcism, disabilities, privacy, impartiality, conduct of interviews, party political broadcasts, terrorism, crime, the Official Secrets Act, charities, religion. With relation to violence in particular, there are four interesting assumptions:

1 that material may offend against good taste or decency
2 that some violence may be psychologically disturbing, especially for the young
3 that violence portrayed may be imitated in real life
4 that recurrent violence may create the impression of 'approval', and may cause people to become 'indifferent' to it.

These assumptions were discussed and questioned in Chapter 9. The code suggests that when considering whether violence is necessary or integral to a programme, producers must also consider:

● the accumulative effects across a number of programmes
● that violence for 'good ends' may be no less harmful than any other kind
● that sanitized or innocuous violence is not necessarily harmless
● that costume violence in a historical context is still violence

- whether the violence is actually gratuitous
- that ingenious methods of inflicting pain or injury are not acceptable
- that 'real' violence in news or current affairs must also be justified
- that depictions of suicide must be handled with great care.

Scheduling also represents a kind of censorship: 'adult' material is only shown after 9.00 p.m. and 18-rated films are held back until even later. Even subscription channels follow guidelines which keep back 18-rated films until after 10.00 p.m.

Indirect influences

Public relations and media management by various interest groups, including environmental groups such as Friends of the Earth, can exert some pressure on television editorial choices. Their possession of information of interest to television, their control of the interface (press conferences), is nothing like censorship as such. But it is something which shapes decisions by producers. For example, environmental groups have become quite good at providing news producers with effective video coverage of protest events, hoping to get such events on the news agenda. Or again, given the value placed on balance in the presentation of issues, producers are still reluctant to cover topics without representatives of more than one point of view. It has been known for organizations to attempt a spoiling operation by refusing to appear or to comment, so that an item will seem wrongly one-sided and will be dropped.

Commercial PR pressures represent a shady area of indirect influence. There may be not direct interference, but it is difficult to believe that sponsorship and co-production deals have no effect on the content and treatment of programmes. Visible product placement is only legal in movies, but the power of the big advertisers must go further. Television companies are not going to produce programmes which will upset them. It has been argued that SKY Television's control of premier-league football screening or of main rugby events is also a kind of censorship in that it denies screen access to these events to many people unless terrestrial channels are willing to pay the price of screen rights.

Government certainly exerts an indirect influence on television. This is discussed at greater length in a separate section below (p. 254). But the power of government to enact legislation, to shape the commercial/financial climate and to interfere politically through contacts and personal influence, all adds up to a considerable pressure on those running television. In the late 1980s the then government let it be known that the BBC had to put its financial house in order if it wanted to go on collecting its licence fee. Swingeing changes followed which resulted in the loss of jobs and the casualization of much of the production workforce. It is impossible to say whether such pressures also led to innovations such as the 24-hour BBC satellite news channel. But it is the new management dating from that period which has led the BBC down a much more commercial road.

> In what respects may constraints on television be both necessary and desirable?

Social norms and dominant ideologies

Censorship in television (or attempts at it) may stem from the interests of certain groups. It may come from the anxieties of politicians and governments. But most of all, it has its origins in the dominant ideology, and in what are perceived to be social norms by those who have the power to control and influence broadcasting.

Consider, for example, the withdrawal of an anti-foxhunting commercial which featured a parody of an upper-class hunter with sado-masochistic undertones; or ex-prime minister Harold Wilson's attempts to suppress material to be shown in the biographical documentary series, *Yesterday's Men* (BBC1, 1972), which he felt reflected adversely on his image. Even after the BBC finally deleted a segment in which he was asked directly about the earnings from his memoirs, still he was threatening legal action. One could also refer to the Thatcher government's management of news in the 1983 Falklands War (see below, p. 248).

The influence of dominant ideology is also evident in the perpetual debate about taste and quality in television, and in the cutting of violent elements from US films screened on British television. BBC1 and ITV1 both cut films as a matter of course, though this fact and the nature of the cutting is hardly publicized. Generally speaking, it is American films and violent scenes that include shots of woundings or suffering which are either excised or made more brief. Specific films such as *Straw Dogs* were kept from television for 20 years before being released in a cut version. Films on Channel 4 or on satellite tend not to be so cut, on the self-regulating grounds that these channels are for specialist or minority interests. The main argument for cutting films which have already been censored has to do with medium and audience. The cinema audience is already controlled (at least in theory!) by the ratings system which keeps children out of 15 and 18 films. The television audience is hard to regulate in this way, for all the 9.00 p.m. watershed. Programmers know that young people do watch after this time, so it is felt that different rules must apply. One might argue that it is the responsibility of parents, not of 'authority', to regulate children's viewing. But in any case, if it is assumed that films being watched at 10.00 and 11.00 at night do have the same adult audience which may watch the films uncut in the cinema, then there is no argument for cutting films on television.

It is in this area of television censorship that one has perhaps the strongest example of the paternalism that is one part of television culture. This is supposed to be a dominant characteristic of 'Auntie BBC' – the Reithian inheritance of giving the people what 'we' think is good for them. But I would argue that it is a cultural thing which is also strong in the commercial/ITC nexus, and indeed in political life. It is something about the 'ruling class' knowing better than 'the people', and therefore justifying the nature and the fact of their rule. Indeed the same assumptions apply to other obvious areas of censorship: sexuality and bad language. *Last Tango in Paris* was screened on late television 15 years after its cinema release, but scenes of full-frontal nudity and buggery were cut.

The conflict in Northen Ireland has always been a problem for television news and documentary coverage, given government sensitivities. There is a long list of programmes which have had material taken out, or have simply been banned. Although it has all the attributes of a war, this conflict has been represented as being about civil unrest and crime and terrorism and therefore not being able to be 'managed' like a war. But government attitudes are revealed in the comments of a former director general of the BBC, Charles Hill (1974). These comments also undermine the myth of impartiality in television news: 'as between the British Army and the gunmen, the BBC is not and cannot be impartial'. The Prevention of Terrorism Act has been liberally applied to censor material. *World in Action* had programmes banned by the IBA in 1971 for wanting to show people from the IRA and Sinn Fein. Things were no different in 1979 when BBC governors banned screening of a BBC *Panorama* programme because it showed members of the IRA. In 1980 the police seized film shot by *Panorama*, showing the IRA out on patrol. In 1986 journalists actually went on strike because they were so incensed that the BBC had banned a *Real Lives* programme about Protestant and Republican extremists in Northern Ireland, under pressure from the government. The PTA was used in 1991 against C4 *Dispatches* because it alleged evidence of an alliance of powerful people conspiring to assassinate Republicans. The IBA (1988) even banned from commercial television the use of a song by the Pogues, which referred to the Birmingham Six and Guildford Four. Ironically, the convictions of these men for pub bombings have since been declared unsafe and they have been released. Ed Moloney (1991) refers to a conversation with a BBC producer which reveals the pressure of indirect censorship: 'the tendency might be to avoid programmes on Northern Ireland, especially controversial ones'.

At the same time, one must not fall into the trap of representing censorship (as I have framed it) as always being about self-interested and unwarranted interference in what is otherwise a fair and open system of broadcasting.

I have already pointed out that the system is, as it were, censored from the beginning. But one must also recognize that broadcasters do try to represent norms and values which are held by a wide range of viewers. The difficulty here – the stimulus for flying a word like censorship – is that it is difficult to find coherent values in a society which is increasingly fragmented. The coherence of beliefs, even of class divisions, of religion, of ethnicity, which existed in the 1950s no longer pertains. There are even divisions within the new sub-cultures of early twenty-first century Britain – among Muslims, for example. The almost inevitable failure of at least some programmes to recognize differing interests and values will lead to dissatisfaction and accusations that views have been censored. This is not to excuse television and the way that it is run. If there were editorializing, if 'biased' documentaries were 'allowed', if the full range of minority interests were represented in programming, then it would remove some of the legitimate complaints about the present situation. If there isn't a consensus in society, television should not pretend that there is. As a medium, it was not established with the remit of trying to create that consensus.

CHANGING ASSUMPTIONS

In all this talk about what is not allowed on television, one loses sight of signs of changing times, even of television taking risks. Some television programmes have provoked political and social debate, in effect about the fact that they were not censored. For example, the drama *Oranges Are Not the Only Fruit* was broadcast on BBC2 in 1990, based on Jeannette Winterson's novel and adapted by her. It criticized Protestant religious fundamentalism, and its story of these influences on a young girl was further layered by her lesbian awakening in a scene with another young girl. A willingness to portray lesbian sexuality can also be seen in the context of lesbian sub-plots during the mid-1990s in two soaps – *EastEnders* and *Brookside*. Ten years earlier it is probable that these themes would have been censored, such is the dynamic relationship between television and society in which television both follows and leads. *Oranges* was also interesting, as Hilary Hinds points out (in *Turning It On*, 1996) because it was contextualized as an 'art' drama within a television play slot which had established itself as potentially controversial. These two factors provided a context which allowed it to push the boundaries.

Sometimes censorship is resisted with some success. In 1968 the writer Johnny Speight responded to censorious pressures from the BBC governors (cuts forced on the scripts) by refusing to write any more episodes for *Till Death Us Do Part*: 'I would write another series for the BBC but only if this censorship was stopped'. This comedy programme was famous for its lead character Alf Garnett, a pastiche of a self-opinionated ordinary man who was both racist and sexist. The character's outrageous remarks either confirmed or exposed prejudices, according to where you were coming from. The series was the object of criticism from the then notorious Mrs Whitehouse and her media-active Viewers and Listeners Association. She objected to the use of swear words. The VLA, which had only a few hundred members, proposed some censorship of television on the grounds that some programmes were too 'liberal' and were offensive. Alf Garnett burnt a copy of her book in one episode of *TDUDP*.

Sometimes television itself fought against censorship. *World in Action* was frequently defended by Granada. For example, in 1980 British Steel won an injunction against the producers to prevent them naming a 'mole' who had leaked documents to the programme which exposed questionable practices in the company. Granada defied British Steel through various stages of legal appeal. In the end BS gave up, though they won their case in law.

Of course, there are plenty of examples of successful censorship, including of *WIA* programmes, which still say a great deal about cultural and political sensitivities. A 1950s *WIA* programme raising questions about defence spending was suppressed by the ITA. In the same decade the ITA also banned a programme that was felt to be critical of the monarchy. Neither programme was going to be particularly intrusive, and they would not have been banned today. In 1964 *WIA* was again banned by the ITA from showing a programme which revealed how poor were the training facilities for British athletes preparing to take part in the Olympic Games. Altogether, there is a strong sense of authorities, of an establishment, of politicians who simply don't like being criticized or exposed through television. *The War Game*, a docudrama which exposed the complacent unpreparedness of the British authorities for a nuclear strike, was banned by the BBC governors in 1965.

Documentaries can be uncomfortable because of the facts they may reveal. Drama can be disturbing for the ideas it may generate and perhaps its implicit questioning of what we do censor and why.

Dennis Potter's play *Brimstone and Treacle* was so contentious in its depiction of the devil's impact on a family and their disturbed daughter (including implied sexual relations) that it was simply banned (1976) even though Kenneth Trodd had completed production. The combination of sexuality and quasi-blasphemy was thought to be too disturbing. It was eventually shown in 1987. In the case of Roy Minton's *Scum* (1977) it was the harshness of life in a borstal that caused a ban. This drama was reworked as a feature film in 1979, but was only shown on television in 1991. The realistic documentary-style exposure of uncomfortable underlying truths caused this play to be pulled. Potter's drama was the opposite in style – mythical, allegorical, unnaturalistic – but still uncomfortable in what it said about attitudes towards disability and sexuality, for example.

Just as contentious in a political sense was the 1975 screening on BBC1 of a four-part drama called *Days of Hope*. This was set in the period 1916–26 and took a critical stance on British conduct of the First World War, the class system and the situation of the working class. Myths about heroism and fair play were attacked. Even at this time, 30 years after the end of the Second World War, there were many who felt uncomfortable with this unashamedly partisan view of oppression and injustice in the British social system. Some comment in the Press and even in Parliament took the position that the play should have been censored in some way because it was 'biased'. The editor of the rightwing *Daily Telegraph*, William Deedes, proposed in a televised discussion that the programmes should not have been shown because they confused art and history (referring to naturalistic treatment and the way that the story was embedded in fact). Such extraordinary comments showed what a sensitive cultural nerve television material of this kind can pluck. The series jarred middle-class sensibilities because it showed both the harshness of working-class life and the intelligence and political awareness of working-class people. The writer, Jim Allen, and the director, Ken Loach, have always created material with a pro-working class, leftwing perspective. Some of their other work on television has also aroused controversy. In particular, Allen has spanned the living social and economic history of those working on the Liverpool docks with *The Big Flame* (BBC1, 1969) through to *Dockers* (BBC1, 1999).

Such controversy and the associated trumpetings about the need for 'greater control' of television output only serve to expose the relatively conservative environment of the medium, and how illusions about impartiality extend beyond factual programming. What some people want to censor and why reflects on British culture and values. Equally, the fact that such 'controversial' programmes appear at all also suggests the capacity of television to challenge the status quo.

The case of *Death of a Princess* (1980) was more overtly political, stemming from the story of an Arab princess who was beheaded for having an illicit love affair. The story reflected real events in the Saudi royal family 3 years before. Pressure was put on the British government to have the programme pulled before screening. The press found out and there was debate over what should happen. The government did put pressure on ATV, who nevertheless insisted on broadcasting the drama.

There was a similar *furore* when the government tried to pressure Thames into pulling a documentary about the shooting by government agents in Gibraltar of IRA suspects who turned out to be unarmed (*Death on the Rock*, 1989). The programme questioned the government's version of events and provided contrary evidence. Prime Minister Thatcher rejected the results of an independent inquiry which cleared Thames of inaccuracy or bias. Such clear examples of political interference, seeking a kind of censorship, reflect the uneasy relationship between television and government. There is a conflict between the need to screen in pursuit of audiences and pressure to contain information to protect politicians.

Attempts to censor material or the work of institutions have even more serious implications for democracy and freedom of speech when they involve documentary and news. This is analogous to concerns about bias in these programme areas coming from within the institutions themselves. The sections below provide two case studies in times of war. But other examples illustrate various attempts to muzzle television and its perceived power in the socio-political process.

In 1986 the Tory government took exception to BBC news coverage of the American bombing of Libya from British bases. The Chairman of the Conservative Party, Norman Tebbit, actually produced a 'report' accusing the BBC of presenting Libyan propaganda, and made scarcely veiled threats about the BBC's position with regard to the setting of the licence fee. The intensity of pressure developed from this sort of political behaviour (the interference of the rightwing establishment), led to the resignation of the director general of the BBC (Alasdair Milne) a year later.

In this same year, 1987, police raided BBC Glasgow offices at the instigation of the government because they objected to a programme in an investigative series called *Secret Society*. The programme was about building and using a military satellite in Project Zircon. Details of the satellite had not been disclosed to the relevant parliamentary committee for debate, though they should have been according to rules about cost and accountability. No one involved in making the programme was charged or arrested under the Official Secrets Act (and the information concerned was freely available in America), yet the programme was censored, and did not appear for 2 years. This was a particularly high-handed example of rightwing government behaviour – deceiving its own parliament, censoring information that was in the public domain and not being put to the test in the process of law which it had invoked.

In 1988 the defence secretary put pressure on the BBC over its drama *Tumbledown*, which suggested degrees of incompetence in the handling of some aspects of the Falklands War. In the event, 2 minutes of the original film were cut. This is censorship by stealth.

> What are the arguments for saying that 'censorship' of television programmes has become either more liberal or more conservative?

CASE STUDIES: THE FALKLANDS AND GULF WARS

Both these campaigns involved British forces fighting in other parts of the world. Degrees of censorship, indeed of propaganda, in wartime are almost to be taken for granted. The politicians and the military defend them on grounds of tactical security, of not giving anything away to the enemy. However, both these wars still raised questions about who was censoring what and why. There were questions about why we got into such wars in the first place, and then about how we conducted them. There were and are questions about why access to information was controlled, and sometimes denied, when that information had no bearing on the tactical conduct of the wars. If the information had something to do with the success of the war (from the British point of view) then the further question was whether debate about fighting the war should have been conducted or, as it was, suppressed in the cause of maintaining public solidarity.

All these questions themselves relate to a cultural shift in which there may no longer be automatic public support for any war that British governments choose to engage in. People are more accustomed to wanting reasons and justifications for major public policy decisions than they were in the mid-twentieth century. With all its limitations, television especially has been an arena of public debate about major issues.

The two wars also happened in the context of fast modern technology which was perfectly capable, given the chance, of bringing back reports for television very quickly. It wasn't allowed to in the case of the Falklands, and was heavily controlled in the case of the Gulf. Behind decisions about controlling television access was a misplaced but deeply rooted conviction among the military and some politicians that television had lost America the Vietnam War. It is interesting how often television seems to be made the scapegoat for 'problems' which actually have other causes. It is blamed for encouraging violence, for cultural dumbing down, for creating a permissive social climate, for undermining family life, for making children stupid. Is it only a matter of time until television will be blamed for natural disasters such as droughts and hurricanes?

The Falklands War, 1983

In the first place it has to be said that the media in general were very responsive to the idea of **news management** in the cause of military security. Indeed some have argued that many of the press showed a distinct lack of backbone in acquiescing to the degree of media management that did go on. Leonard Downie in the *Washington Post* is quoted by John Eldridge 1995, p. 20, asserting that few British newsmen actually tried to pressure government sources for information, and that it was actually the Americans who broke the story about the contentious sinking of the ageing Argentinian battlecruiser, *General Belgrano*. This incident involved huge loss of life (nearly one third of all casualties) from a ship that was not in the war zone at the time and was heading for its home port. But discussion of the affair was effectively suppressed until after the war. Eldridge also documents evidence that attempts by correspondents such as Michael Cockrell to take a more detached, questioning view of what was going on invoked suppression and anger on the part of the government. One rightwing MP accused Cockrell in Parliament of having 'dishonoured the right to freedom of speech in this country'. The BBC became a whipping post for the rightwing government, while the supposedly more amenable ITN commercial news was regarded favourably. It is perhaps relevant that in 1985 a civil servant who leaked information to the media that a government minister had deceived Parliament over the background to the decision to sink the *Belgrano* was prosecuted by that government – and acquitted. Television news concentrated on 'survivors' of the sinking, when the rest of the world was talking about the deaths. The words of one correspondent (Brian Barron) when describing the sinking – 'the tragic incident of the *Belgrano*' – were deleted by BBC editors.

It is known that non-sensitive news copy was changed or simply not sent. In particular there was concern that television coverage might move public opinion against the war if it showed the extent of British losses or instigated debate about what was being done, how and with what success. According to Robert Harris (1983) when Michael Nicholson of ITN wanted to report on the sinking of HMS *Sheffield* he was asked by a military 'information' attaché, 'Didn't you realise that you were with us to do a 1940 propaganda job?'

One should not lose sight of the fact that there was a lot of (perhaps unconscious) collusion of television news people with the view that this was a 'just war', that the British were miltarily and technically superior, that the war had to be won. Interviews, for example, were totally dominated by 'miltary experts'. Diplomats hardly got a look in, least of all around the *Belgrano* sinking, when the president of Peru was trying to broker a peaceful solution to the conflict. The BBC showed footage of an obviously wounded British soldier on a stretcher once at 9.00 – then it was edited out. News and Current Affairs editorial meetings shaped a view of the war as much as did miltary censorship. Dissident comments by relatives of the dead and wounded, questioning the need for the war, were given no space. They did emerge sometimes in local newspapers.

It has been suggested by Philo (1990) and others that another factor which shaped the behaviour of journalists was the pressure of the lobby system, which in effect gives some of them privileged access to political briefings – a privilege that will be withdrawn if those journalists filed reports upsetting to the Whips who arrange the private briefings.

No television film of fighting in the Falklands was seen until the war was over. The British authorities claimed that it was technically impossible to get television pictures back quickly. This was a pointless lie. They had access to military satellite channels and could have asked for access to American channels. The absence of television footage was censorship at source, a deliberate part of the propaganda campaign. It is symbolically significant of the propaganda view of the the war that television resorted to using drawings of action which looked very like frames from a gung-ho war comic.

In the same way, the authorities limited the number of journalists allowed to cover the war. They created a pool of journalists who could be managed and directed away from what they didn't want them to see. They actually fed some lies to the correspondents – disinformation to confuse the enemy, it was later said. Information was fed through 'officials' anyway. If correspondents themselves used the word censorship their material never got out. If they weren't thought to be toeing the official patriotic victory line then not only would material (e.g. voice pieces) be suppressed, but also they would be threatened with withdrawal from the pool. Even the correspondents seem to have been caught up in the web of censorship. Evidence that the RAF hadn't bombed out an enemy runway when they said they had appeared on television and then disappeared again. It didn't fit the mythology. Even more crass was the attempt to assert that film of a shot-down Harrier jet in fact depicted an Argentinian plane.

The accumulated evidence of critical studies of this war makes depressing reading in terms of democratic media models. The Thatcher government was authoritarian by inclination. It was right to be concerned about public reaction, in that opinion polls at the very beginning of the conflict suggested that a majority of Britons did not understand the reasons for the conflict and were not keen to go to war thousands of miles away.

The Gulf War, 1991

In this section the author acknowledges a debt to the works of Kellner (1991) and of Taylor (1992) on news coverage of this war. Some of this material also appears in a different form in another book by the author (Burton 1999).

The Gulf War took place between a consortium of Western forces (the Allies) endorsed by the United Nations Security Council and the forces of Iraq led by Saddam Hussein. As a news event, this war is distinctive in a number of ways. It raises issues about the handling of news and its effects on the audience. It illustrates censorship of television as management at source in a much more sophisticated way than in the case of the Falklands.

A television war

People's perception of news is dominated by the medium of television, as is well attested by surveys of where the public believes it receives its news from. But, as Kellner (1991) puts it, the Gulf War was 'the first war played out on television with the whole world watching it unfold'. It was presented as a **high-tech war**, not least because the toys for boys magic of technology is dug into the discourse of both the military and the television makers. Military publicity managers encouraged presentation of the conflict in terms of 'surgically precise' Western technology dealing cleanly with a world political health problem. Footage from video cameras in the front of aircraft and smart bombs, with (false) accounts from the military of the effectiveness of air strikes, encouraged this view, as well as giving a sense of actuality and truthfulness to accounts of what was going on. This footage was made available to television, where access to the actual theatre of war was often denied. Lies were told about bombing efficiency; after the war it emerged that 70 per cent of bombs missed their targets. Iraqi Scud missile sites were supposed to have been wiped out – then more missiles were fired.

Consistent with this technophilia was the presentation of the conflict as a **clean and bloodless war**. The military were persistent in promoting a view of a clean, effective operation, and many journalists did not ask searching questions about the inconsistencies between what they were told and what they found out. We saw this same phenomenon in Kosovo (1999), but in this case the illusion broke down when television was tougher minded and able to get to sites where technological errors had resulted in deaths on the 'wrong side'. Interestingly, television news nevertheless broadly concurred with the NATO line of these incidents being regrettable errors. The relative lack of censorship resulted in neither a media campaign against the war nor any public outcry other than the objections which already existed against the war in principle. In the case of the Gulf the Americans were particularly keen to promote the 'bloodless' impression because of concern about the effect on public opinion of too many body bags arriving back in the United States. Indeed the American media were barred from entering the base where casualties were flown in. Allied casualties were relatively light, but certainly not as few as the military news managers suggested. Accidental deaths were generally not reported.

It may be argued that as a medium television creates a kind of distance from its subject matter. What is seen is known to be far away and is reduced to the size of the screen. This impression was be compounded in the case of Gulf War coverage by all the detached aerial shots and the lack of real ground-fighting footage. It took a stunning photojournalist's shot of an Iraqi incinerated inside his truck on the road to Basra to bring home the horror of conflict.

It has been argued that this was a **virtual reality war** in which reality became what television news said it was. Pierre Bourdieu (1998) notoriously commented on the war in postmodernist terms which saw form as supplanting substance. He argued that it was no longer possible to see some kind of reality and truth 'out there' as existing distinct from what the media presented. For the audience, media reporting of the Gulf War was the truth. Media reality is inextricably part of social reality. One may say that censorship has the objective of redefining reality in the interests of those in control.

Television coverage of the Gulf War was tribute to the value placed on **picture power**. This was a news drama that dominated screens because there were so many pictures – though little of the actual fighting itself. John Berger in the *Observer* (20 Jan. 1991) remarked that 'the medium's pathological need for moving pictures delivered it into the hands of those who control access'. Journalists would do anything to get their hands on video footage, however selective this might be, and however the facts around that footage might have been concealed.

This was a news war in which notably one heard a lot of **warspeak** – a corruption of language which served to conceal cruelty and suffering, and launched understanding of the event into a kind of reality hyperspace. The bombing of targets was described as the 'suppressing of assets' by the military. Few commentators tried to deconstruct this language and its intentions, let alone its effects. The very title of the operation – Desert Storm – sought to reposition it as a natural (and therefore acceptable) event. Questions about the motives behind and need for the war were in effect made invisible. The war was personalized in terms of justice dealing with the 'butcher of Baghdad'. Economic determinations – fighting to keep Western oil supplies available and regulated – were suppressed.

Satellite newsgathering

This dominated news reporting, especially from those journalists who sought out information independently from press briefings. Significantly, American journalists were not allowed satellite dishes while the British were. The Americans experienced the kind of 'censorship at source' seen in the Falklands. So new technology was important, but only to the extent that it was allowed to be used.

The role of CNN

This 24-hour world news service, and its reporter Peter Arnett, had a unique position in news reporting. They had a base in the Iraqi capital, Baghdad. They had a landline link to Jordan (ironically, running through military protected tunnels) as part of an earlier deal done with the government. The

Iraqis saw the advantage in letting pictures of the war 'behind the lines' (especially pictures of destruction to civilians) out into the world. They tried their own version of news management, but it is also true to say that there was a degree of independence of news reporting. Certainly it is unusual to see a war reported other than from 'our side'. An irony of the situation was that reports taken from CNN were identified as subject to Iraqi censorship. The same was not true for reports 'from the Allied side', for which a pat phrase was 'details have been omitted for operational reasons'. Our side could not be seen to be operating censorship even though they were.

Allied news management

The Allied forces sought to control the movements of journalists and to shape the news that was reported. Only 200 out of 1500 journalists were allowed into what was called the news pool. These people had controlled access to battlefields and were given press briefings by the Allied high command. They were also given video footage. Evidence of disinformation or even lies increased as the war went on. But the majority of journalists reported the military line: they wanted to retain access to sources of information. And then there are the workings of ideology: those who might question the dominant military view of the war would be identified as unpatriotic. However, there were sharp examples of how this might place journalists in conflict with their requirement to tell the truth and to be impartial. One incident involved the mistaken bombing of a baby-food factory. 'Our side' insisted that it was really a chemical weapons factory. There was every evidence – from the cameras at the site, from the Western builders of the factory – that it was not. CNN were sharply criticized by the US government for telling the truth. A more emotive incident was when a missile blew up a bunker in which Iraqi civilians were sheltering. The official view insisted to the bitter end that the bunker was really a military command post. Jeremy Bowen and BBC television news spoke clearly for all the evidence that it was not a military target, that it had been a terrible mistake (which of course the Iraqis exploited on television). It was interesting that ITN fudged the issue in their reporting, saying that Iraqi censorship made it impossible to determine the truth. We are talking here about news management by powerful interests, about the working of ideology in action, and about issues of bias and impartiality in news reporting. There are points at which distinctions between 'news management' and censorship become merely academic.

Binary oppositions

It is no surprise to find the Gulf War being presented in terms of oppositions. News presentation constructs its narrative and its drama in terms of conflict and opposing points of view. Kellner (1991) describes news coverage as setting up a 'dichotomy between irrational Iraqis and a rational West'. One can see something of the discourse of orientalism here – a way of looking at and giving meaning to those who live 'in the East'. There was a clear view of the just versus the unjust, the moral versus the immoral. The nominated and demonized Saddam Hussein was clearly set up as the villain of the piece, opposed to the exnominated Allied leaders. General Norman Schwarzkopf might have been celebrated as Stormin' Norman via his gung-ho briefing appearances, but reporting made it clear that he was just the commander doing a good policing job for 'us'.

Censorship does not of itself create such a structure of understanding and of presentation about the war. But it does create the conditions and provide the selected material which contributes to this bias. The discourse has some of its roots in the handling of press conferences and in the material released by the military.

Issues and contradictions

News coverage and news management by the military also raise some fundamental issues about the functions of news and the exercise of power. In the Gulf War the doctrine of 'the public's right to know' came up against a political concept of 'only what the public needs to know'. Freedom of speech came up against the possible threat that freedom posed to the working of the state (and by extension, its armies). Censorship by definition works against freedom of information and of ideas. The news doctrine of impartiality was contradicted by a sense of patriotic duty to support 'our boys'. The notion of the social responsibility of the media goes out of the window when it declines to question the reasons for and conduct of a war (which has nothing to do with giving away strategic secrets). So the question of censorship, not only in the Gulf War, must refer to both doubts about the use of power by censors and to doubts about the integrity of those who accede to that power.

RELATIONSHIP BETWEEN GOVERNMENT AND TELEVISION

Comments under censorship and constraints above (p. 241), and in Chapter 3 on institutions, have already addressed the power relationship of government with the television industry. What follows will be partly in summary form.

Censorship is one manifestation of the exercise of power. It is clear that there is a dynamic tension between the interests of government and of television. Both of them in their different ways claim to speak for the people – sometimes when they are really speaking in their own interests. Government has material power in that it can mobilize the law, financial mechanisms or even the police in its interests. Television has cultural power in that it can mobilize images and their impact. It has the communicative power of access to the population in their homes. It can gather and edit information about the world. It is this communicative and cultural power which government sometimes envies, uses and censors.

Points of contact

The interface between television and government may be summarised as follows :

- **The law** – which controls the terms under which television operates, and which may be used to change or suppress broadcast material.
- **Party political broadcasts** – which can themselves not be censored, though in theory the ITC could object to aspects of treatment. These broadcasts are a right for the government and for the opposition. The rights of smaller parties and the airtime made available to them are supposed to be negotiated between officials, but in practice allocation is an unregulated fudge in which government gets its way.
- **Finance** – in terms of: Parliament's hold over the BBC in setting the licence fee; the government-established ITC's control over the awarding of contracts for commercial television; government's creation of an arbitrary tax called the levy designed, on a sliding scale of company profits and reach into the audience, to cream off what were perceived to be excessive profits.
- **Patronage** – the fact that government appoints governors of the BBC and ITC. In particular the manner of appointment of the managerialist John Birt in 1989 to 'reform' the BBC went against previous custom and practice. He was clearly 'the government's man'. (This is not to comment on the necessity for or efficacy of his reform of the BBC.)
- **Intervention** – there are a few rights reserved to the government regarding broadcasting, the most interesting of which is the right of the home secretary to insist on access to airtime. Most intervention takes the form of contact on an unofficial basis, perhaps involving telephone calls and memos which only emerge in cases of leaks and scandals.
- **Advertisements** – the government is always in the top ten of advertisers on television, ranked by expenditure.
- **Press conferences and press releases** – are a major source of information from government departments for television journalists. Spin doctors are expert at timing these so that they grab the next news bulletin. They have also used devices such as staged leaks of information.
- **Lobby briefing** – this arcane system of passing on information to selected journalists by the chief Whips of what are perceived to be the two main

parties is yet another manifestation of the 'old boy network'. It is censorious and unjust. It will remain until correspondents have the courage to boycott it *en masse*.

- **Television appearances** – by politicians are a crucial way of getting across to the populace their party's political views and of airing those 'attractive' personalities who will reflect well on their party. The politics of personality through the media is perhaps the most significant feature of political life and power at the begining of the twenty-first century. Camera opportunities and sound bites are constructed by parties as bait to attract television time. What is not said or shown becomes even more significant in the political process.

Consequences

These aspects of the interface between government and television do not always demonstrate that censorship has taken place. Nor should it be suggested that government should have no powers of regulation. But one should recognize that the censorship of television is not just about the overt use of political control mechanisms. If there are kinds of covert control and influence then these exist in at least three arenas – government, commerce and the institutions of television itself. All three in various ways for various reasons have disallowed programmes and perspectives which the audience might have wished to see and hear. Furthermore, all three exist in a state of internal tension between freedom and control.

Freedom of expression, free market, free democracy are all phrases that may be used. But in fact commercial interests don't want a free market; they want one which they can control and profit from. Government doesn't want citizens and the media to have the freedom to know all about what it gets up to. And the people who run television only want freedom of expression so long as it is *their* freedom.

The various examples above of censorship, pressure, exertion of power – whatever you want to call it – are illustrations of the tension between freedom and control, and of kinds of self-interest. The process of making, distributing and viewing television programmes is interesting because it can expose those tensions and inconsistencies. The scope of public access to ideas through television is such that censorship is inevitable at some point. Such access may sometimes threaten the security of the three power players. All three justify such interference by pretending to speak for 'the public'. But the public, the audience, is the one part of the equation which is in reality ignored. They aren't asked to debate or vote for kinds of programme, kinds of access, kinds of changes to programmes. Even at the level of the listeners' and viewers' committees set up by the BBC and ITC, the members are chosen, not elected.

They do not represent the kind of statistically valid cross-section of the population that market researchers might seek out.

At the bottom of 'the problem' is that fact that most people would not wish anyone to be able to make any kind of programme they liked, which anyone at all could receive at any time. One then faces the question of whose interests should prevail, and of who determines whose interests should prevail. Since it is the audience which is supposed (by any kind of censor) to be 'affected' by a programme, it seems reasonable that the audience should be able to decide what its interests are. Examples of television censorship in Britain too often seem to be motivated by the question, What should we allow? A better question might be, Why should we deny?

> In what ways do the interests of television and government coincide, and in what ways are they incompatible?

11

Television History

PREVIEW

This chapter deals with:

- what 'history' may be about
- media technology and change
- critical perspectives on developing media technology
- an overview of key features in the development of television
- a short history of television
- a brief account of key committee reviews and reports on television.

INTRODUCTION

Ideas about what 'history' is will vary according to the critical perspective of the historian. It can be 'read', for example, as being about the exercise of political power, or about processes of social change.

In effect, history is about information and interpretation. **Information** is evidence from primary sources and secondary sources, which can shift according to the object of study. In the case of television production, primary sources might be an interview with a television producer. In the case of televison institutions, it might be a copy of the 1991 Broadcasting Act. This is first-hand information. Secondary sources might be video recordings of programmes from which one infers things about production. **Interpretation** is the sense one makes of evidence, the theories that are constructed about the significance of the information.

Defining television history as an object in itself is difficult because one can look at different aspects of television (organizations as opposed to audiences, for instance). There are different critical positions (postmodernist views of a text such as *Twin Peaks*, say, as distinct from a gender critique of the same series). So there may be different ideas about what history is or should be.

Examples of books which take contrasting perspectives on television among other media are: Brian Winston, *Media, Technology and Society* (1998), which offers a great deal of fact about technology, with for example the proposition that ideas about social revolution through technology (the Internet) are false; James Curran and Jean Seaton, *Power Without Responsibility*, which offers evaluation of ideas about the power of the media in relation to government and audience.

Possible areas of interest in relation to television history are much the same as for other media. They also relate to major topics in this book, not surprisingly.

- The nature of and growth of the power of television (in media institutions), including management and control of the media
- the changing relationship of television with government
- the nature of technological developments as they affect other items in this list, including media products
- changes in television product and form, especially in relation to kinds of realism
- changes in the censorship of television
- changes in representations of social groups
- the relationship between social change and television product
- the expansion of media operations, also with relation to media genres.

Some of these topics in previous chapters have already been given a historical perspective. What follows in this chapter is:

- a brief perspective on developing media technology, including television
- a longer account of key periods in the development of television, bringing together technological, social and institutional change, with some key issues
- a revisiting of some areas such as drama.

MEDIA TECHNOLOGY AND CHANGE

Emergence of new technologies

The arrival of new media technology is neither a happy accident nor the work of lone inventors slaving away in attics. The dull truth is that generally it is military complexes and commercial laboratories that create new developments. Their creations are in the interests of governments and of corporations. An example is that of acetate audiotape recorders, first developed by the German military in the 1930s and then taken further for home-leisure use by various corporations in the USA and in Europe.

Videotape recording, innovated by the US Ampex corporation in the late 1950s, originally for studio use only, was a natural extension of this. So was the Japanese invention of the personal portable tape recorder in the late 1970s. This extension of use of a new technology, particularly for profit in the area of leisure, is typical of media industries.

On this level, the history of media technology is the history of media institutions and of their capitalist drive to expand markets. The effect of technological developments is to:

- **generate some new means of communication** which increases consumption (the video cassette recorder)
- **increase the range** of means of media communication (arrival of satellite channels, e.g. *Discovery*)
- **change the content** of existing media (cable links that allow a couple in their home to take part in a game show such as *Noel's House Party*)
- **change the form** of existing media (lightweight cameras bringing a new mode of realism into documentary, e.g. *Lakesiders*).

It can also be argued that media technology is a part of a **commodity culture** which permeates our society. Some of the technologies are commodities or goods in themselves. The media also are heavily indebted to income from the advertising of commodities. More than this, people become commodities – audience groups are bought and sold through marketing practices; people's stories in news material are bought and sold every day.

Characteristics and issues

Concentration of ownership in media institutions

The notion of ownership includes ownership and control of technology. Innovations cost money, and it is rich media institutions that have the resources to develop and use technology. In this sense there is a relationship between cost/resources and power. If this technology is seen in the context of the kinds of change described above, then it may be argued that technology enhances the power of institutions over the production of ideas which are assimilated by the audience.

Multiplication of types of media

This multiplication extends the reach of institutions into society and into social groups. In turn, this makes possible a reinforcement of effects (whatever it is argued these effects are). The release of a film in cinema, on broadcast television, on satellite television, on videotape and now on DVD discs is an example of multiplication and potential reinforcement of ideas. What is not clear is that more media means more choice – the pluralist argument in support of the media set-up as it is. It can just as easily be argued that developments mean more of the same.

Globalization

Technology has extended communication across the planet. It has extended the reach of media owners. It has extended the ability of people in wealthy societies to talk across the planet. Equally it has excluded poorer nations from this privilege. This globalization ties in with ideas about **media imperialism** – an empire of ideas spreading across the globe.

Creation of markets

It can be argued for example that technology has helped create a youth market, and has helped define 'youth' within society. Audio technology has created the CD single. Internet technology has created websites for music companies and for music groups. Print technology has created colourful magazines targeted at the young, referring to sub-cultural styles in fashion and music. Collectively, these media artefacts construct identities for the young; they help generate a lifestyle.

Exploitation of form

Technological developments often have the effect of changing the way a medium is used. These changes may be comparatively subtle. For example, the innovation of Chromakey (or Colour Separation Overlay) in the 1960s enabled (among other applications) images to be inserted electronically on a screen behind the newsreader. These images had the effect of enhancing the sense of actuality and authority which news wants to project to its audience.

Technology has often been 'applied' to media forms to extend the manufacture of reality. A mixture of models, computer-driven cameras and electronic matteing was used to create shots for the film *Titanic* in which it appeared that the ship had been filmed from a helicopter. It wasn't a real ship, it wasn't a real point of view, but it felt real to the audience because of their previous viewing experience.

Empowerment of the audience

Technology, especially what is loosely called 'new technology' (based on the microprocessor – the chip) has polarities of cost and accessibility. On the one one hand there is a high cost to the production of books like this one, not least in respect of expert electronic compositing. On the other hand it is possible to use the same technology at a lower level – through which this book is being written – to produce all kinds of print/design formats that would have been impossible 15 years ago. It is even possible to go into book production as an individual. So in this sense technological change has given a wide range of social groups the ability to promote their activities, to 'speak' for themselves to others. A positive view would say therefore that innovation equals access to technology.

Convergence of technology

Technologies are coming together in the sense that the 'language' for encoding sound and pictures is now dominantly the digital language of computers. The practical consequences are enormous, from the trivial (removing blemishes from models' faces in magazine photographs) to the obviously significant (huge databases of information about citizens held by state institutions such as the health service and the police). The implications are equally diverse. The models example may relate to representations of women in society and to notions of 'perfection'. The data example may relate to questions of ideology and state control, or for instance to questions of how this technology is used in the policing of ethnic groups.

Control and profit are also issues behind the recent arrival of the DVD disc on which digital technologies are converging in respect of media entertainment industries. Films, music tracks, television programmes, everything can go on one of these discs, including soundtracks in different languages.

The rise and rise of the chip

It is clear that a dramatic change in technology, and therefore in all aspects of society, not least work and leisure, occurred in the last 30 years of the twentieth century. It isn't only the media which can be looked at in terms of being pre- or post-chip. Service industries have expanded hugely. Consider tourism. People are flying abroad for foreign holidays in ever greater numbers. Booking is electronic. Payments may be electronic. The very aircraft fly on the basis of computer controls.

The social significance of these technological facts has yet to be measured. People's understanding of what 'leisure' or 'holiday' means is being modified. Their internal map of the world in relation to other cultures is being redrawn. Family experience is being changed. A generation ago these families would not have been flying to Mallorca; this part of their social experience would have been different.

The revolution started at the end of the 1950s with the invention of the transistor. A few years later the 'trannie' radio – light and portable – was commonplace, and certainly a badge for many of the 'new youth'. There were new music stations, pirate radio stations to identify with, and the trannie meant that young people could carry that part of their culture around with them. The microprocessor or chip, as the next phase, arrived in various applications in the 1970s. The range of these applications has multiplied dramatically. Successors to the trannie have been the ghettoblaster of the 1980s and the Walkman.

The idea of taking your music and your culture with you has been promoted by television adverts (electronically manipulated) which include images of youth with personal stereo, using electronic banking with abandon, having fun with easy money. This encapsulates the meeting of chip technology with media representations. It is a small example of the complex relationship between media and audience – the advert incorporates some behaviour within one group within society, but at the same time it also seeks to modify the behaviour of youth and draw it into a relationship with financial (capitalist) institutions.

The Net

This is a peculiar example of the development of technology in that it is not owned or controlled by a media institution, though many media organizations have websites to promote their activities. It depends on the conveying of digital signals between computers anywhere in the world, using existing telecommunication links which are so numerous and accessible that it is virtually impossible to control its use. To this extent it seems to be a revolutionary example of technology leading to audience power, to unrestrained access. The implications for accessing information across the planet are enormous. People visit websites (information sites belonging to companies and individuals) from their homes. They use the Net to send written messages more quickly and cheaply than letters. They can carry on conversations via their keyboards. They can access live video-camera images. On the other hand, the Internet is also being used for marketing, for the sale of goods, and by the same major media institutions discussed in the rest of this book.

The Net puts issues of power and access, of social change, of effects on social groups, in another context. It does not make them go away.

Critical views of developing media technology

Peter Golding (1974)

Looks at the media and at its relationship with society in terms of a **supply – demand model**. He sees technology as being part of the supply side, affecting production and distribution in particular. He describes the development of media industries and the evolution of audiences as being based on 'supply and demand for two basic social commodities: leisure facilities and information'. The supply side at least partly depends on technical changes – the capacity of technology to deliver information and entertainment.

Raymond Williams (1990)

Talks about the growth of media technology in terms of **economic imperatives** driving companies to create the technology which would make television happen. Williams also refers to the **social significance** of such organized technological development: 'in particular economic situations, a set of scattered technical devices become an applied technology and then a social technology'.

Andrew Crisell (1997)

Traces the development of broadcasting and its technology with an emphasis on **content and form**. For example, he points out that the creation of video recording in the industry dramatically changed the material of broadcasting by allowing manipulation through editing. Of course it also meant that material could be broadcast at any time. Videotape removed a kind of immediacy and truthfulness, though television tries to preserve the illusion of being live even when it is not.

Crisell also refers to more recent distinctions between **distribution and production** in terms of developing technology and control in the media. Cheaper production technology makes it 'easy' to make local programmes for small audiences. On the other hand, global satellite distribution of forms of communication is so expensive that power remains firmly in the hands of rich media owners. Crisell refers (after Hobsbawm, 1994) to the idea that technology develops media imperialism, to 'the increasing powerlessness of individual states against the globalising tendencies of both technology and economics'.

Brian Winston (1998)

Has developed a model of development to embrace technology and 'the **social sphere**'. Drawing on notions from linguistics, he proposes that the development and application of technologies is a kind of **performance** which draws on the **competences** (the potential for performance) which lie in the sciences. What media technology gives us happens in a social context. Winston refers to stages in which prototypes of technology are tried out before more established forms are created. He identifies other concepts about his social sphere which define how technology is developed and how it is used and controlled.

Supervening social necessities refer to any factor which influences the emergence or application of a technology at a particular time. In effect they will have much to do with social circumstances. There is a mutual recognition of need by producers and users. Wireless telegraphy was possible in the 1830s, but it took off in the 1860s because both commerce and the press realized that they needed it.

The **law of suppression of radical potential** is a description of factors which limit, control and delay the introduction of a technology. Winston argues that media technology (and its applications) does not explode into the social sphere because it is regulated in various ways. His example is the 1997 licensing of digital broadcast technology by the government to both new and old media institutions. The self-interest of the old institutions ensures that the introduction and use of digital technology is fairly gradual. In particular Winston argues that his 'law' works to 'ensure the survival, however battered, of family, home and workplace, church, president and queen, and above all, the great corporation as the primary institutions of our society'.

The development of the media in a practical sense has always depended on the development of its technology. There are various characteristics to this development, such as the creation of new types of leisure media. This technology relates to key issues such as who controls it, with what effect on the audience.

Critical views of the development of technology mirror other media criticism. Some views come from Marxist positions, seeing development as being bound up with economic and social conditions. Some views come from textual analysis of form and content (structuralist criticism), seeing development as being about new technologies continuing to be used to construct social meanings and dominant ideologies.

A SHORT HISTORY OF TELEVISION

Key features in the development of British television

Institutionally, there has been a move from the BBC monopoly (1936 to 1954) to the duopoly with commercial television (ITV) from 1954 until the 1980s, and then to a multiplicity of providers signalled by the arrival of Channel 4 in 1982 and of SkyTV in 1984, and finally confirmed by the arrival of digital television (1999).

Geographically, television has spread from reaching only into London (1936–39), to expansion nationally in the 1950s and 1960s, to expansion into the regions in the 1960s and 1970s. This is not to say that it is agreed that the regions are all served well in terms of programming.

Distribution of television is still dominated by land-based transmission, but after shortlived experiments in the 1960s with cable, the 1990s brought fibreoptics and viable local providers such as Telewest. Satellite channels and direct transmission to dish have also taken off since the 1980s. Digital television (see Chapter 12) arrived in 1999 and will replace analogue transmission within 10 years.

In terms of **product**, the programme divisions of television were established early on, based on radio practices – e.g. sport or children's programmes. But the distinctive genres of television such as soaps and quiz shows are of American origin and were introduced through ITV in the 1950s. Western series once flourished, but faded away along with their cinema inspirations in the early 1970s. Talk shows and other examples of the television cult of personalities have been around since the 1950s. Programmes in the 1980s and 1990s increasingly involved the audience in various ways (make-overs and docusoaps).

In terms of **airtime**, television in the 1950s was evening-only transmisson. This gradually expanded into daytime, then later at night, until by the late 1980s we had 24-hour television.

Technical change has of course improved reach and quality. Colour arrived on BBC2 in 1967. Editing became possible with the arrival of videotape in 1958. At the same time, new lightweight 16 mm film cameras with synchronized sound recording enabled news and documentary to achieve actuality and realism through flexible location work. The arrival of satellite links in the late 1960s opened up the global reach of television, as did related innovations such as the jet airliner. Computerized graphics since the 1980s have changed factual television. In the same period, light electronic cameras (Betacam and even camcorders) plus satellite links have revolutionized immediacy and access to events. Domestic video recorders (from the 1980s onwards) have introduced time shifting for the audience.

The **exploration of form** in television has been marked by ways of engaging with the audience and by devices for remaking realism. Engagement is dominated by the use of personal address to camera and by putting ordinary people in programmes of various kinds. Realism is especially exemplified by the rise of drama documentary in the 1960s and by actuality/outside broadcast television. Viewers expect to 'be at' major national and global events in news and sport.

The **cultural context** of changes in British social and political life since the Second World War (1939–45) has been marked by a number of features which have affected television content and how it is understood by the audience.

Postwar austerity was replaced by economic expansion and more liberal attitudes in the 1960s and 1970s. The television industry expanded. Some programmes pushed the boundaries of the establishment, of 'accepted' taste, of censorship. The role and status of women changed with educational opportunities and the arrival of the contraceptive pill in the late 1960s. Prosperity and education brought more jobs and financial independence for women from the 1970s onwards, significantly in the service sector, whereas for males manufacturing and heavy industries have been in a long decline. The feminist movement of the last three decades of the century contributed to changes in the law and in the status of women. Women are a profitable part of the television audience. Education has expanded, especially with the new universities of the 1960s and 1970s and a marked increase in higher-education participation rates. The Open University (1970) and other educational programming reflects these changes. The Tory government of the 1980s and early 1990s spanned a period of recession and economic change which saw the erosion of working-class security and the rise of managerialism. It was in favour both of free-market expansion of commercial television and of controls over the perceived 'power' of television. Economic changes and the extension of education since the 1960s have also produced new kinds of youth culture and new markets for television which are reflected in programming.

All the above changes have blunted but not removed class distinctions in society. The male-dominated manual working class that was still a significant factor in the 1950s and early 1960s has developed into a broader band of what may loosely be called middle class. The notion of authority accruing to some classes or sections of society has also been eroded.

Models of television service have moved away from the paternalistic public-service models of the 1930s through to the 1950s, via debates about commercial funding in the 1950s, and on to a modified market-forces model in the 1990s. This clings to a requirement to serve minority interests, but has shifted from giving the audience what they ought to have to giving them what they want, so long as it makes money. Financing of television production has become a crucial problem: from the 1980s onwards, co-production and sponsorship have increasingly been the norm for major projects.

Changes in the media context have seen television become pre-eminent as the medium of entertainment and of news. Yet it still has to compete with other media for a share of the market. In the 1940s cinema was the major entertainment medium, radio the key to information. The turnround came during the 1960s. But the press still competes effectively with television news and cinema product is still an important part of television diet. The pop-music industry has appeared (late 1950s onwards) and new technology has eaten into television time via VCRs and computer use (mid 1980s onwards). So television both competes with and cannot live without other media.

The **television audience** has changed in ways referred to above, in terms of its economic and social circumstances. It has expanded steadily from peaks of a million in the mid-1950s to peaks of 20 million in the mid 1980s. Until 1964 there were two channels which could depend on more or less equal shares of a growing audience. Now the audience is relatively static in numbers, and has a choice of over 100 channels. It has a huge choice of programmes and, outside the obviously popular prime-time viewing, has fragmented into more specialist groups.

Beginnings of television – the 1920s and early 1930s

This period was marked by:

• technical invention and experimental broadcasting
• commercial development of electronic scanning techniques
• the appearance of the BBC as a public-service radio broadcast medium in 1926.

There are other thorough accounts of the beginnings of television in Britain (e.g. Briggs, 1979), so what follows is very brief. Television, in terms of cameras and transmission, was thought of before it could be technically achieved. From Marconi's radio experiments in the 1890s through the invention of crucial technology such as the radio valve, there were proposals for creating electronic pictures. The commercial potential of such a new picture medium was also realized, even before either cinema or radio had achieved big audiences. David Sarnoff of the RCA Corporation (quoted in Wheen, 1985) said in 1923 that 'every broadcast receiver for home use in the future will also be equipped with a television adjunct'. The Americans, too, were making successful broadcasts in the 1920s: they had 18 experimental stations running by 1928. RCA in America and Marconi/EMI in Britain both had teams of scientists working on the 'problem'. In essence this was to make an electronic camera that would turn images into electric pulses and wavelengths, and to make a receiver which could decode these and turn them back into images. The idea that John Logie Baird created television is romantic but hardly true. He did produce and transmit very poor images in the 1920s and early 1930s, but at the centre of his devices was a mechanical slotted revolving disc which broke down a scene and was matched by a similar disc in the receiving apparatus. This was nineteenth-century technology. It was the corporations that made the cathode ray tube and controlled its ability to scan scenes (and reproduce them) via a beam of electrons. Baird's system was tried out by the BBC during experiments in the early 1930s. It was even used in the first year of broadcasting, alternating with the EMI system. But there was no contest. It was the EMI 405 line system which became the standard. It should however be recognized that Baird substantially contributed to the 'idea' of television. In his experiments he televised the finish of the Derby in 1931 and broadcast to receivers in planes and trains. Newspaper reports embedded the new medium and what could be done with it in the minds of the public.

Earliest pre-war years of broadcasting – 1936–1939

This period was marked by:

- the start of a proper television service on a limited scale in London only
- the development of categories of programmes
- experiments with outside broadcasting
- the interruption caused by the Second World War.

After experiments in the early 1930s with the mechanical and electronic versions of television, the BBC went on air in 1936. Even by 1939, when war broke out, its audience numbered only about 20 000, most in London, in the 25 miles around the Alexandra Palace transmitter. This was shut down because it was believed that it could act as an electronic beacon to German bombers.

All the same, the basis of television programming was established. For 2 or 3 hours a day the new service provided some light entertainment, a magazine programme (*Picture Page*), drama and music performances. Notably, there was no news. Apart from the fact that the fledgling television service had to run on a shoestring, even BBC radio was only just beginning to assert its independence as a news broadcaster that could at least gather some regional news, as opposed to simply reading out bulletins prepared by the Press Association. One thing BBC television did screen, from scanned film recording, was Prime Minister Chamberlain's famous airport speech in 1938 promising 'peace in our time'.

The most ambitious effort of the new television service was its outside broadcasts. George VI's Coronation procession was filmed by three cameras via miles of cable. A musical, *Magyar Melody* (1939), was similarly screened live from a theatre. Other OB involved conventional filming and then electronic screening, as well as early forms of transmitter relay (the 1938 Cup Final). Other events and places covered included London Zoo and parts of Wimbledon tennis championships.

In the studio, presentation was necessarily rather static because cameras couldn't cope with sudden movement, with anything but strong lighting, or even very well with the switching from one to another. It was very much performance before the camera. Television sets were a rich person's hobby, the tiny screen still a novelty. All the same, the production base had been established, the viability of television affirmed and most of all it was clearly going to be a successful entertainment medium. *Picture Page*, consisting mainly of songs, dances and interviews, ran for an hour, twice a week. Drama production expanded. Technical improvements in camera response and definition were continually being made.

Post-war start-up – 1947–1954

This period was marked by:

- BBC monopoly of television broadcasting
- a rather elitist cultural attitude to what constituted quality programmes
- improvements in picture quality and transmission coverage to most of England
- the 1953 Coronation which, with post-war economic recovery and a huge increase in the number of receivers, turned television into a genuine mass medium.

The BBC started its television service again in June 1946. It now covered about 40 miles around London. The pictures were still black and white, with rather fuzzy 405-line definition. Almost imediately television was into OB, covering the post-war victory parade in London. Many other events followed. It is interesting culturally to see how these were dominated by sport, royal occasions and generally 'high-culture' arts events. It is noticeable that popular performers were also favourites of middle-class London theatre – Jack Hulbert and Cicely Courtnedge. Popular pre-war programmes such as *Picture Page* continued, as did drama. There was also expansion in a technical and creative sense. All the same, broadcasting times were limited: 2.00 to 3.00 in the afternoon was aimed at women, 5.00 to 6.00 was the children's hour, evening transmission was from 7.30 to 10.30, finishing with a sound-only version of the news read over a caption card – primitive stuff by modern standards. And the cost of a television set tended to limit the audience to the middle-class and well-off, being the equivalent of 2 months' wages for the average working person.

Within the BBC the television service was not helped by a false perception among senior personnel that it was merely a novel off-shoot of radio. A combined radio and television licence fee had been established in 1946. Television didn't get enough of it. The irony was that by 1955 television viewing figures exceeded radio listening figures. Within 30 years radio listening had shrunk so much that it wasn't worth having the option of a separate radio licence fee.

The Birmingham transmitter started up in 1949, providing Midlands coverage. Television sets were starting to sell in serious numbers – 90 000 licences in 1949. Coverage of the North followed – we had something like a national television service. Multi-lensed cameras with telephotos appeared. It became possible to record onto film from the screen. The BBC moved to a 'proper' studios – the old Gaumont-British studios at Lime Grove. It built its own White City television centre. It had moved away from being a large experiment to providing a permanent service whose popularity was soon to eclipse that of radio. Programmes for children appeared. Cookery and gardening programmes were introduced. The 1950 Oxford–Cambridge Boat Race was covered partly from a camera set up in a following boat. Another technical innovation that year was a special programme from Paris (a compendium of musical entertainment and cultural items) set up through a tortuous sequence of broadcast and cable links.

Other media took the threat of television seriously. The Musicians Union imposed a ban on recorded music. The film industry would not allow the screening of movies or of cinema newsreels. Ironically this gave an impetus to the BBC to expand into its own filming or to buy newsreel material from abroad. However, this news was old, slow and non-contentious. A 10-minute newsreel programme was not news. What the BBC passed for news was the evening radio news with a caption image of Big Ben on screen. And even when something like a proper news programme, news and newsreel, started in 1954 it was still ponderous, with none of the newsreaders in vision. It was thought that their image would interfere with the neutrality of the bulletin.

The significant and watershed event of this period was the coverage of Queen Elizabeth's Coronation in 1953. The viewing audience was tremendous for the time – 20 million in the UK alone. There were relays to Europe, and film was flown elsewhere. This was a precursor of global television for major cultural events, as well as an example of the enduring public fascination with the royal family. It is estimated that the event sold a million new licences.

A year later a metaphorical bomb dropped on the BBC when the Conservative government introduced a Bill to bring in commercial television. There was bitter conflict betwen those who supported and those who opposed the idea. The BBC had been talking about a new channel of its own, and about the possibilities of colour television (which they produced experimentally from 1955 to 1957). But now the debate was about the integrity of PSB versus the dangers of a BBC monopoly in what was clearly an exploding medium. In any case the economy was taking off and it was understood by interested commercial supporters of ITV that television advertising could fuel this take-off. There was a political reaction which caught the mood of ordinary people, against the kind of elitism and paternalism which the BBC, in the eyes of many, had come to stand for. It was argued that competition between the BBC and commercial television would actually bring about more quality in television. It was proposed that spot advertising would avoid the kind of interference with editorial freedom which had been seen with whole-programme sponsorship in the USA.

Arrival of ITV and of competition – the late 1950s and early 1960s

This period was marked by:

- the arrival of commercial television and the creation of a duopoly
- expansion from evening to daytime television
- the establishment of proper television news services
- a flood of American imports and the establishment of the range of television genres as we know them
- expansion into national television coverage
- the arrival of video editing.

When ITV arrived in September 1955 it was hedged about with controls. The Independent Television Authority (like the present ITC) acted as moderator of the new commercial companies. The Act enabling ITV insisted that programmes should be 'predominantly British in tone and style and of high quality', and nothing was to be included which offended against good taste or decency. Rediffusion and ATV started broadcasting in London, respectively for weekdays and the weekends.

Their first commercial was for toothpaste. Other products that dominated a rather basic consumer list were soups, butter, soap, petrol, beer and newspapers. Advertising was confined to specific slots, with no more than 6 minutes in any hour. The ITA monitored the quality of advertising. The list of prohibitions included advertising of matrimonial and dating agencies, and women modelling underwear, except in silhouette (allowed after 1971). This was a very controlled commercial system. As Crisell points out, what is advertised provides an interesting social and cultural commentary on the times. The list above is all about post-war austerity. But soon other products emerged, notably an array of washing powders aimed first at the traditional manual washday, then at the less labour-intensive laundering of the washing-machine age.

In 1956 ITV companies opened up in the Midlands and the North. Others followed, until by the end of the 1950s 90 per cent of Britain was covered, including Ulster Television (1959). In spite of its success with the viewers, ITV broadcasting was still hugely expensive – companies were losing money until 1957. But when things did turn around, they did so dramatically. By the end of 1957 it was estimated that ITV had a 73 per cent audience share. The fact was that, given a choice, the audience rejected 'quality' programmes, as defined by 'high art' (Shakespeare and concerts). As the programme controller for Rediffusion put it, 'The public likes girls, wrestling, bright musicals, quiz shows and real-life drama. . . . From now on, what the public wants, it's going to get' (quoted in Black, 1972).

Competition from ITV caused the BBC, to revamp in a populist manner. Francis Wheen (1985) refers to this time in terms of 'the BBC's nervous conservatism and commercial television's early adventurousness.' Peter Black refers to the negative effects of elitist programming, including whole evenings devoted to operas. The BBC did have some good programmes, but it needed to learn about competitive scheduling and promoting its product. Commercial television brought American or US-influenced material, particularly game shows such as *Double Your Money*, Westerns such as *Rawhide* and cop series such as *Dragnet*. This was partly a result of needing to buy in programmes to fill rapidly expanding schedule time. It was also about the ethos of competing and trying to attract an audience. Indeed, by 1965 the ITA was moved to limit American shows in the prime-time 8.00 slot to no more than two out of five in the weekdays.

Costume action series such as *The Adventures of Robin Hood* were very popular. ITV also nurtured new British television drama through its Armchair Theatre. From 1958 its new producer Sydney Newman commissioned original material which was simply excellent. Commercial television was by no means the cultural wasteland which its enemies had threatened it would be. Granada produced a version of John Osborne's then daring contemporary play *Look Back in Anger*. The BBC thought it was too provocative and not suitable for a television audience. A few years later, however, the BBC persuaded Newman to leave ABC and continue his innovative work with plays commissioned for television in what was called the Wednesday Play slot.

ITN news also blew the BBC out of the water for a few years, with its brisk pace, original reporting, emphasis on location film footage and ability to get where the action was. Under pressure the BBC actually showed its newsreaders for the first time, just before ITN went on air. But the ITN newscasters were named, were fluent and rapidly became personalities in their own right. Where BBC interviewers were deferential, ITN people were forthright and could ask difficult questions. ITN used vox pops. They also introduced synch. sound taken from location recording, rather than laying a sound commentary over pictures in documentary style. The effect of immediacy and actuality was powerful.

ITV light entertainment such as *Sunday Night at the London Paladium* both alluded to theatrical variety-show roots and became a weekly cultural fixture for many families in the UK. It launched (from 1958) the career of comedian/compère Bruce Forsyth, who is still fronting shows on British television. A measure of the success of ITV is that in December 1955 84 per cent of London viewers were watching this Sunday-night show. Indeed, the top 10 programmes measured by the proportion of London viewers, from 1955 to 1961, were produced by ITV. New genres such as the hospital drama, represented by *Emergency Ward 10*, were hugely successful, the start of a line that leads on to present times and the equally successful hospital soap *Casualty*.

ITV also introduced admag programmes such as *Jim's Inn* (1957) – this was a kind of sitcom/soap, a shallow front for characters to present, use and praise all sorts of products. In this case the product placement was pretty clumsy. The possibilities for misusing such programmes were clearly seen by the government and the ITA, which banned them in 1963.

The BBC did fight this competition, with success after a few years. It introduced the first soap opera – *The Grove Family* – in 1955, as well as the very English cop show *Dixon of Dock Green*. Both were successful – certainly in the top 10 if there had been proper audience measurement on a national scale. Even factual programmes succeeded through their 'characters' – the cult of personality – with examples such as Philip Harben, the television cook on BBC, or Armand and Michaela Dennis on ITV, whose *On Safari* series was a great favourite with children. One great success for the BBC from 1957 on was the 6.00 weekday magazine and news programme *Tonight*, which established a new format on television and blended hard news with 'gossip' items. In the same slot on Saturdays the BBC introduced *6.05 Special*, a rather tame pop-music show. But it, and similar commercial programmes, did recognize the new power of rock music and of an emerging teenage market.

Both channels gradually introduced more films in the early 60s, as the technical problems associated with telecine were overcome. The British film industry couldn't stop television companies buying from America. Movie screenings rapidly became an essential part of audience appeal and programming, as they still are.

An interesting political episode occured in 1956 when Prime Minister Eden threatened to impose controls on broadcasting, largely because of (Sir) Robin Day's ground-breaking interviews for ITN with President Nasser of Egypt, who was a political enemy at that time because of his take-over of the formerly British-controlled Suez Canal. This intervention backfired. The Suez crisis and British invasion was a failure for Eden's government. And the previous agreement (known as the 14-day rule) with politicians that television would not discuss political business just before it was due to be discussed in Parliament was abandoned by defiant broadcasters. What is noticeable is that it was ITN which broke the ground. Previously, the BBC, with the establishment affiliations of its governors, had hardly discussed political matters and had never been contentious.

Other developments within this period included the start of a schools television service in 1957, the same year when the early evening broadcasting break between 6.00 and 7.00 was ended. By 1959 more than half the homes in Britain had a television set. This year saw the first coverage of a general election. This was the beginning of politics by personality. Even then, candidates were being advised to drop the mass public oratory style and to work with the intimacies of the medium.

Coronation Street arrived in 1960 and has been in the top-10 ratings ever since. ITV advertising was earning the companies a million pounds a week. However, advertisements for tobacco products were gradually squeezed by a series of bans on what they could promote and to whom, until they were finally banned altogether in 1965.

What tobacco companies did instead, from the 1960s onwards, was to turn to sponsorship. Embassy sponsored a world snooker championship from 1978, largely as result of the decision by the BBC to cover the sport, which then became an immediate ratings success. Cornhill Insurance sponsored test cricket from 1977. Advertisers rapidly picked up on the fact that coverage of sports such as football meant that hoardings and the grounds were in shot. Even the BBC found itself unable to avoid giving free promotion of products in this way, if it wanted to get the viewers by covering such events.

Within this period, television was in some ways technically retarded by an unresolved debate over line standards – Britain's 405-line black and white was inferior to what was used elsewhere. Colour needed better definition. On the other hand, from 1958 onwards videotape recording became possible. Both the BBC engineers and the Ampex corporation in America produced machines that, although clumsy and limited at first, rapidly revolutionized television by making possible pre-recordings and repeats, as well as making it possible to compose programmes through editing. Film recording was all right for archiving material, but not really good enough as a source for rebroadcasting so until this time, for example, if a drama was to be repeated it had to be staged all over again. Also, of course, videotape (and then a videodisc) created the instant replay, which is a staple of sports coverage.

Commercial television continued to encroach on the previous monopoly of the BBC in the early 1960s, as it opened up companies such as Border television in more remote parts of Britain. The BBC itself opened up a new Welsh service, competing with TWW (Television Wales and West) and later HTV (Harlech). 625-line improved definition arrived with BBC2 in 1964. The first satellite pictures were sent across the Atlantic in 1962, though, as with most technical developments, it took several years for this to become commonplace and economically viable.

An age of expansion and of controversies – the 1960s and 1970s

This period was marked by:

- expansion and innovations in programme form (the rise of drama documentary)
- the appearance of some contentious subject matter (programmes adopting political positions and taking a critical view on social issues)
- the rise of costume drama and of big documentary series
- the arrival of BBC2, of colour television, of satellite links, of teletext, of electronic newsgathering
- programmes which pushed back the boundaries of taste and of censorship, mainly with regard to the depiction of sex and violence on television
- labour disputes and the effects of recession towards the end of the period.

It was a time also defined by continuing expansion in coverage by television services (broadcasting hours were not controlled after 1972), by the consequent need for more programmes, by the relative liberalism of the Wilson Labour government (1964–70), and by the cultural explosion of a youth market defined through swinging London, new pop music and new fashions.

In particular, the BBC under the liberal regime of a new (1960) director general, Hugh Carleton Greene, clawed back a half share of the audience. The 1960s were innovative times for television in general. But the 1970s brought a gradual change as the recession bit. The BBC was especially hard hit because inflation meant that its licence fee was worth less. Latterly, programme projects had to be cut. However, good and cutting-edge programmes were made in the 1970s, thanks to the innovations and energies of the 1960s. One form which went into decline was the one-off play. In a sense it was a theatrical concept. What sold on television, including abroad, were series and serials.

But back in the 1960s docudramas like *Cathy Come Home* (1966) jostled for popularity with the authenticity of *Z Cars* (1969–78), the soap-opera naturalism of *Coronation Street*, the ironic spy chic of *The Avengers* (1961–9), the satire of *That Was The Week That Was* (1962–3) and the anarchic cultural stabbing of *Monty Python's Flying Circus* (1969–74). This latter series was followed by John Cleese's now famous sitcom *Fawlty Towers*, balanced on a knife edge between acute observation and surrealism. *Cathy Come Home*, about homelessness and incompetent bureaucracy, was a notable example of television which sparked public debate and ruffled political feathers. It had a lot to do with establishing Shelter as a key charity looking after the interests of the homeless. *That Was the Week That Was* might seem satirically tame now, but in 1962 it was outrageous stuff, making fools of some politicians and needling an establishment that had been protected within the British class system until then. With peak audiences of 10 million it is clear there were a lot of people out there who also thought that 'authority' needed a good goosing. The cult SciFi children's series *Doctor Who* started in 1963. The comedy double act that made the *Morecambe and Wise Show* first appeared on screen in 1961 via ATV, though it was the BBC series from 1968 which established the duo in a British cultural heartland. Their format was relatively conservative – sketches on stage and the involvement of celebrity guests. But the comedians' sense of whimsy and the absurd, plus the evident affection within their banter, made them special, to the extent that compilation repeats in 1999 still pulled in huge audiences. *World in Action* (1963) is still running as a current affairs and documentary programme taking on strong issues. Also still running is *Top of the Pops* (1964). It is hardly at the cutting edge of British pop music any more, but its safe formula of using chart hits has given it a long life among such programmes. Sport was established as a major feature of television programming. In particular, the BBC's *Grandstand* (1958 to date) had a strong hold on Saturday afternoons. The corporation had exclusive contracts with major sports, which it hung on to for many years.

The second round of general-election coverage on television came in 1964, when many commentators believed that Harold Wilson's practised television manner helped Labour win by a narrow margin over the Tories, led by the televisually gauche Alec Douglas-Home. 1968 was a year of contractual bloodletting, when a number of commercial companies lost their licences to broadcast, including Rediffusion, which had opened on air in 1955. This was also the point at which the ITA forced the production of a common listings magazine – the *TV Times* (1967). This and the *Radio Times* are Britain's top-selling magazines.

ITV continued to be strong in news and current affairs, and in starting *News at Ten* it borrowed the two-newscasters format from the USA. This programme remained a successful anchor in the schedules until 1999, when it was replaced with earlier and later news programmes, freeing up more prime time. There was an ironic sense in which ITV, cash-rich, could increasingly afford to move upmarket to prove its credentials, whereas the BBC had to move into more popular programming to get its audience back – which it did.

In this period of expansion, among other formats borrowed from American television was the talk show or chat show. David Frost was a combative interviewer in the 1960s. Michael Parkinson was immensely successful in the 1970s and 1980s. The genre is still very popular, but there is a distinction between programmes like his, in which interviewing brings something out of the interviewees, and those such as Clive Anderson's shows in the 1990s which really depend on repartee and the star status of the guests. Television continued to put on huge outside broadcasts with great success. The marriage of Princess Anne in 1974 was seen by more than 500 million around the world. The football world cups of 1966 and 1970 saw huge coverage operations mounted, the scale of which we now take for granted. Similarly, British coverage of the Munich Olympic Games in 1972 was the biggest to date. The moon landing in 1969 was a huge television event in which normal programmes were simply abandoned. Mega events of this kind attracted audiences and sold television sets, not least in the new colour format.

Blockbuster documentaries also enjoyed world-wide audiences through the increasingly important sale of programmes abroad – *The Ascent of Man* (1973), *Life on Earth* (1979), *The World at War* (1973–4). Similarly the rise of the costume drama was associated with its equal popularity in societies as diverse as the USA and Soviet Russia, as illustrated by the huge success of *Elizabeth R* (1971) and *I, Claudius* (1976). In 1970 the BBC sold 8000 hours of television to other countries.

It was a sign of how culturally conservative times had been that not until 1971 was a television commercial allowed to show a toilet bowl on screen. The 1970s produced some tough, violent and realist crime thrillers which were a stark contrast with the tongue-in-cheek ritualized violence of *The Avengers*. *The Sweeney* showed police corruption and violent treatment of criminals. *The Professionals* (ITV, 1977–83) was less realist but equally bone-crunching.

British television finally reached the colour age in 1967, on BBC2, though the sets cost the equivalent of £1500 and it wasn't until 1977 that more colour than black-and-white licences were sold. As an aside, one may note that commercial local radio started in 1972, with immediate success. Closed-circuit educational television was opened up experimentally in Glasgow via cable systems in 1965. Teletext started on BBC in 1973 and on ITV in 1975. Global television coverage (see sport above) became relatively commonplace through developments in satellite technology, which also affected news and current affairs. Newsgathering was also revolutionized by the arrival (*c.* 1976) of portable video cameras. Cassette material could be fed directly into satellite links and sent back to BBC and ITN London centres immediately after the recording of events. Open University programmes began in 1971. The ITA was revamped as the IBA (Independent Broadcasting Authority) in 1972, with an expanded remit to monitor commercial radio and projected cable channels.

The underlying economic difficulties and the tensions between management trying to keep labour costs down and workers trying to protect their positions, also affected television. The BBC was literally blanked out on one day before Christmas 1977 by a dispute which was a foretaste of the downsizing and management–union battles of the 1980s. Even more dramatic was the much longer 11-week commercial television strike in 1979, when managers struggled to keep any kind of programmes on air. The unions got their pay rise in the end, but their companies lost millions in advertising revenue. The long-term effect was a steady shedding of full-time staff – part of the casualization of the industry.

Consolidation and market forces – the 1980s

This period was marked by:

- some consolidation of services and of programming as affected by rising costs and an economic recession
- the arrival of Channel 4, of limited cable services, of satellite broadcasting, of breakfast television, of 24-hour television
- serious questions about the future of the BBC as a public-service model of broadcasting
- an acceptance of market forces as driving television, not least with reference to co-productions and to populist programmes (the expansion of soaps and the interbreeding of the soap form in prime-time television)
- the televising of Parliament
- the growth of independent production companies, and the shedding of many full-time staff by the big contractors and the BBC
- an increasing stretch between the search for cheaper programmes and the creation of big-budget productions which would appeal to an international market
- the development of electronic newsgathering, of time-based (computerized) editing, of computerized visual effects.

By this time most homes in Britain had a television set; by 1990 three out of five homes had two or more televisions. Geographical reach was nearly total. Television schedules had expanded to fill the day and night. To this extent television had reached saturation point. The British economy in the 1970s had become unstable and marked by high unemployment as global winds blew in competition that demolished much of its strength in traditional manufacturing. The television industry wasn't looking to take on more staff or to spend vast sums on original programmes. It was looking to consolidate its audience and seek new markets by inventing new brands. Inflation had eaten into the value of the BBC licence fee, but the commercial system was still flush with cash. In any case, the 1980s brought the Thatcher government which was sympathetic to competition and economic self-sufficiency. So the 1980s was marked by the arrival of new kinds of television for new kinds of audience, and by a lack of government sympathy for what was seen as the old-fashioned and complacent BBC that had been having too much of a free ride. The irony is that it was still the BBC that was seen as setting standards for PSB in television. Even the Chairman of the IBA expressed this view (quoted in Hood, 1994).

The 1980s also brought cable, satellite television, breakfast television, Channel 4, and S4C for Welsh speakers which could take programmes from either the BBC or commercial systems.

The commercial C4 came in 1982. It was initially a subsidiary of the IBA, paid for (until 1993) by a forced levy on the established contractors, who also sold its advertising. Initially, it suffered a huge problem with Equity, the actors' union, which refused to agree to reduced fees for the cash- strapped newcomer. There was blank screen between some programmes – anathema for television with its belief in continuity. The problem was that everyone had come to believe that the medium was an unfailing milch cow. But minority-interest television will never be especially profitable, so wages and percentages will always be an issue as operators open up a proliferation of channels on shoestring budgets. C4 has now achieved independence and financial self-sufficiency. It has justified its remit to seek out minority audiences and to encourage independent production. In particular it was enjoined to serve cultural, sports and ethnic interests. Through a shrewd mixture of imaginative foreign-programme purchase and a lot of good, cheap original programming from independents it took television to audiences and through subjects which BBC2, with the same mission, had in the end failed to do. Most of all, it funded independent film production, now to the tune of some £6 million a year. It is no exaggeration to say that C4 has transformed the British film industry.

Both the BBC *Breakfast Time* and the commercial TVAM (now Good Morning Television) were started in 1983. Programming experiences and lost franchises have established the fact the public won't buy serious television at this time: that personality-led, magazine-format chatty and fun television is what sells. This is what happened to TVAM. It was started by a prestigious team including Anna Ford and Angela Rippon, well-known newscasters. But the serious, newsy approach of early TVAM didn't appeal to viewers. A lack of audience meant a lack of advertisers and therefore a lack of income. The company's 'dream team' resigned. TVAM went downmarket, including the introduction of Roland Rat the puppet. Roland became a cult. Ratings and income went back up. Such is the power of advertising.

The market is what dominated the 1980s, whatever the public talk of standards and high-quality television. The BBC was left in no doubt by the Tory government that if it wanted its licence fee then it had to be attractive to the audience. This is the government that placed in power a chairman of governors of the BBC – Marmaduke Hussey – who then took the unprecedented step of sacking the director general, Alasdair Milne (in 1987). Milne was seen as representing an old-style independent BBC that would not fit in with Tory cost-cutting and managerialist ideas and which had upset the Tories a few years earlier with its Falklands coverage. Milne was followed briefly by Michael Checkland, an accountant by background, and then by John Birt. Equally the government eventually backed away from ideas about a BBC funded by commercial sources because it became clear that there simply wasn't the money in the 'advertising pool' to pay for this.

Cable has also had problems in finding its niche. Local cable companies were given franchises and monitored by a new Cable television authority in 1984, under the Cable & Broadcasting Act. The problem was and is to find material that consumers want. Technically clean versions of existing channels have some attractions. Bought-in material, mostly American, provided other possibilities. But in the end, originating television material is expensive. The most successful source was the new satellite broadcasting – Sky and BSB. Cheap local community or educational television has limited appeal. In spite of the plea for programmes which would 'appeal to the taste and outlook of people living in the area', few of the present 60-odd franchises do provide locally made programming. Limited city cable systems (based on wires which couldn't carry many channels) went back to experiments in the 1960s. But what counted was what was on offer, which at that time was mainly the major broadcasters. In the 1980s the cable itself wasn't there or was expensive to put in. But in the early 1990s there was a major wiring-up of Britain with fibreoptic cable, largely because American companies like Nynex and United Artists were allowed to buy into cable in order to restart it. They were also technically able and now legally allowed to provide interactive services and independent telephone operators. But in the 1990s cable was taken up by barely 20 per cent of its potential customers, and still cannot be seen as significant in the distribution of television. The fact of the matter is that buying into its packages costs too much for many consumers. But the charges need to be there to make it pay: a classic commercial dilemma. Even attractions such as MTV (1987) were soon to be hijacked by the satellite DBS system. MTV made the pop video an essential feature of the 1990s, where in the 1980s it had cut its teeth on programmes like *The Tube* (1982–7).

Satellite television had similar start-up problems in 1982, and required enormous investment. In 1989 Sky launched four DBS (direct broadcast) channels, including the staples of sport, news and films. Sky was selling dishes and signal converters to homes (it was losing a million pounds a week in its early stages).The BBC also made a start in the satellite business with its UK Gold channel. By 1990 Sky had a competitor – BSB (a consortium of television and communication companies including Granada, Virgin and Pearsons). Murdoch kept his nerve with Sky, using his enormous income from successful British newspapers to subsidize costs, including inducements to people to fit dishes and choose Sky. In 1991 he drove BSB into a merger in which it disappeared. Sky retains a considerable and profitable audience in Europe.

One example of the lateral expansion of television in the 1980s into specialized channels and niche markets was the start of the televising of Parliament in 1989. MPs had made a great fuss for many years about this potential intrusion into their privacy, a curious position to take in a democracy. There was reason to suppose that they were more concerned about some of their wilder behaviours appearing on screen before their voters. In spite of Prime Minister Thatcher's opposition the idea was approved via a select committee. Parliament does not make for riveting television, but news pictures and compilation programmes do bring the public sphere of political affairs into the private sphere of our homes.

Economies meant that the glory days of original television drama were largely over. Those writers with a track record, like Dennis Potter or Jack Rosenthal, could still get on screen. Potter's *Singing Detective* was one of the creative events of the 1980s, mixing film noir with the musical. Big-budget costume and period dramas still made money. *Brideshead Revisited* (1981) (costing £4 million and taking 2 years to make) and *The Jewel in the Crown* (1984) were fine examples of these. *The Edge of Darkness* (1985), a paranoid thriller concerned with misdemeanour and cover-up in the heart of the state, had things to say about the political times and remains the most exciting television. *Boys from the Blackstuff* (1982) and *The Monocled Mutineer* (1986) showed that pungent realist drama about British class and economic conditions could still make it through television. The controversial *Death of a Princess* (1980) has already been discussed (see p. 246). Heavyweight documentaries were still being made – for example, *The Living Planet* (1984). The controversial fly-on-the-wall documentary series *Police* (1982), on the Thames Valley force, actually came from BBC Bristol, which has also established a world-wide reputation for the quality of its wildlife productions. The now top-rated soap opera *EastEnders* burst onto the screen in 1985 with immediate success. *The Bill*, set in a London police station and combining soap and police-drama qualities, appeared in 1984.

Big events, especially royal ones, still pulled in audiences. In 1981 750 million people around the world watched the marriage of Prince Charles and Lady Diana Spencer. In 1985 the *Band Aid* charity concert event to raise funds for areas of poverty and hunger in Africa was watched by an estimated 1.5 billion people world-wide.

There was also a vogue, starting with the American drama *Roots* in 1977, for the mini-series, in which two or more long episodes are broadcast on consecutive nights, rather than being spread over weeks. This is as much a scheduling ploy as anything else. It continued through to the 1990s, with similar devices used by *EastEnders* to both surprise and attract the audience by screening extra episodes or longer episodes as a special event. In 1983 Central Television made a mini-series about the American president John F. Kennedy, and sold it to NBC in the United States.

In 1986 C4 tried to deal with persistent, well-publicized protests about sex and violence on television from Mary Whitehouse and her small Listeners and Viewers Association. They put up a red warning triangle in the corner of the screen. Not surprisingly, it just served to boost ratings and was dropped a year later.

In the budget-conscious 1980s co-productions became increasingly common, as did the appearance of film arms of the major ITV companies: Zenith for Central Television in the Midlands; Euston Films for Thames Television. Euston was the co-producer with C4 of the drama series *The Nation's Health* (1983), which took a critical look at doctors in much the same way as the writer's (G. F. Newman) previous series *Law and Order* (1978) had taken a critical view of the police and the law. Goldcrest Films (an arm of the media giant Pearsons) co-produced with HTV a series called *Robin of Sherwood* (1984–6). The dramatized biography of Nancy Astor (1982) was a BBC2/Time-Life co-production. The soap opera *Brookside* (1982) was an example of an independent production (by Brookside Productions) for the new C4, in which Phil Redmond used his bankability from his enormously successful children's series *Grange Hill* (1978) to build real houses for the filming.

The 1980s was also a period when the development of technology affected television in many ways that the audience came to take for granted. Electronic cameras became the norm for newsgathering, with their ability to feed back live pictures of events. The new Sony Betacam system meant that you didn't need a wrestler's physique to lug the camera around. Time-based editing meant that video editing became quick and straightforward, again especially useful for the quick turnaround times demanded by news.

Portable satellite-link equipment was developed in the late 1980s, meaning that news teams could beam up pictures and sound from any location without needing to find a ground station. The electronic insertion of graphics and images became a matter of course for factual programmes. It could be used, along with the first serious computerized image manipulation such as Quantel, to produce fantasy effects in children's programmes (e.g. *The Chronicles of Narnia*, 1988–90) as well as for illustrating information behind such events as elections.

The video recorder became commonplace in the 1980s: it was present in 40 per cent of households in 1985 and in 60 per cent in 1990. People could now use television at their convenience, recording minority-interest programmes such as the Open University ones which were broadcast at night and watching them when they wanted to. They could also store their favourite programmes on the shelf, like books.

Audience research was rationalized in 1981 when the BBC and ITV agreed to drop competing systems and jointly support BARB (British Audience Research Board).

New technology and a cold global climate – the 1990s

The last decade of the twentieth century was marked by:

- a new broadcasting act and its consequences
- mergers and take-overs which put television institutions firmly in the global marketplace
- an expansion in the number of channels available
- a consequent adjustment in the relationship of television to other media
- the arrival of digital technology and its consequences for distribution
- a blurring of lines between genres and between modes of realism
- the development of programmes which involve the audience in one way or another
- continuing debate over whether the BBC gives value for money and justifies the licence-fee system.

The Broadcasting Act (1990) and subsequent amendments was driven by a political will to increase competition in the industry. Both the BBC and ITV systems were required to commission 25 per cent of programmes from independents. The BBC rapidly introduced 'producer choice' which smashed the hitherto secure production base and its sometimes protective practices by allowing (forcing) producers to put together production teams from any source. The BBC embarked on a savage cost-cutting exercise at the beginning of the 1990s, saving £70 million in 4 years. Many people lost their jobs or went freelance or formed new production companies – not just from the BBC. All the same, it is true that costs have been held down and innovative material has come through from companies such as Tiger Aspect and Hat Trick. For example, the latter has produced *Drop the Dead Donkey* (1990 onwards), a sitcom set in a television newsroom. Thanks to rewriting and the insertion of topical items up to the last minute, with late production and the advantages of video editing, this programme is a good example of how the medium can be used effectively, even to satirize itself.

The 1990 Act replaced the IBA with the ITC (and a new Radio Authority). The ITC was given responsibility for satellite television and for cable. The act also forced a new round of bids for ITV licences, the fees from which go to the government. There was bloodletting: Television South West lost its contract to West Country Television; Television South lost to Meridian; Thames lost to Carlton; TVAM lost to Good Morning Television. There were rightful concerns about the setting of financial benchmarks for these bids –

namely that the ITC should be taking the highest bids. Pious statements about 'quality television' meant nothing if bidders were prepared to say anything in order to get the contract. In any case the definition of quality in television has always been problematic, not least with regard to those who actually oversee the system. Corner, Harvey and Lury (in Hood, 1994) summarize the ITC definition in 1990 as being about:

- aesthetically valued, high-culture programmes
- the provision of public information
- production values related to technical quality
- what was popular.

The rules about mergers and cross-media ownership were relaxed through the act, allowing a 25 per cent holding of shares in other television companies. Not only did Yorkshire merge with Tyne Tees, but Granada took control of Yorkshire Television via LWT (which also had 14 per cent of Yorkshire). Granada now owns the franchises for these three companies. Granada also has 13.5 per cent of shares in Sky, plus 20 per cent of ITN. Carlton has emerged as a major player. It has a 20 per cent share of GMTV and a controlling interest in Central Television, which also owns 20 per cent of Meridian. The company also owns Zenith Productions, Quantel, The Moving Picture Company (influential in advertising) and the Technicolour Labs in Britain. (See also Chapter 4 on control of British television.) Ownership has been concentrated on a national and a global scale. The government has squeezed more revenue from commercial television. The influence of the broadcasting unions has been largely diminished and production costs for some types of programmes brought down by the forcible creation of a place for new independents. Television now is all about profitability and 'value for money'. How far we have seen any increase in programme quality is another matter.

The BBC had its charter renewed in 1996, but the managerialism of its ex-director general John Birt (1992–2000) forced through changes which effectively mean that the BBC is playing the commercial game dressed in PSB clothing. It has expanded its satellite operations with 24-hour news and UK Gold. This last was a deal with Thames Television, which although it had lost the London weekday contract continued, like other rejected contractors, to 'trade' in the media. BBC Worldwide has expanded enormously in its business of programme sales, spin-offs and tie-ins. The BBC is in a deal with the successful American Discovery channel for factual and educational broadcasting. The corporation is also offering a new digital service. It is appropriate that the new director general, Greg Dyke, made his name in commercial television. Commercial opponents of the BBC continue to argue against the licence fee, paid by all viewers for a service which on average only 40 per cent of them use. Many of them want pay-as-you-view to come in.

Others have criticized the dumbing down of television and of the BBC in particular, in the competition for audiences, for ratings, for the approval of governments who set the licence fee. There is a central political/fiscal argument here which is in many ways mirrored by the debate over the health service. It is agreed that all kinds of people should have access to health and to television – both public services. But when it comes to paying for this access the government gets cold feet and the rich get selfish.

Channel 4 was very successful in the 1990s under the shrewd programming leadership of Michael Grade (1988–96), who introduced successes from the United States such as *Friends* and *ER*. Indeed C4 got to the point of popularity where under its original agreements with the main ITV companies it had to pay them a large share of its advertising revenue. The 1996 Broadcasting Act stopped this – but C4 now really does have to go it alone.

The 1990s also saw the arrival of the new commercial Channel 5 (1997). It is owned by a consortium of media giants such as United News and Pearsons (who also have holdings in Sky). It has an uncertain sense of identity and relies on a lot of cheap imported programming. Its news programme, with bright, pacy, fairly informal presentation, is probably the best index of the young browsing audience which it is hoping to attract for its advertisers. It looks for cult hits from elsewhere, like *Xenia, Warrior Princess* – a piece of mythic strip cartoon brought to life.

Digital television arrived in 1999 with a variety of competing providers, notably the BBC and Murdoch's Sky. The industry intention (backed by government) is that within 10 years analogue television signals (and sets) will go. Everything will be broadcast or carried in the universal computer language of numbers. Quality will increase. High-definition television at 1200 lines can be brought in. We already have wide-screen television (since 1997), though there has not been much take-up of this because of cost. The question is what will be carried by the digital providers. There is access to more and more channels – about 200 on digital. Providers are hoping that specialist interactive services such as shopping channels will take off, though it seems likely that web shopping will compete fiercely here. Typical of the Murdoch approach is subsidy of the new technology (the set-top conversion box) in order to get people to sign up. Since all providers will have to offer the dominant channels anyway, if they want subscribers, there isn't much difference between the services on offer. So it is a question of who will get most of the audience committed to their service. What does seem to be the case from the American experience is that new channels can't easily generate new audiences or new programmes. What is likely is that the existing audience will be spread more thinly, more programmes will be recycled, the same genres will be remoulded.

Sky itself has moved into considerable profit – £63 million in 1993. Murdoch is also a key player in the attractive areas of film and sport. His

Movie Channel has often outbid the previous main players of BBC1 and ITV1 and attracts customers by showing newer films. He has the advantage of being a Hollywood figure as well – the owner of Twentieth Century Fox Films, Searchlight Pictures and Fox Television. C4 has also started (1999) its own subscription channel to generally more upmarket movies – Film Four. But Sky has caused the most cultural upset through its sport channel and a predatory approach to buying up rights. Sky Sport is now a standard feature of the bar television in many English pubs. The channel has the rights, co-owned with the BBC, to screen premier-league football. (Sky owns the rights to whole matches; the BBC could only afford highlights.) During the 1990s the BBC lost its dominance in respect of screening major sports events to both ITV and Sky.

In terms of programming, a number of trends emerged in the 1990s. One is the wooing of the after-school and teenage audience. Australian soaps such as *Neighbours* (BBC1, 1986 onwards) and *Heartbreak High* (BBC2) have been very popular. Several of the stars, such as Natalie Imbroglio, have moved on to pop-music careers. Mainstream soaps such as *EastEnders* (BBC1) have strong strands involving young people. Soaps have crossed with sitcoms, notably the American *Friends* (C4), to keep the younger audience viewing later on. There has been a reflexive stream of programming in which television pastiches or parodies itself. Steve Coogan made a series – *Alan Partridge* (BBC2) – about an absurd self-regarding television chat-show host. *Vic Reeves' Big Night Out* (BBC2, surreal and sometimes tedious) was a parody of a variety show. *Never Mind the Buzzcocks* (BBC2) is a comedy quiz show about pop music which like *A Question of Sport* (BBC1) makes fun of its more serious quiz-show antecedents. *Drop the Dead Donkey* (C4) has been referred to above (p. 284). *Brass Eye* (C4) satirized types of documentary and current-affairs programmes. *The Day Today* (BBC2) satirized news. *Have I Got News For You* (BBC2) is a quiz show which encourages outrageous comment on news events and news personalities. This is postmodernist television in which the medium becomes self-referential, confident that its audience is so televisually aware that it will see the joke.

There has also been a development of programmes featuring viewers themselves in various roles, riding on the technology of newer lightweight video cameras. Docusoaps and video diaries have already been discussed (p. 156). The point is that here the audience is in some cases behind the camera, providing raw material, in other cases in front of the camera, providing, as with *Paddington Green* (BBC1), cheap footage of everyday life which is moulded into the dramatic structures of fiction. Light cameras – Hi8 and now digital – have made it ever easier to obtain authentic news footage under 'difficult' circumstances. Indeed, many editors now have ethical problems to deal with, in that anyone with any point of view to promote can employ the cameras and offer usable material on, for example, domestic demonstrations in some ethical cause or wars in foreign places. Some such material was taken from the Baltic states in 1991, in the turmoil surrounding their breakaway from Russia and given the inability of Western news teams to get on location. This newer pattern in newsgathering is enhanced by more reliance on such sources because they are cheaper. The increasing affordability of satellite time and of link equipment has brought even more immediacy to the news. The conversation in real time between the newscaster and the reporter on location has become *de rigueur* – even if there is nothing new to say.

Discussion-type programmes involving a studio audience go back to the 1980s, when the American *Oprah Winfrey Show* brought a gossipy frankness to the screen that was very different from the serious issues based *Question Time* put out by the BBC. The 1990s brought us *Jerry Springer*, also from the United States, which is orchestrated entertainment, not discussion.

It could be said that 'event television' was a feature of the 1990s, developed from earlier examples of major coverage and hyped through sophisticated trails. The Glastonbury pop festival has become a television event, to be previewed, given live coverage and dissected afterwards. The same is of course true of sport. There is a kind of self-fulfilling prophecy here – Formula One car racing is hyped as an important cultural event; up to a point it achieves that status because of the hype and the extent of coverage. Drama is promised, though the macabre sub-text is that it will not exist without crashes. In-cockpit cameras have appeared, which at least break the tedium of watching from afar. And yet nothing can disguise the fact that what is in vision is fundamentally a bunch of cars travelling very fast round and round the same stretch of track.

Since its expansion to becoming the dominant popular medium in the 1960s, television has always had a close relationship with other media. Movies are a crucial part of its programming and its appeal. Its programmes are viewed and approved (or not) in newspapers and magazines. It showcases the pop-music industry, which also provides it with invaluable material. In the 1990s the web of media industries was woven tighter, binding television within a package of entertainment and information. This happened through ever more complex ties of ownership and was emphasized through interdependence of product (for example, the number of chat shows and quiz programmes which depend on personalities from other media for audience appeal). But television also remains unique by virtue of its instant access to the whole population in their homes.

GOVERNMENT COMMITTEES AND REPORTS IN THE HISTORY OF TELEVISION

Selsdon committee and report, 1934

This report on the future of television recommended that the Baird and EMI systems should be tried against one another. It also proposed that television should be paid for out of the existing radio licence fee and that advertising should not be used to raise money.

Beveridge committee and report, 1950

This review of the BBC and its charter had the effect of maintaining the monopoly of the BBC, but referred to the option of a commercially funded service. It was actually quite critical of the BBC monopoly. It recommended the development of regional services, but these were a long time in coming. In failing to develop such services, the BBC undermined its position a few years later compared to the growth of regional ITV companies.

Pilkington committee and report, 1961

This review of where broadcasting was going was very critical of the commercial sector, in a political climate in which Lord Thompson's infamous pronouncement that having a commercial television contract was like having 'a licence to print money' hadn't gone down too well. It was as a result of the perception of excessive profits that the ITA imposed a surcharge tax on ITV companies, on a sliding scale related to profits, which was known as the Levy. This arbitrary tax actually had to be reduced later, when profits fell.

Ideas about the ITA selling advertising were never put into action. But the recommendation for a second BBC channel was acted on, with the arrival of BBC2 in 1964. 625-line definition and colour eventually came in as new standards, also as a result of the committee's ideas. The government was further persuaded to toughen up the ITA's quality-control powers over programmes in the commercial system. However, the snobbish tone of the report with regard to popular television, the definition of quality as being about minority, elitist interests and the eccentric recommendation that ITV be started again with tougher rules, backfired. The press and many politicians were rightly angry about the report, which ran counter to the growing liberal mood of the times and of the electorate.

Annan committee and report, 1977

In spite of various expectations of this committee (the heralding of a new commercial channel) and despite its actual recommendations (the creation of a new Open Broadcasting Authority to run such a channel) nothing much came of it. Its most important pronouncements were to endorse the idea of public-service broadcasting, however funded, and to endorse the licence-fee system for the BBC.

Peacock committee and report, 1986

This was mainly taken up with the future of the BBC and its finances, with the future of PSB and with ways in which new technology was likely to shape broadcasting. Although the Tory government had set up the committee with some animus against the BBC's supposedly biased reporting of the Falklands War and against the 'privileged' finances of the BBC, in the end the committee recommended that advertisements or sponsorship should not be brought in to help pay for the BBC. However, it did recommend subscription television in the long run, including for the BBC. Whether this comes through as monthly fees or pay-as-you-view, it does mean that the audience pays only for what it wants. But at the time of writing this still hadn't happened for the five dominant terrestrial channels. Peacock was pro-consumer choice and free-market inclined, but it didn't deal with what would happen if the market did not see as profitable what a section of the audience might want to watch, given the chance.

12

Television Futures

PREVIEW

This chapter deals with:

■ likely developments in terrestrial, satellite and cable television, especially those that relate to the industry and to technology

■ the importance of emerging digital television

■ global pressures on British television

■ the changing form of television programmes

INTRODUCTION

There won't be too much speculation in this chapter, because this is a dangerous game. In particular, although technology had a great influence on television in the 1990s and will certainly influence its future to some extent, it is easy to overestimate this factor. The history of technology from Baird to website portal providers is one in which the prophets promise a new world tomorrow, but actually it takes a little longer to arrive and doesn't look quite as they described it. As Jeannette Steemers says (1999), 'there is little certainty that the public will 'buy into' the new services on offer'. We still have a duopoly of the BBC and ITV, in terms of audience share and of income, but this is being steadily eroded by Sky, C4 and C5. Global competition and new technology has changed and is changing what television looks like and how it gets to the audience, but slowly. Government ensures that commercial interests will not prevail unrestrained. It also seems minded to protect the BBC, revamped as it is in its new commercial clothing.

ITV

The terrestrial commercial television system is relatively healthy within Britain, but is not secure in the global marketplace ('Television in the Global Marketplace', p. 298 below). It has an inferior record to the BBC in terms of producing and selling programmes abroad. It is having to work harder for its share of the advertising 'pool', given the competition from other media, including satellite television. But the relaxation of merger and take-over rules controlling television in the early 1990s created contractors at the centre of the system that have financial clout.

The system remains monitored and quality-controlled by the ITC. The smaller companies remain beholden to the giants, Carlton, Granada and UNM. Yet they are also protected by the system. And the middle players like Harlech (HTV) have both developed their own niche programming and are substantially owned and controlled by other media giants – UNM in the case of Harlech.

The realignment of and tensions in power among ITV companies and the conglomerates behind them was illustrated by a row over the screening of prime programmes through Ondigital (1999). This pay-television service is owned by Granada and Carlton. They proposed showing top-rating programmes such as *Coronation Street* and *Morse* through Ondigital before they were seen on the main network. In the event, compromises kept such shows off prior 'release' but allowed lesser-rated programmes such as the game show *Gladiators* to be shown 'early'. Ondigital is fighting for its share of a new market with Sky digital and the BBC. The dispute involved power play between the three dominant ITV companies and the regulatory power of the ITC.

The ITV system is moving to compete abroad. There was a *furor* in 1999 over the decision to move the flagship programme *News at Ten* and provide later and earlier news. This represented such cultural upheaval that the ITC nearly blocked it. But ITV needed to clear space in its evening schedules to let in more films and 'made for television' material (including its own). Ironically, a new threat to ITV's security (and to that of the BBC) is likely to come from commercial global players who are not necessarily seen as television providers. Media giants such as the German-based Bertelsmann (coming from a publishing base) have started looking for niche markets through digital channels – in Bertelsmann's case, sharing ownership (with Kirch) of a package of television channels known as DFI.

BBC

In spite of the considerable public debate (i.e. among politicians and in the media) about the future of the BBC, it has remained substantially intact. There have been arguments as to whether the BBC has been dumbing down in the face of competition, as to whether it still represents a benchmark for public broadcasting, as to whether it is valid for it to go on charging a licence fee in the face of sliding audience share. It was even reported by those close to government in the late 1980s that Prime Minister Thatcher was then minded to break up the BBC in its traditional form. But it is still with us – and that Tory government is gone.

The BBC has changed internally, having lost great numbers of full-time staff and much of its centralized in-house production base. It has embraced new technology, with its 24-hour satellite news channel, with new channels BBC Prime and BBC World (1995), and its digital online service. It has done this by entering into deals with American digital and cable companies – Flextech and TCI. It has even persuaded the government that it should have a top-up fee to pay for its digital service. It has moved into global alliances to get distribution in the USA – BBC America – and to obtain access to more programming. It has sold off its transmitters (1997) to an American group in an act of privatization which raised £244 million.

The BBC is good at selling its product. It has been seductive and loud in providing 'Infomercials' about its own merits, on its own channels. One of these, *Perfect Day*, became a marketing sensation because of viewer response, because the Lou Reed song of the 1970s went to number one in the charts, and because the major artists who appeared in the video asked for only very basic fees – simply because they actually supported the PSB principle of the BBC and approved its programme quality. The corporation's image, its reputation, its cultural iconography within the context of public service helped it, rather ironically, to promote itself in the most commercial fashion. There are indeed those who argue that now that the BBC has embraced the marketplace and commercial practices it is not the traditional BBC and is not doing what it was set up to do. Its commercial rivals continue to snipe at its apparently privileged position – it can play in the marketplace on the back of a universal public levy called the licence fee. But the fact is that for the moment that fee seems secure. No one can think of a better way to fund some television and keep it free of the obligations which go with reliance on advertising.

The remaking and commercialization of the BBC at the beginning of this new millennium is typified by its commercial division, BBC Worldwide. This has an income of £1.25 billion and is rated the fourteenth largest UK media company. A major part of its activities is related to publishing books and magazines, not least the *Radio Times*. But it is now, for example, moving into web promotion in a big way. Freebeeb.net disks are being distributed through post-offices and small chain stores. New web users will be seduced into BBC sites to do with programme topics such as gardening – and the sale of spin-off products will follow. Similarly, promotion of the major series *Walking with Dinosaurs* mirrors the practices used in Hollywood. Not only the use of computer animation/simulation, but also the marketing via a website and the production and sale of a video, toys and books, precisely replicate the methods used to promote Spielberg's hugely successful film, *Jurassic Park*. Indeed one problem for the BBC is that with Worldwide making so much

here is a sound argument for saying that these profits should be taken
ount for when setting the licence fee.

'viewer share in relation to licence fee' debate, as it could affect BBC
income, is now more complicated. On the one hand, BBC1 has only a 30%
share of viewers, which might be an argument for trimming the licence fee.
On the other hand, BBC2 has a further 10% of viewers. And in any case ITV
– the only other programme maker of volume to be compared with the BBC
– also only has a 30% viewer share – quite a change from its 43% to BBC
33% in 1991. For ITV the change also suggests that there is a relatively
limited commercial market in Britain, since its percentages have been eroded
by C4, C5 and Sky.

PUBLIC–SERVICE BROADCASTING

The survival of PSB pivots on what is happening with the BBC, even though
I would argue that it has been by no means the only home to PSB for some
years now (see references to PSB and C4 in Chapter 4). All the broad-
spectrum broadcasters can only serve the 'public at large' if they go on getting
the money to pay for challenging programmes. ITV1 and the BBC are losing
audience share. The BBC has a unique funding base, but it is called into
question when the corporation uses the cash for essentially commercial
practices – even if it has been politically pushed in that direction. Yet again, it
has to use those practices in order to compete and to hold on to audience
share.

Granting a digital licence fee to the BBC suggests that the government is
prepared to make people pay to keep a PSB choice alive. It is ironic that the
threat to broad-spectrum quality programming comes from (apparently)
greater consumer choice. It is a classic problem – if the majority choose
dedicated subscription channels (film, comedy, sports, etc.) then what is left
for the rest of the population? (See also Chapter 3, on PSB.)

Siune and Hullen (1998) have produced an interesting table of old and new
media structures. The old structure describes key characteristics of a PSB
model, as well as the original position of the BBC. The new structure is very
much about the market model which dominates television today. The question
is how far the PSB ideal, perhaps still embracing goals of democracy and an
audience as citizens, can hang on to these goals while also meeting
competition and taking an individual and global perspective on its remit and
on its audiences (see Fig. 12.1).

	OLD MEDIA	NEW MEDIA
Broadcasting	Monopoly	Competition
Goals	Democracy	Survival/success/profit
Means	Programme production/ selection of material	Selection of material/ programme mix
Logic	Responsibility	Market/economic
Criteria for selection	Political relevance	Sale
Reference group	Citizens	Consumers
Focus on	Decisions taken/ power structure	Processes of policy-making/ new conflict dimension
Perspective	Nation/system	Individual and global

12.1 Old and new media structures with reference to public-service broadcasting. Source: Siune and Hullen, 1998

CABLE TELEVISION

Cable in Britain is dominated by NTL and Telewest. It is not a major provider of television, though this service is expanding. Cable is as much a provider of telephone services, in competition with British Telecom. Its initial problems in the early 1990s were about getting in cables fast enough to provide a service at all. Ten years later it has high penetration to urban centres but is trying to turn round a rather poor record of reliability and faults servicing. Its picture quality for television has not always been even as good as broadcast reception – and superior quality should have been its key selling point. The arrival of digital should change this. The cables now in place should also allow for the kinds of interactivity that pundits promise, for example in community networking. Otherwise, the fact is that at the moment cable provides few local television services and has not revolutionized the distribution of television, as first predicted. But it does seem secure, with companies claiming up to a third of potential customers in their areas. It does have the potential for interactive uses. And it will benefit from the digital television revolution that is bringing pay-per-view services at the same time as the growth of telephone, Internet and E-commerce which all want to use the cable systems. BSkyB, ITV and the BBC all want cable customers to take (and pay for) their services. Already the BBC has edged Sky News off cable by offering its 24-hour news for free.

Cable is typical of media industries moving towards a situation of near monopoly – NTL is trying to buy one of its few remaining rivals, CWC Communications. This accepted bid has been referred to the Monopolies and

Mergers Commission to see if it is in the public interest. The arguments over this are again typical for the media industry as a whole. On the one hand a duopoly in the cable television business doesn't seem to be in the public interest. On the other hand it needs some commercial clout to face off BSkyB, which does have a monopoly of satellite broadcasting and dominates cable by virtue of its programming power. BSkyB now controls the rights to top football matches and to most of the good boxing, golf, cricket and rugby. Cable badly needs to be able to carry these events – and is being made to pay for it.

SATELLITE TELEVISION

BSkyB had a successful decade of expansion and profit in the 1990s, but is now struggling with the costs of digital and of paying for the programming which holds the viewers. It has pulled in over a million new digital subscribers, on top of its existing 3 million customers. It needs to be a service which the cable companies want to carry because Sky makes money for them. Cable carriers (as opposed to DBS to customer dishes) are becoming more and more important for Sky, so Sky is now investing more money in programming, while holding on to its dominance in sport screening rights – premier-league and Uefa Cup football, Ryder Cup golf, etc. As far as the consumer is concerned, the distinction between satellite and cable television is blurred.

DIGITAL TELEVISION

(See also Chapter 3.) This is about the transmission code, not the channel on which it is carried. So the information that is the television programme is in effect turned into the numbers language of computers and can be distributed through any of the existing carriers. It will replace analogue broadcasting. It does offer advantages such as picture/sound quality and the capacity for manipulating the information carried. So, for example, sports watchers can now choose camera angles on a game in progress or can give instructions for their own replay.

As Britain goes digital there are huge amounts of money to be made from providing the services. In the commercial sector this means BSkyB and Ondigital. Viewers need decoder boxes. The boxes are free, to bring in the viewers who then provide the serious money through their subscription payments. The providers of each box and cable package figure that once they have got the consumer to buy their system they will hold on to them for a long time. Being locked into one package is against the notion of consumer choice, but the government that should protect consumer choice is also keen to get digital technology up and running – and someone has to have a reason to foot the huge investment bill. It has been suggested that the digital market, including other services such as telephones, will be worth £17 billion by 2006.

The broadcasters offer digital-to-air services now. In addition to its main channels the BBC offers 24-hours news, and the BBC Knowledge, Choice and Parliament channels. As broadcast, these services are free. As a part of satellite/cable subscription services, they cost, but are on offer along with the plethora of other channels.

There is a war of words and of political lobbying between commercial programme producers and the BBC over the £24 top-up fee for digital users, in addition to the licence fee. Indeed, commercial television didn't want the BBC in digital television at all. It sees the licence fee as a kind of free subsidy, which then enables the BBC to offer its News 24 on cable for nothing. On the other hand, it may be said that the BBC is doing exactly what political pressure and critics have said it should do – to be more effective, cost-conscious and competitive along commercial lines. Digital television is expanding the viewer experience, and is also finally destroying the myth of the captive generalist viewer. Already people surf the channels in a way that is unattractive to advertisers. People can select into interests. We will see more 'dedicated-interest' channels, what are called thematic services – for example, Rainbow Television for gay people.

Digital makes pay-television likely as the norm in the future, so some channels will live on the income from a committed and interested audience. ITV and BBC1 will probably survive as the big providers because there is enough range of interest on their channels that people will still think it worth paying for them. However, two concerns will arise if the weight of funding shifts towards subscription or pay-television services. One is that media giants will buy up saleable events (the obvious example is sport), commodifying them for sale on their channels only. This is already happening with BSkyB. The other is that anything which is experimental or of interest to an audience below a certain size will never make it to the screen because of the tyranny of the market.

Digital television gives more power to the distributor who controls these new gateways to audience/consumers. Distribution is no longer dominated by the BBC and ITV. The same is true of production. And comments about the rise of the television distributor need to be balanced against the consequent demand for product to fill the new channels. Where the new (and old) distributors will achieve more power is if they start to buy up the successful independent producers or small distributors. Carlton has bought out Planet 24 Television (1999), makers of the *Big Breakfast Show* on C4.

The demand for product will continue the trend towards repeats (Granada/BSB channels), and again the big players will benefit because they have large back catalogues of programmes. This trend will also benefit Hollywood, which is in a similar position of strength with all its movies to sell. So there will be more of the same, more of the old and just possibly more experiment as expanded digital television chases its viewers.

TELEVISION IN THE GLOBAL MARKET PLACE

Here, British television is having a tough time. The media giants of American television are juggernauts. In spite of the rules about home-grown product, the fact that so many more channels and hours have become available since the 1980s means that the quantity of foreign (mainly US) product coming in has increased hugely overall, not least in prime time. Home-grown British product is often made on low budgets, aimed at particular audiences or channels (like C4) and not exportable. Between 1989 and 1997 the import–export television trade balance moved from parity to a state where the value of imports (£600 million) was double the value of exports.

The Americans sell television in bulk, some of it by whole channels. So children have Fox Kids or Nickelodeon (Viacom). There is Discovery's Animal Planet or Time Warner's Cartoon Channel. The Americans package up big series or collections – 26 or more programmes at a time – while the British tend to commission only 6 to 10 programmes at a time, so they don't have the volume of product that is wanted overseas (though some longer series are now coming through). The problem for British television in competitive terms is therefore one of directed investment and commercial practices, not necessarily a lack of raw cash. The effect of this situation is very evident in the case of young viewers. The kid's satellite channels have moved from having about half the number of viewers achieved by terrestrial channels (in 1994), to having about the same number. And child viewers can be sold a lot of spin-off and tie-in products through the commercial breaks.

If the British have been slow to adapt to American marketing needs, there are other and growing potential markets. We have the central advantage of speaking a major international language, so it is likely that the British television industry will expand into those markets, with and without the use of dubbing. Already we sell strongly to countries like Holland. English-speaking satellite channels already have a European market, and can expand. Such changes won't affect the English viewer's experience of television as it is watched, but they will change the institutions which make the British programmes as a part of their range of activities. In this respect it is instructive to look at the tables produced by Meier and Trappel (1998) which show that while British media/television companies are a strong presence among European media firms measured in terms of sales, on a global scale measured by revenues the best ranking for any British Company is for the BBC at only twenty-first in the list. A further table of transnational European media corporations emphasizes the importance of diversification across media, for strength and for survival. It is noticeable that British companies have a long way to go in expanding the range of their interests.

It would also be misleading to suggest that British television isn't aware of the need to go global. BBC World Service television started as long ago as 1991. It did its deal with Flextech over the Discovery channel in 1996. The problem lies in a combination of factors: the force of competition, finding the right alliances, producing the right material for given markets and finding huge sums of money. The Carlton/UNM merger is one example of how things are moving. So is the fact that BSB has a 24 per cent stake in Premiere, a European digital channel and part of the German Kirsch pay-television company, itself part of a larger media empire.

BOUNDARIES OF FORM

The form of television in terms of its overall programming and provision has changed in a pattern that is much like that for other media such as the press or the magazine industry. That is, only a few providers can afford to provide a mixed bag of programming which can attract relatively large audiences. Otherwise the trend is towards specialist channels – narrowcasting – and towards specific audiences. This change, from few to many channels, from general to more particular audiences, is one that is still going on. What is available, what people call to mind from the term 'television', is very different to what it was in 1970. Steemers (1999) suggests that the new narrowcasting could 'reduce the significance of both the generic broadcasting service and the scheduler'. People will create their own viewing schedules, as indeed inveterate users of the video recorder already do.

Form in the more specific sense of programme treatment and structure is also changing, largely in respect of the construction of realism and of a relationship with the audience. Television programmes used to show a pretty clear division between the conventions of the factual and the fictional. Each programme used to be a finished artefact that was presented to the audience as a 'thing to be watched'. Increasingly television has blurred the lines between fact and fiction and has brought in programme forms which are 'things to be participated in'. There is the kind of infotainment programme which, for example, presents clips from motorway video recordings as a form of pleasure for the viewer. This is in line with the type of programme that reconstructs real crime as drama. There are the 'neighbours from hell' and 'holidays from hell' type programmes, which film real people, impose a dramatic structure on the material and then sell actual footage as a kind of entertaining fiction. Viewers have their gardens or the house 'made over' –

and this is turned into entertainment. In such ways viewers also participate in programmes, just as other programme forms involve them phoning in responses to quizzes and questions, or meeting a partner and going off with them. These trends seem likely to continue, given the economics of documentary-type, viewer-involved television, as well as the arrival of cheap (and sometimes intrusive) cameras and the growth of interactive technology. The line between life and the screen is fractured. The provision of crafted, expensive, made-for-the-screen set pieces either in the form of drama or of documentary will remain, but only in prime time and in the hands of the big spenders.

INSTITUTIONS AND TECHNOLOGY – CONVERGENCE AND CHANGE

It is clear that control of television is being concentrated in fewer and fewer hands. It is also true that technology encourages this concentration as companies find that they have increasingly common interests, either as carriers/distributors or as providers of the content that is carried. Above all other types of technology it is the digital encoding of information which underpins the convergence, enabling the systems and the devices to 'speak a common language'. The convergence of multi-nationals, as much through agreements and mergers as through outright take-over bids, continues rapidly. For example, BSkyB has monopolistic deals with Nynex the cable operator and with Kirch in Germany (which has interests in television, film and newspapers).

Roger Fidler (1997) proposes that there are six principles relating to technological change. These may be applied to television.

1 **Co-evolution and co-existence**: new forms of media and of media use all develop interactively. The close relationship between cable and satellite television is an example of this. Satellite originally depended on cable for distribution; now cable depends on satellite for much of its product.
2 **Metamorphosis**: new media grow out of old forms. Broadcast television was a predicted development out of broadcast radio, for example.
3 **Propagation**: emerging media carry on dominant traits of earlier forms. The programming divisions and PSB tradition of radio, for instance, strongly influenced the way television developed in this country.
4 **Survival**: media adapt or die. Consider the BBC, which has adapted to a commercial environment and has adopted commercial practices to counteract market-driven political pressures.
5 **Opportunity and need**: media are adopted as much because of social, political and economic needs as for the merits of their technology.

Commercial television arrived at least partly as a response to cultural changes creating an audience which wanted something less stuffy than the BBC, and to economic growth which welcomed a new medium through which to carry advertising and stimulate further growth.

6 **Delayed adoption**: new media take longer than expected to become a commercial success. Commercial, satellite and cable television all lost a lot of money at start-up, before becoming widely accepted and profitable.

TECHNOLOGICAL FANTASIES AND REALITIES

Digital television is with us, and it is expanding its audience reach rapidly. What is less clear is how far its technological potential will be realized. A lot of this potential rests on its ability to engage the viewer interactively. Home shopping is already available. The home television is just a screen with which to do things.

There are a whole range of experiments going on with digital which may affect how television is made, as well as what we actually see. For example, Cambridge University is working on virtual-reality applications. In one of these the actors for a drama meet to rehearse in virtual space. In another the television audience reach out to construct their own drama. The line between virtual-reality devices and television is becoming blurred. The nature of viewing is changing.

This kind of digital application is specialized and still perhaps a little fantastical. What is real is the expansion of the number of channels made possible by digital and continuing year on year. Pay-television is likely to expand – the principle of paying for specialized services, such as sport and movies, that you really want to watch. This is likely to affect the BBC as well. The answer to commercial critics will be for the BBC to provide a basic package through its licence fee but to ask viewers to pay for added value – just as happens with subscriptions packages to other services.

More practically, there has been talk of interactive demand-led viewing for years. Given DVD technology, we are nearing a situation where (with pay per view) audiences could call up a film or even a favourite past programme from a provider. This would not be broadcasting so much as electronic purchase. Nor would there be any obvious reason for regulating such a provider in the same ways as traditional broadcasting. Time Warner's Full Service Network, based in Orlando, Florida, has made this future happen now. It provides four services on demand via digital technology: movies, video games, shopping and banking services. This experiment for several thousand people is likely to lead to a widespread normal service.

Another experiment on a New York channel centres on a soap, *East Village*, in which you can go back over parts of programmes, discuss material with other viewers online, and provide feedback which influences how the narrative develops. Interactivity not only may change television viewing as we know it, but it introduces a host of other activities on screen. Equally, given the examples of the healthy survival of other narrative media such as books, it does seem likely that the reception of entertainment material will continue to be a valued function of new television services.

OTHER TRENDS

The demand for product is likely to to cause producers to dig more deeply into other media. This isn't just about the appearance of specialist music or documentary channels. It is and will be about producing programmes, especially in blockbuster mode, which are drawn from novels and drama (e.g. *Gormenghast* on BBC2, Jan.–Feb. 2000).

Television is also likely to perform social functions, most obviously in respect of education. We already have the Learning Channel, but the larger possibility is for television to 'publish' learning material on-air, for all kinds of education courses. (This will cause a fuss among traditional book and video publishers.) Providing that educational channels can get the viewers to pay enough money they are unlikely to care about the fact that viewers are recording material for later re-use.

To conclude, it seems that there will be:

- more integration of production and distribution interests
- more of this and other kinds of merger on an international scale
- more diversification by companies across other media
- an expansion in the number of channels available, mainly via satellite
- an expansion, with this, of pay-television
- a fragmentation of audiences into specialized interests
- an improvement in picture quality
- the development of widescreen television
- the development of choice, pay-television and interactivity on the basis of new digital technology
- the development of hybrid forms of programme
- further experiment with kinds of audience involvement in programmes and with devices for creating a greater sense of 'reality' in television. These devices will range from playing with the conventions of form to the development of widescreen television and of large display screens in the home.

Bibliography

Adorno, T. 1991: *The Culture Industry*. London: Routledge.

Allan, S. 1998: *News from Nowhere*. In Bell and Garrett (1998).

Allan, S. 1999: *News Culture*. Buckingham: Open University Press.

Allen, R. (ed.) 1992: *Channels of Discourse Reassembled* (2nd edn). London: Routledge.

Althusser, L. 1969: *For Marx*. Oxford: Blackwell/Verso.

Alvarado, M., Gutch, R. and Wollen, T. 1987: *Learning the Media*. London: Macmillan.

Ang, I. 1991: *Desperately Seeking the Audience*. London: Routledge.

Balzagette, C. and Buckingham, D. (eds) 1995: *In Front of the Children*. London: British Film Institute.

Barthes, R. 1957: *Mythologies*. London: Vintage.

Barthes, R. 1977: *Image, Music, Text*. London: Fontana/Collins.

Baudrillard, J. 1988: Selected Writings. Ed. M. Poster. Cambridge: Polity Press.

Bell, A. and Garrett, P. 1998: *Approaches to Media Discourse*. Oxford: Blackwell.

Black, P. 1972: *The Mirror in the Corner*. London: Hatchinson.

Blain, N. and Boyle, R. 1998: *Sport as Real Life: Media Sport and Culture*. In Briggs and Cobley (1998).

Bourdieu, P. 1984: *Distinction*. Cambridge, MA: Harvard University Press.

Bourdieu, P. 1998: *On Television and Journalism*. London: Pluto.

Bourne, S. 1998: *Black in the British Frame*. London: Cassell.

Bourne, S. 1999: A People Denied Its Great Expectations. *Times Higher Educational Supplement*, 25 June 1999.

Briggs, A. 1979: *History of Broadcasting in Britain: 4, Sound and Vision*. Oxford: Oxford University Press.

Briggs, A. and Cobley, P. 1998: *The Media: An Introduction*. Harlow: Longman.

British Film Institute 1994: *British Television*. Oxford: Oxford University Press.

Brunsdon, C. 1998: What is the 'Television' of Television Studies? In Geraghty and Lusted (1998).

Brunt, R. 1990: Points of View. In Goodwin and Whannel (1990).

Buckingham, D. 1990: *Watching Media Learning: Making Sense of Media Education*. London: Taylor & Francis.

Buckingham, D. 1995: On the Impossibility of Children's Television. In Balzagette and Buckingham (1995).

Burton, G. 1997: *More Than Meets the Eye*. London: Arnold.

Burton, G. 1999: *Access to Sociology: Media and Cultural Studies*. London: Hodder & Stoughton.

Chibnall, S. 1977: *Law and Order News*. London: Tavistock.

Clarke, A. 1992: Television Police Series and the Fictional Representation of Law and Order. In Strinati and Wagg 1992.

Cohen, S. 1973: Mods and Rockers. In Cohen, S. and Young, J., *The Manufacture of News*. London: Constable.

Collet, P. and Lamb, R. 1986: Watching People Watching Television. Unpub. report to the IBA.

Corner, J. 1995: *Television Form and Public Address*. London: Arnold.

Corner, J. 1996: *The Art of Record*. Manchester: Manchester University Press.

Corner, J. and Harvey, S. (eds) 1996: *Television Times*. London: Arnold.

Crisell, A. 1997: *Introduction to British Broadcasting*. London: Routledge.

Cumberbatch, G. 1989: Violence and the Mass Media. In Cumberbatch, G. and Howitt, D. *A Measure of Uncertainty: The Effects of the Mass Media*. London: John Libbey.

Curran, J. and Gurevitch, M. (eds) 1996: *Mass Media and Society* (2nd edn). London: Arnold.

Curran, J. and Liebes, T. 1998: *Media, Ritual and Identity*. London: Routledge.

Curran, J. and Seaton, J. 1997: *Power Without Responsibility* (5th edn). London: Routledge.

Daniels, T. 1998: Television Studies and Race. In Geraghty and Lusted (1998).

Dickinson, R. Harindrinath, R. and Linne, O. 1998: *Approaches to Audiences*. London: Arnold.

Docherty, D. 1990: *Violence in Television Fiction* (BSC annual review). London: Broadcasting Standards Council.

Dovey, J. 1998: About News. Working paper, University of the West of England.

Downie, L. 1983: The Washington Post. In Eldridge (1995).

Drotner, K. 1992: Media Panics. In Skovmand and Schroder, K. (ed.) (ibid.).

Du Gay, P., Hall, S., Janes, L., Mackay, H. and Negus, K. 1997: *Doing Cultural Studies*. Berkeley, CA: Sage and Buckingham: Open University.

Eldridge, J. (ed.) 1995: *Glasgow Media Group Reader Vol. 1: News Content, Language and Visuals*. London: Routledge.

Elliott, P. 1970: Selection and Communication in a Television Production. In Tunstall 1970.

Ellis, J. 1992: *Visible Fictions: Cinema, Television, Video*. London: Routledge.

Erikson, E. 1950: *Childhood and Society*. London: Triad/Paladin.

Fairclough, N. 1995: *Media Discourse*. London: Arnold.

Feuer, J. 1992: Genre Study and Television. In Allen (1992).

Fidler, R. 1997: *Mediamorphosis*. London: Sage/Pine Forge Press.

Fiske, J. 1987: *Television Culture*. London: Routledge.

Fiske, J. 1989: *Understanding Popular Culture*. London: Routledge.

Fiske, J. 1991: Moments of Television: Neither the Text nor the Audience. In Seiter et al. 1991.

Galtung, J. and Ruge, M. 1970: The Structure of Foreign News. In Tunstall 1970.

Gauntlett, D. 1998: Ten Things Wrong with the Effects Model. In Dickinson et al. (1998).

Gerbner, G. 1972: Violence in Television Drama. In G. Comstock and E. Rubinstein (eds), *Media Content and Control: Television and Social Behaviour*. Washington DC: Government Printing Office.

Gerbner, G. 1986: Living with Television: The Dynamics of the Cultivation Process. In Bryant, J. and Zillman, D. (eds), *Perspectives on Media Effects*. Hillsdale, NJ: Laurence Erlbaum.

Geraghty, C. and Lusted, D. (eds) 1998: *Television Studies*. London: Arnold.

Geraghty, C. 1996: Representation and Popular Culture. In Curran and Gurevitch.

Gianetti, L. 1993: *Understanding Movies*. Englewood Cliffs, NJ: Prentice Hall.

Gillespie, M. 1995: *Television, Ethnicity and Cultural Change*. London: Routledge.

Glaessner, V. 1990: Gendered Fictions. In Goodwin and Whannel (1990).

Goffman, E. 1979: *Gender Advertisements*. New York: Harper.

Golding, P. 1974: *The Mass Media*. London: Longman.

Goodwin, A. and Whannel, P. 1990: *Understanding Television*. London: Routledge.

Graddol, D. and Boyd-Barratt, O. (eds) 1994: *Media Texts: Authors and Readers*. Buckingham: Open University Press.

Gramsci, A. 1971: *Selections from the Prison Notebooks*. London: Lawrence & Wishart.

GUMG 1976: *Bad News*. London: Routledge & Kegan Paul.

GUMG 1982: *Really Bad News*. London: Routledge & Kegan Paul.

GUMG 1999: *Message Received*. Ed G. Philo. Harlow: Addison Wesley Longman.

Gunter, B. 1987: *Poor Reception*. Hillsdale, NJ: Lawrence Erlbaum Associates.

Gunter, B. 1994: The Question of Media Violence. In Bryant, J. and Zillman, D. (eds), *Media Effects: Advances in Theory and Research*. Hillsdale, NJ: Lawrence Erlbaum Associates.

Habermas, J. 1989: *The Structural Transformation of the Public Sphere*. Oxford: Polity.

Hall, S., Critcher, C., Jefferson, T., Clarke, J. and Roberts, B. 1978: *Policing the Crisis: Mugging, the State and Law and Order*. London: Macmillan Press.

Hall, S., Hobson, D., Lowe, A. and Willis, P. 1981: *Culture, Media, Language*. London: Hutchinson.

Hall, S. 1995: The Whites of their Eyes: Racist Images and the Media. In Dines, G. and Humes, J. (eds), *Gender, Race and Class in Media*. London: Sage.

Hall, S. 1996 (1971): Technics of the Medium. In Corner and Harvey (1996).

Hall, S. (ed.) 1997: *Representation*. London: Sage/Buckingham: Open University.

Hargrave, A. 1993: *Violence in Factual Television*. Report for the Broadcasting Standards Council.

Harris, R. 1983: *Gotcha: The Media, the Government and the Falklands Crisis*. London: Faber.

Hartley, J. 1982: *Understanding News*. London: Methuen.

Hartley, J. 1992: *Tele-ology: Studies in Television*. London: Routledge.

Hartley, J. 1998: Housing Television. In Geraghty and Lusted 1998.

Hay, J. 1992: Afterword. In Allen (1992).

Hebdige, D. 1979 *Subculture: The Meaning of Style*. London: Methuen.

Hill, C. 1974: *Behind the Screen*. London: Sidgwick & Jackson.

Hinds, H. 1996: Fruitful Investigations. In Baehr, H. and Gray, A. (eds), *Turning It On*. London: Arnold.

Hobsbawn, E. 1994: *Age of Extremes: The Short Twentieth Century*. Harmondsworth: Michael Joseph.

Hobson, D. 1982: *Crossroads*. London: Methuen.

Hood, S. 1994: *Behind the Screens: The Structure of British Television in the 1990s*. London: Lawrence & Wishart.

Horkheimer, M. and Adorno, T. 1972: *The Dialectic of Enlightenment*. Oxford: Blackwell/Verso.

Huesman, L. and Eron, L. (eds) 1986: *Television and the Aggressive Child: A Crossnational Comparison*. Hillsdale, NJ: Laurence Erlbaum.

Jensen, K. 1995: *The Social Semiotics of Mass Communication*. London: Sage.

Kaplan, E. 1992: Feminist Criticism and Television. In Allen (1992).

Katz, E. and Lazarfeld, P. 1995: Between Media and Mass. In Boyd-Barratt, O. and Newbold, C. (eds), *Approaches to Media*. London: Arnold.

Kellner, D. 1991: *The Persian Gulf Television War*. Totawa, NJ: Westview Press.

Kellner, D. 1995: *Media Culture*. London: Routledge.

Klapper, J. 1960: *The Effects of Mass Communication*. Glencoe: Free Press of Glencoe.

Kozloff, S. 1992: Narrative Theory and Television. In Allen (1992).

Kuhn, A. 1985: A History of Narrative Codes. In Cook, P. (ed.) *The Cinema Book*. London: British Film Institute.

Levi-Strauss, C. 1968: *Structural Anthropology*. London: Allen Lane.

Lodziak, C. 1992: *The Power of Television*. London: Frances Power.

Lorimer, R. 1994: *Mass Communications*. Manchester: Manchester University Press.

Lusted, D. 1984: The Glut of the Personality. In Masterman, L., *Television Mythologies*. London: Comedia.

Malik, S. 1998: Race and Ethnicity. In Briggs and Cobley (1998).

McQuail, D. 1983: *Mass Media Theory*. London: Sage.

McQuail, D. 1992: *Media Performance*. London: Sage.

McQuail, D. and Siune, K. (eds) 1998: *Media Policy*. The Euromedia Research Group. London: Sage.

McQueen, D. 1998: *Television: A Student's Guide*. London: Arnold.

McRobbie, A. 1994: *PostModernism and Popular Culture*. London: Routledge.

Meier, W. and Trappel, J. 1998: Media Concentration and the Public Interest. In McQuail and Siune (1998).

Milliband, R. 1973: *The State and Capitalist Society*. London: Quartet Books.

Moloney, E. 1991: Closing Down the Airwaves: The Story of the Broadcasting Ban. In Rolston, B. (ed.), *The Media in Northern Ireland*. London: Macmillan.

Moores, S. 1993: *Interpreting Audiences*. London: Sage.

Morley, D. 1980: *The Nationwide Audience*. London: British Film Institute.

Morley, D. 1986: *Family Television*. London: Comedia/Routledge.

Morley, D. 1992: *Television, Audiences and Cultural Studies*. London: Routledge.

Morley, D. 1991: Changing Paradigms in Audiences Studies. In Seiter et al. (1991).

Mulvey, L. 1975: Visual Pleasure and Narrative Cinema. In *Screen 16* (3).

Mumford, L. 1998: Feminist Theory and Television Studies. In Geraghty Lusted (1998).

Muncie, J. 1987: Much Ado About Nothing: The Sociology of Moral Panics. *Social Studies Review* (Nov.).

Murdock, G. 1992: Citizens, Consumers and Public Culture. In Skovmand and Schroder (1992).

Newson, E. 1994: Video Violence and the Protection of Children. Report of the Home Affairs Committee. London: HMSO.

Nightingale, V. 1996: *Studying the Television Audience*. London: Routledge.

Noble, G. 1975: *Children in Front of the Small Screen*. London: Constable.

O'Shaughnessy, M. 1990: Box Pop: Popular Television and Hegemony. In Goodwin and Whannel (1990).

Palmer, P. 1994: The Lively Audience. In Graddol and Boyd-Barratt (1994).

Philo, G. 1990: *Seeing and Believing: The Influence of Television*. London: Routledge.

Postman, N. 1986: *Amusing Ourselves to Death*. London: Methuen.

Propp, V. 1968: *The Morphology of the Folk Tale.* Austin: University of Texas Press.

Reith, J. 1992: Broadcasting over Britain. In Skovmand and Schroder (1992).

Schlesinger, P. 1987: *Putting Reality Together.* London: Constable.

Schlesinger, P. and Tumber, H. 1996: Television, Police and Audience. In Corner and Harvey (1996).

Schlesinger, P., Dobash, R. and Weaver, K. 1992: *Women Viewing Violence.* London: British Film Institute.

Seiter, E., Borchers, H., Kreutzner, G. and Warth, E. 1991: *Remote Control: Television, Audiences and Cultural Power.* London: Routledge.

Selby, K. and Cowdery, R. 1995: *How to Study Television.* London: Macmillan.

Sheldon, L. 1998: The Middle Years: Children and Television. In Howard, S. (ed.) *Wired Up, Young People and the Electronic Media.* London: UCL Press.

Silverstone, R. 1994: *Television and Everyday Life.* London: Routledge.

Siune, K. and Hullen, O. 1998: Does Public Broadcasting Have a Future? In McQuaill and Siune (1998).

Skovmand, M. and Schroder, K. (eds) 1992: *Media Cultures.* London: Routledge.

Sparks, R. 1992: *Television and the Drama of Crime.* Buckingham: Open University Press.

Steemers, J. 1999: Broadcasting is Dead: Long Live Digital Choice. In Mackay, H. and O'Sullivan, T. (eds), *The Media Reader.* London: Sage/Buckingham: Open University.

Strinati, D. and Wagg, S. 1992: *Come on Down.* London: Routledge.

Taylor, P. 1992: *War and the Media: Propaganda and Persuasion in the Gulf War.* Manchester: Manchester University Press.

Thwaites, A., Davis, L. and Mules, W. (eds) 1994: *Tools for Cultural Studies.* Melbourne: Macmillan.

Todorov, T. 1976: The Origin of Genres. *New Literary History* 8 (1).

Tolson, A. 1996: *Mediations.* London: Arnold.

Tuchman, G. 1979: Women's Depiction by the Mass Media. In Baehr, H. and Gray, A. (eds) *Turning It On.* London: Arnold.

Tulloch, J. 1990: Television and Black Britons. In Goodwin and Whannel (1990).

Tunstall, J. 1970: *Media Sociology.* London: Routledge.

Tunstall, J. 1993: *Television Producers.* London: Routledge.

Van Zoonen, L. 1994: *Feminist Media Studies.* London: Sage.

Van Zoonen, L. and Meier, I. 1998: From Pamela Anderson to Erasmus: Women, Men and Representation. In Briggs and Cobley 1998.

Von Feilitzen, C. 1998: Media Violence. In Dickinson et al. (1998).

Wagg, S. 1992: 'One I Made Earlier': Media, Popular Culture and the Politics of Childhood. In Strinati and Wagg (1992).

Wayne, M. 1994: Television, Audiences and Politics. In Hood (1994).

Wheen, F. 1985: *Television*. London: Century Publishing.

Williams, G. 1996: *Britain's Media*. London: Campaign for Press and Broadcasting Freedom.

Williams, R. 1990: *Television, Technology and Cultural Form*. London: Routledge.

Williamson, J. 1978: *Decoding Advertisements*. London: Marion Boyars.

Winston, B. 1998: *Media, Technology and Society*. London: Routledge.

Index of companies and channels

This is compiled as a single list because a number of companies also give their name to channels, e.g. Carlton or Sky (BSkyB). Detailed references to the BBC in general (BBC1 and BBC2), and to ITV in general (channel 3 and the various commercial companies generically), are not given below because they appear so frequently in the text. The chapters on institutions, history and futures in particular will yield the greatest number of comments on these two main organizations of British television.

Index of programmes

These are cited when there is significant comment in the text. However, programmes referred to in historical sections are not cited because of the volume of entries involved. These sections are as follows: documentary, 163–9; youth TV, 190–2; race and changes, 198–202; history of TV, 265–88.

General index